Sylvie A

From wannabe to racer:
The long road to racing.

Contents

Introduction

Part 1: The Journey To The Grid

Chapter 1   Starting Out.

Part 2: "Let's Go Racing!"

Chapter 2   Round 1: Brands Hatch Indy.

Chapter 3   "Homework on the bus".

Chapter 4   Round 3: Cadwell Park.

Chapter 5   More to do, more to spend, more to worry about.

Chapter 6   Prepping for Snetterton.

Chapter 7   Round 5: Snetterton 300

Chapter 8   More fixes, more worries.

Chapter 9   "The Big Meet" – return to Brands Hatch.

Chapter 10   Cadwell Park: The Mountain beckons again.

Chapter 11   Final round preparation

Chapter 12   The Finale (Brands Hatch Indy)

Epilogue

Appendices

Dan Thomas

Introduction

When I first sat down to write this book, I envisaged a tale about an apparent no-hope, unambitious and middle-aged man, known for a lifetime of unwise decisions (and who thus remains the butt of many a joke) who got through a racing season, shaken but intact and with a huge grin on his face, having achieved a lifetime's ambition: racing a motorcycle in a proper race series and gaining a Clubman race licence on the way.

For the most part, that's how it went and I hope that, in the telling, I have done it in a suitably engaging, light-hearted and entertaining manner. Within these pages, you'll see how even someone as disorganised as me can still make it through a racing season. I could always have done it better, of course and hindsight has proved that with a little more patience and preparation, I could have done a lot better but it was still brilliant. I have also included a detailed list of all the costs incurred, from the very beginning in 2016 to the final round at Brands Hatch in October 2019.

The ultimate goal is to encourage readers to have a go themselves, especially if they think they're too old. I was 56 when I started the season but my friend Alan Hensby was 59. We both had birthdays by the summer, so finished the series aged 57 and 60 respectively. Some of the riders I met in my rookie season were well into their 60s. Really; if someone like me, a proficient (but slow) rider managed this, even if it was mostly at the back, then perhaps you can, too.

Readers will, however, note a change of mood within these pages as the story unfolds. Racing is exciting and great fun but it is also very dangerous. For all the highs, there can be deep, deep lows. When a rider is injured, it can be bad but sometimes a rider will pay the ultimate price for following his or her passion.

To that end, this book is dedicated to my very good friend Dan Thomas, a man I knew for all too short a time but whose friendship I will cherish for the rest of my life. A percentage of all the profits from sales of this book will go to the Kent Air Ambulance in his honour.

Addendum: Since I started writing this book, the one person who had most encouraged me to enjoy my biking, my dad Bob, was lost to us. Had he not passed on his enthusiasm or rather, his obsession with bikes and included me in so much of his life with them, my ambition to race and this book would never have happened. As a result, the book now gets dedicated to two of my favourite riders, Bob Male and Dan Thomas.

Part 1: The Journey To The Grid

Chapter 1:
Starting Out

I have been a biking fan for most of my conscious life. What follows is the account of how I went from Barry Sheene wannabe to genuine (if slow) motorcycle racer, at the crusty age of fifty-six and a half. The main story started in 2015 but the initial seed was sown in 2004. Earlier than that really, if I take my father's influence into account.

It was Dad who first introduced me to motorcycles and it was he who took me to my first proper races (the Transatlantic Trophy at Brands Hatch in 1977, followed by the 1978 Manx Grand Prix). Thanks to him, I have been obsessed with motorcycles ever since. I have owned no end of junk but also some pretty good machinery and have loved all of them (except that CX500, which I'll ignore).

I only became a regular racing spectator in later adulthood, around 2004. After being introduced first to British Superbikes (BSB) and then MotoGP, I soon became an avid viewer.

As time passed, my obsession grew. In 2007, I met a young racer who had joined Bemsee (the British Motorcycle Racing Club) and was looking for help, so I offered to buy the back protector he needed. To say, "thank you", he gave me a ticket to a meeting at Brands Hatch. A weekend spent in the paddock had me hooked at a completely new level.

Over the following years, I'd visit UK race meetings with friends, following our heroes in British Superbikes. For the smaller Bemsee meetings, I would travel to Brands (my local circuit) or Lydden Hill in Dover where I established firm friendships with many of the racers. The paddock was friendly and the guys I hung out with, all racers in the Yamaha Past Masters (YPM) series, were a close-knit bunch of wisecracking, mickey-taking people. On track, however, they were serious rivals.

The club seemed to consist of mostly young riders but the paddock was open to anyone with an ACU (Auto Cycle Union, the UK motorcycle racing's governing body) licence and included people of pensionable age. I was nowhere near that old (back then, at least) but it did set my imagination running. I was frequently encouraged to have a go, rather than just sit on the side-lines as a spectator. Frankly, I didn't think I had the nerve or the skill. I certainly didn't have the finances to race and quickly dismissed such thoughts.

The idea of racing never left me completely, though and I maintained that fantasy of being, if not a racing god, at least an ACU licence holder who had raced. I had started GP Future, an online racing advice site about that time and felt I should get some proper experience myself because, without being able to offer first-hand knowledge, I felt a fraud.

"To race, first find your steed."

With the seed sown, I began to consider what I might race. My immediate thought was a Yamaha TZR250 and the Past Masters series as I was familiar with the class and the riders, if not the bike. Two-strokes are simple (important for a mechanical klutz such as me) and I had already spent a long time in that section of the paddock and was confident of getting plenty of support. The problem was that by this time, the bikes were all 30-plus-year old, fragile machines; a significant downside of the two-stroke set up. Frequent engine rebuilds were commonplace and the bikes could seize without notice. When I looked at photos from the races, most of the riders could be seen with their left hands poised over the clutch lever, ready to catch the engine before it nipped up.

I considered pit bikes; miniature motocross bikes. I had friends in those circles too and would visit local karting tracks to see grown men thrashing these tiny bikes around, all of them having a ball. For this level of racing, I wouldn't even need an ACU licence and the bikes were relatively cheap to buy. There were lots of kart circuits within easy reach and both bike and gear could be thrown in the back of a car. I also reasoned that if I fell off, there was not so far to fall.

I attended a number of mini bike race events with FAB Racing or British Minibike (BMB) championships, mostly at Lydd in Kent or Angmering in Sussex and was keen to go with this option but procrastination and lack of funds got in the way, so the idea withered on the vine. However much I talked about it, I was convinced that it wouldn't happen.

At a Bemsee meeting in 2015, someone suggested Minitwins; a series created ostensibly for the Suzuki SV650, so I asked around to get an idea of costs. Buying a race-ready bike was probably cheaper than converting a road bike (more of that later). Running costs were lower than many classes; the engine is bulletproof, road tyres were used and, because of the forgiving nature of the bike, it was a popular series for novices. The racing is still highly competitive and the Minitwin grid is often oversubscribed. Minitwins looked like a potentially affordable option.

"HOW much?"

Aside from my advancing age (and the associated recognition of both my mortality and lack of flexibility), my other major obstacle was being able to afford to race. This is probably the largest factor for anyone who considers racing but if I wanted to truly appreciate what all aspiring racers have to face, I had to start with a bike. Even at the lowest club level, motorsport is eye-wateringly expensive. You always need to improve yourself, the bike or probably both. All this comes at significant cost.

To get started, I had two options: I could buy a road bike and convert it, learning (a lot) about the bike as I went, or I could source a race-ready bike and just ride it. The best time to buy a bike is in the winter, as road bikes tend to get mothballed and race bikes are either retired or just stored until next season. Either way, they are generally cheaper to buy in the darker months so, if I waited until

October, there was likely to be a number of track or race bikes appearing.

Of course, from October until March I had no funds at all but eventually scraped together £800, which got me a perfectly good (and local) Generation 1, carburetted SV. I collected the bike using a borrowed trailer and put it in my garage.

Less than a week after buying it, another Gen 1 bike appeared. Ironically, this one was only a mile away from where I had bought the first bike but, unlike that first one, this had already undergone a lot of conversion: race bodywork, rear-set foot pegs, minimised wiring loom, aftermarket radiator, hefty brake calipers and a very trick race clock. The price? £1400.

I spoke to my new Minitwin friends through social media and all agreed that the work that had been carried out on the track bike were worth more than it would cost to convert a road bike. After a very generous conversation with my other half, she lent me the £1400, I bought the track bike and sold the original road bike to pay her back.

The first track sessions.

I had now blown all my money, so the bike sat in the garage. For my birthday in July, my other half Cheryl once again generously bought me a bike trailer, offered by a friend at silly money. In September, I booked my first track day at the Brands Hatch Indy circuit.

I'd like to say that the day was a resounding success, that the bike and I gelled immediately, that I found some hitherto unknown racing mojo and wiped the floor with everyone. Sadly, it was at the track that I discovered the first of what would be many issues with the new bike. Specifically, it would splutter on tight right bends. Every time I went out on track, at some point, the bike would refuse to play ball. My abilities also showed a woeful lack of talent. Still; that was the whole point of the day; to see what the bike and I were capable of. At this point, it wasn't much. However, I still had a great day.

It wasn't all negative. For a start, other than my first time around, Paddock Hill was not as terrifying as I had expected and I was enjoying taking the bike on track and wringing its neck. When I had booked this track day, the one thing I decided I had to have was instruction. I had done a couple of track days a few years ago where I had simply been left to get on with it, so there was nothing done that would help us actually learn the track. Instruction may have been available but my friends and I knew nothing about the process, so we had simply bimbled around. This time, I had a proper race bike and I wasn't going to waste the day. So, with the aim of learning to ride at pace, I paid my £25 and rolled up to Garage 1 for my post-lunchtime lesson.

My instructor Steve took me out for a couple of laps with him in the lead, showing me the racing lines. He waved me through and followed me for a few laps before passing and signalling me back into the garage.

"Generally, you're positioning is good," he started. "You're moving around freely and I see you have the balls of your feet on the pegs, which is great." So far, so good.

"Your positioning on the track is erratic, though. You're fine in some places but not so good in others. You were crap at Clearways but then Clearways catches lots of novices out. Is this your first time here?"

I told him that it was.

"OK, you can always improve your bike position but your biggest issue is that you're cruising. In racing, it's either full gas or full brakes; there is no in between and cruising is a big no-no. As you came out of Graham Hill, I saw you change up and thought, 'here we go' but then you changed back down when you got to Surtees. Do NOT do that. Keep it on the gas. Remember, the bike will take much more than you can give it.

"The Indy circuit is probably the best track in the country for an SV. It's short, with no long straights for the bike to run out of puff and you don't need to change gear often because the SV has so much torque. Tell me; were you being passed much?"

"There was an R1 and Fireblade that would both wipe me out on the start-finish line," I said.

"Yes, I've been watching those two. This is a novice-only day but they're on the ragged edge and have both had some very close calls. I wouldn't be surprised if either of them has their bikes swept up before the day's out.

"So, this afternoon I want you to build up that speed, hit more apexes and NO cruising. If you take on board what I've shown you, I guarantee that you'll be using fourth and fifth gear, maybe even sixth before the day is done and, if you do get overtaken, it'll only be once."

I doubted his confidence but, true to his word, that's exactly what happened. I did lap after lap and, as the final session ended, I realised that I'd not been passed since the third lap and I was doing those laps robotically, without thinking about it. It had been money very well spent.

There was still the issue with the bike's performance, though, especially the spluttering so, when I got home, I asked my online biking friends for advice. Much centred around the fuel outlet being on the left of the tank and me riding with a half-empty tank and the potential for fuel starvation. Something to bear in mind next time out.

Of course, funds ran out again so that was the only outing the bike had in 2016. I still wanted an ACU licence but knew that the bike had to work properly before I should consider troubling the grid. I saved what little money I could towards another track day. That didn't come until October 2017, again at the Brands Indy circuit.

This time I had booked two instruction sessions. The plan was to get one in the morning so I had something to work on and use the second session as a check up on what I'd learned, plus further pointers.

I met up with my instructor Mike and we had the same initial brief. We let the other riders go out and then set off from the pit lane and on to the track. Sadly, the SV played up from the off; so much so that, on my third lap, it died completely as I turned into Paddock Hill and I rolled gently onto the grass, leant the bike up on the Armco, jumped over and watched the rest of the session from the sidelines. Once recovered and back at the garage, I decided it would be best to call it quits, as I didn't want to risk breaking down again.

Sorting the bike.

Once in the garage, I phoned Steve Jordan Motorcycles. Steve specialises in bike tuning, mostly Suzukis and especially the SV650. Both he and his wife Sarah have competed successfully in Minitwins and have a reputation for excellence. Sarah offered to check my bike over for me if I could get it there, so I abandoned my second instruction session, loaded the bike and drove to Leatherhead.

Leaving the bike at Steve's with instructions to sort out the gremlins and fit emulators to the front forks while they had the bike, I went home, a little dejected. Still, the bike was in good hands. It just meant I would be postponing any more riding for another season.

("Emulators"? Put simply, these are devices that are fitted inside the otherwise non-adjustable front fork suspension and go a long way to improving the handling. I have a road SV as well as the track bike and, once I'd had the emulators fitted and the track bike set up for me, the road bike felt horrible. That'll be a purchase for another day, though.)

I got a phone call from Richard at the workshop telling me that he couldn't fit the emulators because the forks were bent. Terrific.

Motoliner in Maidstone could straighten them for about £150 but I said I would source alternative forks for now. Richard had fixed the stuttering though, which was mostly down to a butchered wiring loom; the first of a number of issues I would find with this "bargain" bike. He had stripped it back and removed all dodgy connections before taking out the ignition switch, rewiring the loom through the kill switch and connecting the race clock into the main loom (it had originally been powered by a PP9, 9-volt battery). There was a lot of work done to it (around £800 worth, actually) which used my entire 2017 budget and then some. This was proving far more expensive than I had anticipated and I hadn't even started racing. In hindsight and, based on what I'd spent, I'd have been better off waiting until the end of the season and buying a Minitwin-compliant bike. Still; there was always 2018.

Getting the racing licence.

2018 dawned. The bike was much better but I had no money for the Bemsee race school in February. Undeterred, I scraped enough together for the MSV/ACU assessment day at Brands in May. This would also be a new opportunity to test the newly fettled bike. The Friday before the event, I fired the bike up.

Nothing.

I took the battery out (a real pain in the neck, as it was located in a bespoke housing, tucked under the fairing) and charged it overnight. The next morning, I tried again and the bike roared into life. Fantastic. I switched it off, reassembled the bodywork and tried again, just for good measure.

Still nothing.

I couldn't believe it. I'd only pressed the starter button three times and the battery was dead again. A quick call to my local dealer had a replacement battery purchased and on the charger. I was really worried this time, as the assessment day was in a couple of days. I packed a set of jump leads and a charger, just in case. I needn't have worried as the bike performed flawlessly. Thanks to the work carried out by Steve Jordan's team, the bike had been completely transformed. My confidence was returning.

The assessment test was in the afternoon, so I set up in one of the three garages allocated for the ACU riders. We had our classroom session, which consisted of common-sense safety information and flag recognition. The instructor made a point of highlighting areas in the presentation that, in his words, **"WE WOULD HAVE TO KNOW"**, before handing out test papers.

The ACU test is designed to be easily passed. Nobody failed.

Once done, we took our bikes to the grid to perform a practice start. We were positioned in formation where we'd be sent off at pace. We would then come back to the grid for another start and single flying lap, after which the red flag would come out.

We lined up on the grid and set off, row by row. The aim was to make a fast pull away without stalling or crashing, the latter of which would mean an instant fail. I passed the test with no issues and, while not flawless, my race start was deemed good enough for me to get the licence. Or so I thought.

Let's go back to 2004, when I had what is called a transient ischemic attack (TIA); colloquially, a mini-stroke. I was referred to St Thomas' hospital in London, where the doctors found three holes in my heart and fitted an occluder (a miniature, double-ended umbrella) to close those holes off. Two weeks later, the hospital outpatient department discharged me with a clean bill of health, the surgeon telling me that, within a month, it would be as if nothing had happened and I could carry out a normal life and be as active as I wished. Since then, I had taken up cycling again and participated in two long bike rides; one from London to Brighton and one from London to Eastbourne.

Back to 2018, I filled in the ACU application form and sent it off to ACU headquarters in Rugby. A few days later, I got a letter saying the ACU cannot issue me a licence until I have a full GP medical, including complete MRI scans, to satisfy them that there was no risk of me having any heart-related episode. So began months of arguing that my surgeon had discharged me, all to no avail. My GP wanted £150 to perform the medical or, more accurately, he sent me a form and told me to fill it in, after which he would sign it and charge me £150.

That was it; I had come to the end of the road. Despondent, I contacted a Bemsee friend who put me in touch with one of the club's medical team. Dr Rosie played an absolute blinder, contacting the ACU after getting the relevant history from me and chasing them up regularly. She understood why a doctor with no racing experience might be reluctant to sign a health declaration form but, as a race doctor, she recognised that the risk was negligible or, at least no worse than it would be for anyone my age planning to scare themselves to death. The ACU agreed, so Dr Rosie performed the medical and my licence arrived in July. As one door closes…

Too late to start.

We were by now well into the year and, although I had just about enough money to pay for a single meeting entry, I decided not to enter the 2018 season. It was halfway through and Tracey Ringrow (Bemsee Secretary) pointed out that even the rookies would now be very fast, so starting in 2019 would be more sensible and I'd probably be better off getting in a few more track days. She was right, of course, so I booked another MSV day, this time at the Snetterton 300. I'd done three track days at Brands by now but needed to widen my experience. I knew I'd be embarrassed on the long straights but hoped the SV would perform well enough in the infield section.

The bike was brilliant, if slow compared to everyone else. There were a few Rossi wannabes, a couple of whom were on the Yamaha

R1 rental bikes. Conscious of my SV's lack of speed and my abilities, I kept a weather eye out for potential incidents but kept mostly out of trouble.

Snetterton was fabulous. As predicted, I looked stupid on the straights but those fast road bikes had one major disadvantage over me: brake lights. I would catch them at the Agostini hairpin, they'd lose me coming out but then brake at the 300m marker leading up to Hamilton. I would simply schmooze past, brake near the 100m marker and not see them again until they blasted past me on the Bentley straight. That whole exercise would be repeated at Brundle/Nelson and the Bomb Hole. I succeeded in pissing off some flash riders that day and I was elated; the bike was performing better than ever and my confidence was boosted no end. Again, double instruction sessions provided me with plenty of invaluable pointers.

In the meantime, it occurred to me that I needed more stuff. My aging leathers were not CE approved, which was a requirement from the 2018 season. In fact, all my riding gear needed replacing. I'd need a van, a generator and a gazebo, not to mention a serious upgrade of the cheap, monkey metal tools that I currently owned.

The bike needed a new radiator, as the one fitted was not Minitwin compliant. (Bemsee has subsequently relaxed this ruling. So long as the radiator is the same capacity, aftermarket units are now permissible). I also needed to fit a front brake guard. I had two front wheels, both of which had dings on the rims, so would they need sorting. The chain and sprockets had not been changed since I had owned the bike and I had no idea how long they'd been on. I bought a chain and sprocket set and a used radiator, with a view to fit them in the new year, ahead of the last track day I'd have at Brands before the start of the 2019 season.

I bought an old Ford Transit van and a generator (in time for the Snetterton trip), courtesy of a small tax windfall. I started as a self-employed contract engineer in 2018 and was able to buy a gazebo through my company. The helmet was bought at the last 2017 Bemsee race at Brands and gloves and boots the day before my

ACU assessment day. A racing friend sold me his spare, unused leathers for a song. Things were now falling into place.

I booked a dyno test at the last Bemsee meeting. Minitwins allow a maximum of 72 horsepower which, for a carby is generally achieved by adding cams from an injected SV650, re-jetting the carbs and fitting a full race exhaust system. I knew my bike was old and likely to be in the low 60s but was horrified when it came out at 59 HP. I never expected to bother the top end of the pack but it seemed the entire grid would be able to laugh at my asthmatic wheezer's expense. All that was likely to happen was that I would be getting in the way as everyone else lapped me. Some serious thinking and work was needed.

I renewed my Bemsee and ACU membership anyway (licences run from January to December). Cue the next obstacle. I got an email saying that I couldn't have the new licence until I submitted the results of a new eye test. I was not happy, as I'd had one in May, following my ACU assessment. Riders over 55 have to have an eye test every year. My existing test would expire before the end of the season, so it had to be renewed. Bugger.

A phone call resulted in an eye appointment in the middle of the optician's "full eye test for £10" period, so I didn't complain. My mother has glaucoma, so I am actually entitled to free eye tests but, because my last one had been less than 12 months previous, I had to pay for this one. Ironically, the UK Government has since changed the rules to allow only one free test every two years. Still, if I can get another £10 test, it won't matter.

2019: new year, new plan.

The bike had been sitting in the garage since October and had not been run at all. In the interim, I had replaced the front forks (from my road SV, which had rather inconveniently died) and had emulators fitted. I rolled the bike out one January weekend, pulled the choke out and pressed the button. The bike started on the third button press. The battery was still fine.

I was elated. Well, briefly. There was a lot of white smoke coming out the fairing. Initially, I thought it was smoky because it was on choke but, on closer inspection, I saw a pool of oil in the catch tray. I hit the kill switch, let the engine cool and looked inside. I could see drips that looked like they started at the top of the rear cylinder. There was no oil but there was petrol, so it looked like I also had leaking carburettors to deal with. This was not getting better. The last thing I needed was the bike catching alight while racing.

I took the bike over to my friend Steve Shrubshall's workshop. He did a compression test, which showed the front cylinder was holding 120 PSI and the back 80. Not good. Steve had a spare engine that ran which I could buy if I wanted. I agreed and we arranged for me to return later in the week so we could swap engines.

Steve phoned me the following day. He had been suspicious of the compression test so had retested my engine and found that his tester had been faulty. The second test showed both cylinders holding 130 PSI so the engine swap wasn't necessary. I'd still need to sort the oil leak (from the clutch cover, by the look of it) and service the carbs but that was considerably less of an issue.

The next few days were spent in Steve's workshop, dealing with the leaks and carrying out final little checks ahead of my next track day at Brands, booked for 16 February. With the knowledge that I might soon find myself among racers, I booked a place in the Intermediate group. Up until now, I had only ever run with the novices but, if I was to make any progress, I had to get out of that comfort zone.

All that would be left after that was to enter a race. At nearly 57, this was a significant bucket list item but I had set myself a very low bar to ensure some achievable goals:

1. Enter one race meeting.
2. Take part in at least one race. The SV650 is eligible for Minitwins and Thunderbike Sport but I reckoned four Minitwin races in a weekend would be more than enough for a first outing.
3. Complete at least one race.
4. Stay on board, i.e. don't crash.
5. Try not to finish last, although I wasn't really worried about that one.
6. Don't kill myself. I should probably have put this one a bit higher up.

I had no unrealistic ambitions for glory. My goal was to have had a go and to have had fun trying. This had already been an eventful journey, some forty years in the making and I'd hardly started. I was never going to be a major player but wanted to say I had taken part and properly, not just as a wannabe.

I'd had countless doubts, endless disappointments and obstacles to face, delays due to finances (mostly) or circumstances but through all this, both the bike and I had slowly improved and should at least be able to make an appearance. After this first foray, I would either have scared myself so much that I'd say, "Never again", run out of money or scare myself and say, "I want another go!"

I knew that if I pursued it further, I could spend a little more to get the bike competitive or sell it as a very good track bike and source another Minitwin. It had been ridiculously expensive already but the pleasure it had afforded me made it priceless. There is an itemised list of costs to date in the appendices.

In December 2018, I attended the Bemsee open day, where I was encouraged by the fantastic, friendly atmosphere that greeted me. I met Bemsee staff, retailers and the Minitwin reps, all of who provided plenty of invaluable information and support. Grant, the Minitwin rep, told me, "I've been doing this for eight years. It's expensive but I haven't regretted a single penny spent on racing; not even where the bike failed me and I sat the weekend out. It's the best thing I have ever done."

It's difficult to argue with such enthusiasm. All I had to do now was wait for the email inviting me to pay my first entry fee. That email arrived in the first week of February. I applied for my race number and paid my entry fee: £300 for the racing and an additional £85 for practice day. I was allocated racing number 20. All I had to do was wait until race weekend. Suddenly, it was becoming real.

I contacted Grant again who put me in touch with Kevin Lilley, a seasoned racer who was also my age. Kevin would be my paddock buddy at Brands, showing me the ropes, where to go and when. Bemsee operates a very good (and friendly) buddy system, so no one is left to fend for themselves. Even if you are alone, everyone else in your class is happy to help out, lend tools or parts to ensure you can get out on track. I cannot recommend the club highly enough.

In order to get as much information as I could, I joined a number of social media groups, where I was able to ask countless questions in preparation for getting to my first race. There still seemed so much to understand and to learn. I learned about even the little things, like having two 20 litre jerry cans, rather than the single one I had bought, plus a separate five litre can for the cheap fuel to be used in the generator or remembering to take pool shoes for the showers. Knowing when you could turn up (read the "Final Instructions" document sent by Bemsee is the advice there), so joining the group was certainly worthwhile.

Joining the social media groups also allowed me to contact members of the 2019 Bemsee Rookies group. This covered every class and I contacted other riders who were starting out in Minitwins for the first time. It was here that I "met" Matt Wetherell, Alan Hensby, Sam Kent and Dan Thomas. Of these guys, Sam lived a long way off but Matt and Alan were all within visiting distance.

Dan had also booked the February track day, so we agreed to meet at the circuit. I would be able to get there sooner, so I told him I'd try and keep a spot for him and his van. Although I had entered the intermediate group, Dan was a more seasoned track day rider and was in the advanced group. This would be great for both of us, as we could help one another out and provide feedback.

Dan and I hit it off from the start. He was quiet and humble in the garage but when I saw him out on track, I wondered where that speed demon had come from. I knew two things from that point; we were going to be good friends and I would never see him on the race track (except when he would inevitably lap me, of course).

Once again, I had booked instruction and once again, Steve was my instructor. I met him prior to starting my first session to tell him that it had been about six months since my last track day and that I was nervous about getting back on the circuit, although it was not my first visit there. Armed with that knowledge (although I didn't tell him about my racing aspirations), we went out on track.

After following Steve for a couple of laps, he waved me through and followed me for about five laps, passed me and we pulled into pit lane. Pulling up at garage 1, Steve removed his lid.

"Well, that wasn't bad. Despite you saying you were nervous, I'd say you were in the right group. You're too good for the novices but some of those advanced guys are really quick."

I told him about Dan who was riding a similar bike. I had marvelled at his pace but was comfortable with my pace and group.

"To be honest, you're not really doing much wrong. Your body position is good, I see you're using the gearbox fairly well, although you should still be able to get into sixth if you give it a go. You need to work on your corner speed, though. If you look at the tyres, there's a good fifteen millimetres of untouched rubber there. Believe me, the bike won't drop and WILL go that extra few degrees. You just need to have a bit more faith in yourself. We'll see how it improves this afternoon."

I returned for a few more sessions before having my last instruction period in the penultimate intermediate round. Steve seemed pleased that I seemed to have smoothed out and that my pace was marginally quicker now.

"OK, so you're more competent but what do you intend doing with the bike? It looks like a fully set up race bike, as far as I can see."

I told him, "I've entered the next Bemsee Minitwins race, here in March. That's why I joined the Inters, as I knew I needed to up my game. It was bloody terrifying at first but I began to get used to the idea of picking up the pace and don't feel anywhere near as scared now as I thought I might."

"That's fantastic," he said. You know, I've seen so many people of your age, what, mid-fifties, come to a track day and then do nothing about it. Has this been a long-term ambition?"

"About forty years, I guess. I've watched bike racing for years and helped some riders out and never thought I'd get to do it myself but I've paid my entry now, so I'm committed."

"Awesome. Well, wherever you end up on the day, you'll have done more than 99% of the armchair expert wannabes so, well done you."

Cue a big grin. Steve's enthusiasm was a great fillip to my confidence. Sure, I'd probably embarrass myself but he was right; I was actually going to have a go. Not at a track day, where I'd not really learn or prove anything but at a proper, genuine race meeting. Suddenly, it was all becoming real.

To add to the sense of expectation, Rod Harwin was at the circuit, selling his usual array of racing wares. He had offered free race numbers to any Bemsee rookie starting that season, so Dan and I both rolled up to collect a pair of numbers 34 and 20 respectively.

We spent the rest of the afternoon thrashing our bikes and passing comment on each other's' pace or style ("Man, you're quick into Surtees, Dan/You're really getting the hang of Graham Hill now, Steve") before helping each other pack the bikes away, as ready as we were going to be for that first meeting.

I looked back at a Facebook comment I'd posted around that time:

"I've been reading some lively banter on the Bemsee Rookie FB page this morning, as everyone psychs themselves up for the opening event in March. I am very nervous about "having a go" at racing but am still looking forward to it, I think. I've made so many friends through racing, at all levels and will for the first time, be with many of those friends not as a spectator but as a fellow (very green) racer which, for me, is unbelievable.

"Setting up in the paddock will be a real opportunity for me to live out a lifelong fantasy/ambition. Yes, I'm scared witless; I've spent a lifetime never really taking risks and this is likely to be my first real test of character. I am woefully unprepared and unfit but my friends wouldn't expect anything less from me, really. Brands Hatch will be a baptism of fire. I have the bike (also woefully uncompetitive), I have a racing number and I am just waiting for the email telling me I can send in my entry request.

"Of course, it being me, I have managed to make my life even harder. My other half and I run a wedding props supply business and yes, we are booked for a wedding on 10 March. The challenge will be being in Brands Hatch and in Battle at the same time, using only one van. So long as timetables are OK, we will sort it.

"I am immensely grateful to both my other half Cheryl and her brother Andy, who are helping me fulfil both commitments. It's important that I have my race head on and that I don't get distracted, as that could be disastrous. Cheryl and Andy are both great organisers (far better than me) and we have already had lots of discussion as to how everything can be sorted.

"I will be writing about all of this in detail before, during and after the weekend. Expect plenty of mishaps, disasters, mistakes, misery and euphoria."

...and so it started.

Part 2: Let's Go Racing!

Chapter 2:
Round 1: Brands Hatch Indy (Wrotham, Kent)

Thursday: Arrival.

My planning skills might at best be described as "disorganised", so today was going to be a challenge. I had taken time off work to load the van, so I could get to the circuit in plenty of time to set up. To complicate matters, I had other commitments to fulfil on Friday, which only left the afternoon to collect the caravan, get to the circuit and set up.

I arrived at about 3:45 to find the sheltered, back wall of the paddock already full, so set up in the main paddock area. This might not have been a problem but there was a gale blowing and setting up the gazebo became a real issue. It's sturdy, so I wasn't concerned about it collapsing but there's only so much you can do by yourself. Fortunately, with help from neighbours Jim, Grant and Kevin, we had the gazebo erected.

Mother Nature had plans for the weekend, with rain and wind forecast. No sooner was the gazebo erected than I had to use webbing storm straps to fix it to the van and caravan, which brought another challenge. I had initially intended to set up today and then go home, leaving the gazebo and caravan in the paddock. I would buy food on the way and bring it with me tomorrow morning but there was no way I was going to risk the wind blowing the gazebo away so it, the van and caravan were now as one. I was going nowhere.

Cheryl phoned me, wanting to know when I expected to be home. Once I told her about the wind problem, she told me to send her a shopping list and she would bring the stuff up to me. What a star.

I waited for her in the caravan, which was still swaying in the breeze (the wind had settled a little but it was still raining). I still had plenty to do before I was ready to race but it would have to wait until Friday. I would do the last-minute prep for the bike between my practice sessions.

I would have to up my game considerably if I intended to do another round. I wasn't miserable (yet) but this really hadn't been the start I had hoped for. With a bit of luck, once other riders arrived and had set up around me, I'd get a bit more shelter and the van and gazebo would become less mobile.

What HAD I taken on?

Friday: Practice Day

Despite the terrible weather that night, I managed to get some decent sleep but was still awake well before the 6:30 alarm. It was going to be busy, as we had to go through all the formalities before being let loose on the track for 9:00.

Kevin came over to my gazebo at 7:45. My spare wheels were already having wet weather tyres fitted and I'd had a shower. Before getting into what needed to be done, the talk started on the events of the previous day. There had been a track day running as the Bemsee riders arrived. We had been allowed to set up in the lower paddock, as the track day customers were using the garages. However, as one Bemsee rider was setting his gazebo up, someone had come along and hitched his trailer, loaded with a brand new R1 and Fireblade and driven off the site. No sooner had it been noticed, word went out and social media and Club Sport News (well done guys) put the word out. Some people complained about the lack of security but who was going to challenge someone riding out of a track day, towing track bikes? It had left a bad taste though and everyone was gutted.

The next morning, both bikes were found, completely undamaged and the owner would be racing after all. This was brilliant news and lifted the paddock mood considerably.

For Kevin and me, the first job was signing on, getting our stickers (one for the bike, one for the helmet) and making the bikes ready for first practice.

Before being allowed on track, there were two more jobs to be completed: getting the bike noise tested and fitting the race numbers on the bike's bodywork. The rules require one to be fitted to the nose of the fairing and one on either side of the seat tail unit. The marshals often comment that they can't see the tail numbers easily, so we are encouraged to apply them to the side of the fairing, too. Fortunately, when I couldn't sleep on the Wednesday night, I had made a set of numbers, which I could now fit to the bodywork.

Back at home, I couldn't find the yellow Gaffer tape I'd used for the number background, so needed to get some more. A&R, who had fitted the tyres, didn't have any yellow, so I would see if Rod Harwin had. However, I couldn't see his set up and presumed he would turn up later in the day.

Back in the gazebo, I was giving Kevin plenty of reasons for concern. The first issue was a big pool of oil in the belly pan.

"Got any paper roll?" he asked.

"Er, no." came the lame reply. Kevin grabbed a roll and, once we'd removed the belly pan, he laid paper inside to soak up the lake.

"The problem with the carby," said Kevin, "is that the clutch cover is plastic and has a tendency to warp. Try nipping it up a bit more to see if that sorts it."

Taking another look, he pointed out that the clutch cover and alternator cover had no casing protector. Not only that but neither the oil filter nor the oil filler cap had been lock-wired in place.

"Got a Jubilee clip?"

"No." (This was getting uncomfortable).

"Right; we'll get one sorted and I'll lock-wire it on."

I did at least have lock wire, so I didn't need Kevin to use his stuff this time around. As we were looking over the bike, Sam Kent, another rookie, bowled up.

"Have you guys got a fire extinguisher?" We both had.

"Bugger. I've just been challenged because I don't have one. I'll see if anyone has a spare or if I can set up with someone who does." Looking at my bike, he said, "Ooh; you can't have your transponder there anymore," pointing at my fork-mounted transponder cradle.

"Really? I checked with a Minitwin rider at the track day last month. His was in the same place."

"Nah; it has to be mounted on the frame now."

I went to the tool chest to locate a pair of scissors to cut the cable ties holding the cradle.

"No, I'll do that," offered Kevin. "You concentrate on sorting that clutch cover. One job at a time, otherwise they'll all be half-finished."

"As far as I was aware," I said, "they're not available for carbys. I know others have asked."

"They are now," he replied.

"Great. So; my weekend might be over before it's begun."
"Well, let's ask Mike Dommett (Bemsee CEO) for advice."

We walked over to the office to sign on and approached Mike.

"Hi Mike," said Kevin. "This is Steve. He's here starting out in his rookie year. Today is his first race weekend and he's riding Minitwins."

"Shitting yourself yet?" Mike offered, helpfully. I smiled meekly.

"Yeah, Steve's carby has no engine protectors and we're not sure if we can get any. Another guy is bringing some in but we'll not sure if they'll fit."

"Go and find Mark (Dent, Chief Tech). Let him know the score and see what he says. We'll make every effort to get everyone racing if we possibly can."

We left the office to find Mark Dent, stopping at Rod Harwin's stall to buy yellow gaffer tape to finish off my "number board" and a jubilee clip for the oil filter. We found Mark in the noise test area and Kevin highlighted the issue.

Mark said, "That's fine. There are so many riders who've not been able to source engine protectors, so you're not alone, Steve. We're making a note of all the bikes without and making sure they are fitted in time for the next round. Give me your bike number."

For me, that would be Cadwell Park; round 3. I would therefore have a bit of breathing space.

We made our way back to the paddock. Kevin recommended that I get to noise testing but to get kitted up first as, although I wasn't on until 9:45, time would pass before I knew it.

After donning the leathers, I pressed the starter button and was relieved to hear the bike start up on first press. After the problems I'd had at my last track day, where it had backfired continuously, I was worried about noise testing but took it up anyway.

Rolling up to Garage 34, I was told to set the revs to 5,500 and hold it there. There were a few pops but the marshal said I was well within the limit, even with the backfires. A noise test sticker was applied to the fairing and I rode back to the paddock. Another box ticked.

The weather was cold but dry and, while there were still damp spots, by the time I was due to go out, there would at least be a dry line so, after discussion with Kevin, I decided to stick with the dry tyres. I picked up my wets on wheels (and a roll of blue paper tissue, while I was at it) and dropped them into the back of the van.

The bike now had its blue "I'm allowed on track" and green "I'm not too noisy" stickers applied. I put the bike on its paddock stands; my rear stand and a headstock stand for the front, borrowed off Kevin (naturally), as the front stand I had didn't suit the forks. I owned a headstock stand but needed to get a new pin fitted as none of those supplied with it were suitable for my bike, either.

"Don't forget your numbers, Steve," called Kevin from across the road. "They won't let you on track without them!"

I had time, so offered the number to the front of the fairing. There wasn't enough yellow to make a full border, so I added more gaffer tape and then the number.

I went to the van to get the numbers I'd cut the day before. Bugger - four zeros but only three twos. Where the hell was the fourth? I knew I'd put them in the van but decided to just fit them to the side of the fairing, as per the marshals' preference. Applying more yellow gaffer tape to create the background, the numbers went on. I finally located the missing number and set about making the tail yellow, too. As the first 20 went on, so did the first call for the blue group, which I was in. I couldn't leave the bike with a number only on one side, so continued working. I got the last one on just as the third (and final) call went out.

I grabbed my helmet and gloves, removed the tyre warmers and took the bike off its stands. It's a delicate balancing operation trying to hold the bike, move the stand out of the way and getting on without dropping it but I was on board and on my way to the pit lane tunnel and onto pit lane.

We were ushered out almost immediately but, as I joined the track, I realised that I'd not put my orange rookie bib on. I didn't want to lose the session; going to my gazebo, fitting the bib and coming back would have cost me valuable track time. I decided to risk it and, as it turned out, got away with it.

Holy cow but those guys were FAST. I had been surprised when I went on my first intermediate track day session but this was on another scale. The Minitwins were out at the same time as the 600s and Thunderbikes (which included a number of Honda Fireblades and Ducati Panigales). I was definitely the slowest of the slowest group. The first session passed without incident though, although I had a number of overcooking moments that had woken me up. However, I made a point of finding a line that I was comfortable with; one that also allowed others to pass safely.

In racing, it's the responsibility of the passing rider to do so safely, not of the overtakee to let them do so. "If you can't pass safely, wait until the opportunity arises and THEN pass" is the rule. Suffice to say I was passed a LOT of times but I didn't care. I was learning shed-loads and was circulating among some seriously quick riders, watching their lines and body positions to determine how best to get around.

I soon learned to follow lines taken by instructors as they passed and realised I must have been going way faster than I'd ever taken the bike before. I only hit the rev limiter once, mind; on the Brabham Straight. Other than that, my progress must have looked positively pedestrian.

An incident at Clearways brought the red flags out. As I rounded Graham Hill bend, I was directed to leave the track via the midway exit gate, rather than return to pit lane.

Back in the paddock, after getting the bike on the stands, I could see another pool of oil. Now I was worried. Once again, the fairing lower came off and I used more paper to soak up the oil. I nipped the cover up a little tighter but also the engine casing that it was bolted to, as I also noticed a minor weep there. The fairing went back on and then the tyre warmers. The leak looked to have been sorted for now, so I could relax.

Not too much though as, taking Kevin's advice, I tidied everything up. Tools went in the tool chest and any detritus (used gaffer tape, lock wire and cable ties) all went into the rubbish bag. "A tidy space is a safe space". I threaded some twine through the paper roll, hanging it up in the roof space of the gazebo.

Session Two came and again, there were no major incidents for me. An R1 took a trip into the gravel at Clearways, the final corner, bringing out the yellow flag (no overtaking) and then the yellow and red flag (low adhesion) as marshals realised there was gravel on the track where the rider had pitched off. I completed the session without being completely terrified (at least not all the time) and completed another incident-free fifteen minutes on track. I rode back to the paddock where a check on the engine seemed to indicate no more oil escaping.

It occurred to me that I'd not eaten but I was running short of time before my final track session of the morning. I could grab something to eat once that was over. While thinking about food, Jim from next door popped his head in." Everything all right?"
"Seems to be. I had an oil leak but it looks sorted now."

Jim owned a wealth of carby spares. He would make a list and was willing to bring anything up to my next round if I was interested. I was indeed, so said I'd give him a shout nearer the time.

By now, an old friend, Martin Cross, had turned up to spectate before going to work. I suggested he watched from Paddock Hill. It was a short walk and he'd see most of the circuit from there.

Sure enough, the call came for Blue Group, Session Three. I was out by the first call this time and made my way to join the queue of bikes waiting to go out. An official approached and asked, "Are you aware of the red flag, end of race ruling? Is there a reason you went off the track at pit lane entrance?"

"In the first session, I had been directed to leave the circuit early," I said. "Last time, when the flag went up, I pointed to the first gate and, when the marshal didn't react, I assumed I should get off there, as I was so far behind everyone else."

"Ah. No, you only need to leave at a non-standard point if a marshal directs you to do so. In the first session, a rider was down before the pit entrance which is why you were sent off early. Last time, the red flags only came out to signify the end of the session. We'd only expect you to come off early if you'd got a problem. Otherwise, next time, all the way round to the Clearways exit point. It's your track and your money. Make the most of it."

A schoolboy error on my part but it was another lesson learned. I don't know why I did it, as that ruling was no different to what happens at a track day. Still; it would be remembered this time.

I went out again but struggled and couldn't get my head in the right place. However, I did become aware of what might be considered the equivalent of what golfers call "hitting the sweet spot", when they catch the ball in the exact point of the club to make it take the best possible trajectory. When you complete a lap and realise you hit all the apexes as you expected, it feels fantastic. Sure, I wasn't fast (although I was convinced that I was improving) but just completing a couple of perfect (for me) laps was brilliant.

I did get a bit ahead of myself, though, with three incidents in this third session. First, I went into Paddock Hill too hot and the bike drifted further left than I had planned, which had me heading for the gravel. I managed to get myself together but what I wasn't aware of was a Panigale homing in on me and he ended up on the kerb, with me very nearly on them too. His gesticulations made it clear that he was not happy but, talking to the guys afterwards, I was told, "It's the first round and you have a bib on. He should have made allowances. Don't worry about it. It's done now and you can't do anything more about it, so just concentrate on your next session."

The second incident was also at Paddock, where I missed a gear and temporarily forgot that I had a race shift set up (1 up, 5 down) and, instead of kicking down, I tucked my boot under the gear lever and clicked up. The bike reacted instantly, putting me into a slide that had me looking at the inside of the track rather than along it. I started down Paddock Hill without actually steering, having just slid into the right direction. I gently closed the throttle and tootled slowly down Hailwood Hill before taking a deep breath, regrouping and getting around Druids in a better position.

The third and final issue involved forgetting gear positions again, with me already being in too low a gear, clicking up and locking the back wheel briefly as I approached Druids. I quickly pulled the clutch in, went back into third gear and continued on my way.

That last session had taught me a lot; not least where my limits were. I was still not leaning over enough but the one thing I realised was how often I had stopped breathing. I found myself "in the zone" so often that it took a moment on track for me to take a sudden breath in; something I would need to keep an eye on.

Session Three would be my last, as I had to get back home that afternoon. That meant missing scrutineering. Kevin offered to take the bike for me, so long as I signed my tech inspection card and left it on the bike before I left.

With the bike back on stands (and the tech card stuck under the screen), I drove home to fulfil a previous commitment before returning to the circuit around 6:30. This also meant missing the track walk but I'd make a point of doing that the next time I came to Brands.

"Next time"? I'd not even done a race and I was already thinking I might keep this up at least for a couple more rounds. I had already set myself that low bar and, at my age, I am conscious that I am unlikely to bounce as well as I once might have. I wasn't in this to win a title; I was aware of my limitations and just wanted to get the experience, enter as many rounds as I could afford and hopefully become a better racer in the process.

The Bemsee Paddock Buddy system is a major boon here. Without Kevin's remarkable patience and guidance, I'd simply be a lost soul, wobbling dangerously around the track and being clueless in the paddock. It also meant that, when I did return, the completed (and approved) scrutineering card had been signed. Kevin had been an utter star.

I was absolutely knackered and ached all over but on Saturday, everything would go into hyperdrive. Before all that, I'd need to get my riding gear checked by Scrutineering. After that, it would be qualifying (I was expecting "dead last but finished") and then a brief pause before the first race at 11:50. Cheryl would be coming to watch, so I'd have my first proper audience in my first proper race. I needed to sleep but I was still buzzing and I hadn't even started.

Saturday: RACE DAY!

So, the years of, "Will I/won't I?" had finally come to an end. I was going to take part in my very first, genuine motorcycle race. If being nervous about the whole prospect wasn't bad enough, the forecast was grim and meant that, on top of everything else, I might have to try riding on wet weather tyres for the first time.

Before I could get to that, I had to get my riding gear checked by scrutineering. Thanks to my lack of exercise and poor diet choices, the leather suit was, shall we say, a little snug. Still, after some assistance from Kevin's wife Jo, who rammed my back protector down when I zipped up the suit, I could finally walk to scrutineering, even if breathing was a challenge.

The gear passed muster with no issues. A sticker was applied to my crash helmet and my yellow tech card was signed off. Tick one box for no dramas.

Discussing with people in adjacent paddocks, the general mood was that rain was imminent. The track was still damp in many places, so wets would be the order of the day. I asked Kevin if he'd lend me his headstock stand again but he had needed it because he now had both his wet and dry set up bikes prepared with tyre warmers fitted so he needed both front stands.

I walked to the A&R Racing truck. All their stands had been sold. Rod Harwin was set up by the garages, quite a distance from my paddock space, so I borrowed Kevin's bicycle (I owed that man a lot of beers) and cycled up the long, steep hill to the pit lane tunnel. Without realising it, I was exposing myself to lots of unplanned exercise. That cycle ride took forever and, while Rod didn't have a headstock stand, he did have an alternative one on offer. I needed to make sure it fitted, so cycled back, measured the distance between the centres of the SV's forks, popped the tape measure into my leathers and cycled back once more.

The stand was suitable (more on this later), so I draped it over the handlebars for the final ride back to the paddock. I hitched the front wheel up onto the stand; a careful balancing job. The stand was very narrow and I didn't want to risk the front end falling off if the wheel was out.

While I had a set of wheels with wets fitted, the back wheel had a disc brake but no cush rubbers and the front had no discs. Swapping discs was going to take some time, so I decided to deal with that before fitting the wet rear, which would be simpler. If you're going to race, it really pays to have everything properly prepared. This includes two complete sets of wheels; one pair with dry weather tyres, one with wets.

There's something wonderful about the Bemsee paddock because, just as I was looking at the required job to sort the front wheel, Barry Mantell, who had set up behind me offered me his spare front wheel, complete with discs. I was genuinely gobsmacked to receive such an offer and, with time pressing, I accepted gladly.

I'd only ever taken the front wheel off this bike once and that was in Steve Shrubsall's workshop, so hadn't needed any of my tools. Today, however, I was missing a 12mm hexagonal tool to remove the wheel spindle. Barry did, though. His young spanner man Doug helped me get the front wheel off and we swapped it with Barry's wet-shod one.

Getting that wet wheel fitted was an issue, though. The pins in the paddock stand were too long and stopped the spindle getting back in. Doug held the bike while I added some washers to the stand pins to give clearance for the spindle and we were back in business. With the front wheel fitted, another hurdle had been overcome thanks to the kindness of strangers.

The back wheel came out easily. I fitted cush rubbers into the wet wheel, ready to reassemble the rear end but could I get the spindle back in? Of course not. Everything seemed to be misaligned. I called Kevin over but no amount of cajoling, swearing and brute force would move it. In fact, by now it was jammed solid, supporting only 25% of the wheel but refusing now to go in or out.

The call came to get to the collecting area for qualifying, so Kevin had to go. Without qualifying, I was convinced that my weekend was over before it had begun. Things were looking bleak. Barry also had to go but Doug stayed as we tried to get the spindle moving. After a couple of minutes, Jim appeared.

"You not going out, Steve?"

"I want to but we can't get the back wheel sorted." I was calm now, beyond panic because I knew that worrying about the qualifying wasn't going to help. With no back wheel, I couldn't even get the bike back into the van. All I could do was try to overcome this new hurdle and see if I had any options afterwards.

Using a mallet and an extension bar as a drift, we finally got the errant spindle out. There was no apparent damage, so it was treated to a soaking in WD40 and an Emery cloth (a fine-grade abrasive cotton-backed sheet) to polish it up. While the rear end was clear and accessible, I cleaned out the years of grime in the inner faces of the swinging arm, leaving Doug to polish up the other fittings.

"The biggest difference between race bike and road bikes," said Jim, "is that race bikes tend to be pristine, especially the wheels because they come off at every race meeting. Being clean also lets you see if there are any problems"

While my bike was definitely not pristine, it was now looking a lot better. We tried a dry fit of everything before reassembling it with no problems. I now had a bike set up with wets, ready to roll and face up to Mother Nature's soaking.

The sun came out and I watched as the steam began to rise from the tarmac.

Jim looked at the track and outside the gazebo. He smiled, recognising my frustration. Had I not changed those tyres, I would have been out for qualifying. "If you go out on wets now, you'll destroy them. For Brands, if it's dry in front of your pit space, it'll be dry on track. Even if the track is a little damp at first, by the time everyone has done warm up, a dry line will have formed and before you know it, it's all dry. Let's get those dry wheels back on."

Returning the bike to its dry set up was much faster. I knew what to do now and everything was clean, so fitted quickly. With Doug's continued help and advice, the wheels were changed in five minutes. Once again, I was saved thanks to a combined effort of other people in the racing family.

Kevin returned from qualifying. I told him what had happened and how everyone had helped get it back in place. He told me to go to the control office to ask for advice about my lack of qualifying.

Borrowing his bicycle again, I rode to the office and spoke to Tracey, the club secretary. As soon as I said that I'd missed qualifying, she said, "Steve Male?" I was the only one who'd not made it. "Have a word with the Clerk of the Course, Tony MacBride. He's up on the first floor."
I found Tony and told him what had happened and if that was it and my weekend was over.

"Absolutely not. We want to make sure everyone gets their chance on track. Missing qualifying only means that you'll start from the back of the grid but you need to get your practice in. Let's have a look. You're in Minitwins, right? Let's see what's still to run. Ah, here we are. Get yourself into the Thunderbike Sport session. That's the closest group to yours that's not been out yet. Speak to Mike (Dommett, Bemsee CEO) and we'll have you out there."

I could see why people speak so highly of this club. The officials run a very good series and really look after the riders, which allows even rank amateurs like me to have their day in the sun.

I relaxed a little and made sure everything else was in place. Doug and I pumped the front brake to get it biting again, having pushed the caliper pistons back to refit them when we put the front wheel back in. When Doug pumped the rear brake pedal though, nothing happened. It's rare for anyone to use the rear brake when racing but you'd like to know it's at least operational in case you do need it. Barry came in and said, "Take the cap off the breather pipe and pump it again."

Sure enough, when Doug removed the cap and pressed the pedal a couple of times, the fluid level dropped and we had a working back brake again. I fitted the tyre warmers and waited for the call for the Thunderbike Sport practice.

Practice was rather like a track day session. I had standard tyres on and the track was now dry. The fifteen minutes passed without incident. I watched to see where passing riders went and replicated their lines as best I could. The bike was running all right in the main but every once in a while, I found myself riding a bike with a gearbox full of neutrals. Whenever that happened, I would invariably not know what gear I was in and so coasted until a suitable one presented itself and I could get going again.

There was still about 45 minutes to go before I was due on track, so I rode to the main gate to hand over a couple of tickets; one for Cheryl and one for my friend Mike Wake, who was coming down for the day. Once I got to the gate, the woman in the kiosk said,

"Nah; you need to go to the lower paddock entrance. They keep all the tickets." So; after another long ride back, I handed the tickets to the staff in the paddock gate shed.

Race 1
(Row 13, grid 39)

"Attention Paddock. First call for MRO Minitwins and Rookie Minitwins. Please make your way to the collection area. That's first call, Minitwins and Rookie Minitwins."

This was it. I fitted some earplugs, put on the helmet and gloves before whipping off the tyre warmers and the stands. I'd fired the engine up ten minutes before, so it was well up to temperature now.

I rode out of the paddock, through the pit lane tunnel and up to the collecting area. One marshal was holding a sign that read "Rain lights ON", so I leaned back and flicked the switch to turn on my rear red light. Maybe we were still due some rain. I hoped not as, like the rest of the grid, I didn't have wet tyres fitted now.

The marshal tested the bike transponder for a signal (all good) and checked my number.

"Row 13, number 39, please."

I looked ahead and saw signs for positions 1-30, so waited behind them. As we moved off, I became aware of a second group of waiting riders; positions 31-39. Oops. I let everyone roll out and followed behind.

I saw a chalk mark on the tarmac that read "Row 13", so stopped with the front wheel on the line. It was a long way from the start/finish line. So far back, in fact, that I could barely make out the start lights. Martin Tomkins, riding the only Ducati on the grid, pulled up next to me.

"What's your grid position?" he asked.
 "39'" I replied. "I was told row 13."

It was only when seeing the massive gap to the next row that we realised our error. On the left of the start/finish straight were a number of tiny marker flags that read from 1 to 13. THOSE were the grid places, so we rolled up and took our correct places. I was still very green but was learning all the time.

The marshal lifted his flag, pointing to the lights as he stepped away from the track. The lights went out and we were off on the warm up lap. I believed that there would be no overtaking in warm up, so kept my position as we made our way round and back to the grid. I waited, holding the bike in first gear, staring intently at the lights.

I told myself, "Lights on, wait. Lights off, GO!"

The bank of lights illuminated and then went out.

We were off! I was riding among some racing gods and trying to keep my head together. Martin had got a bad start, so I got ahead of him until he regrouped and we peeled into Paddock Hill together. The combination of asthmatic bike and terrified rider meant that I wasn't ahead of him for long. Still, I just concentrated on what I was doing; talking myself through each section to build confidence and get round in one piece, still breathing. Having missed qualifying, I knew that gaining ground would be difficult at best so, once the rest of the grid had disappeared into the distance, I set myself the goal of trying to maintain constant race lines.

I'd love to report that everything clicked, that I roared around the track, picking off riders as I worked my way through the field. I'd love to report that but we know that wouldn't be the case. I was angry about missing qualifying but reminded myself that I was at least out there, even if it was 39th of 39 racers.

It was three laps before the first wave lapped me and boy, did they fly past. I was assaulted from both sides but kept to the maxim that it is the following rider's responsibility to pass safely, not mine to get out of the way.

It was terrifying. My lines were all over the place and there were times that I just wanted it to end but I got through the nine laps (because I had been lapped, I got to see the chequered flag one lap early) without crashing and without causing anyone else to crash.

By the time I returned to my paddock space, Cheryl had turned up at Scratchers Lane, so I walked up to the shed to get her ticket. Mike Wake knocked on the caravan door a little later and, over bacon sarnies and coffee, we discussed how well or otherwise I had done. It would be a while before I was next out so I went to the race office to get my results sheet and the programme that I should have picked up when I signed in.

The results sheet didn't make for good reading. Aside from coming home last, my best lap was 1 minute and 15 seconds; utterly woeful but I was pragmatic. Both bike and rider had survived and I had completed a race without crashing. I was knackered and felt like I had gone 10 rounds with Mike Tyson.

Let's put a positive spin on this first race. I had finished 36th but I had at least completed the race. Three riders didn't, crashing out before the end.

Race 2
(Row 12, Grid 36)

Lunch came and went and, at 3:00, it was time to go out again. Cheryl helped me get the leathers on before I went out to warm the bike up.

"Attention Paddock. First call for race 12, MRO Minitwins and Rookie Minitwins. Please make your way to the collecting area."

Mike took the tyre warmers off and removed the rear paddock stand once I'd mounted the bike. Meanwhile, Cheryl videoed the moment for me to watch when I got back.

In the collecting area, I knew where I needed to be this and stopped the bike in the correct place before we rolled out onto the circuit. After the initial warm up lap, we lined up to watch the lights. It felt odd not being at the back but I concentrated on those lights.

The lights went out and we shot off. This time, my start was better and, although a couple of the Race 1 fallers passed me before the first corner, I wasn't dead last. I maintained my third-from-last position for about three laps this time, so was feeling much better in myself. The fast boys didn't pass me until lap four, so I had improved on the first race already.

The reason for the improvement? Mike had provided pointers for lines and apex positions and I felt this second session was going much better. I had also taken the advice of local rider Carl Bell who had told me, "if you get passed, try to keep up with the overtaking rider at least to the next corner if at all possible. You'll find yourself being dragged forward and making progress before you know it."

I did try to do that, honestly I did but my bike's terrible power disadvantage, coupled with my lack of confidence, made it more difficult than I care to admit.

Come lap three, I was barrelling along the McLaren straight when I hit a false neutral again. I pulled the clutch in quickly and coasted round Paddock Hill until I found a gear. Too high a gear, as it turned out, so I had to go back down the gearbox, by which time the two riders behind me were able to pass, leaving me dead last again.

Returning to the paddock, Cheryl was beaming, really proud of me. Mike said I looked more relaxed and that, while I was still not hitting the apexes every time, it was already better.

I had still come last and my lap times were still laughable but I had taken three seconds off my previous best time. My goal was now to get below 1 minute and 10 seconds if at all possible. However, the rain had returned. If it was still raining tomorrow, all bets would be off.

I had completed two races and, despite feeling wiped out, I was buzzing. It could have been so much worse had I not had the help from others in the paddock. Knowing Cheryl was there to witness my second race was brilliant, too. I didn't want to look for her although I gave a cursory look across at Hailwood Hill on the warm down lap, where I knew she was watching with Mike.

I chatted briefly with Kevin who was pleased that I had enjoyed it and that I'd managed to improve the time in the second race. He did say that I needed to work on my body position, though as I had spent far too long sitting upright, rather than tucking in under the screen. Again, I had something new to work on.

Tomorrow, I would be going through it all again. Thanks to everyone in the paddock, I survived my first day. Thanks to Cheryl, I had been able to eat and, more specifically, I had been able to fulfil this lifetime's ambition. It had been a grand weekend so far.

Sunday: Races 3 & 4.

I was exhausted from yesterday's activities. I had been walking, running or cycling around the paddock all day, with little time to actually stop until the final race was over. Even then, there had been jobs to be done in preparation for today. The weather was still not looking promising, which was going to mean an early start again, so I could get my wet setup ready.

I was awake by 6:00, looked out the window and groaned when I saw leaden skies and steady drizzle. Still, it had been forecast, so I got up and walked to the showers. I even managed to get a shave, something I'd not done for four days. I hate being scrubby but had been a little preoccupied these last couple of days.

I got to work on swapping the wheels. As I had no spare discs for the front, I started there, removing the discs and fitting them onto the wet wheel. I was getting quicker at wheel changing and had learned the need to be organised. A common recommendation from riders is to reserve the top drawer of your toolbox or tool chest for stuff used in wheel changing. For an SV, that's two socket wrenches (one with a 22mm socket, the other with a 17mm socket), a 12mm hex head socket, 5mm and 6mm Allen keys, a tyre pressure gauge, a block of wood (to support the rear wheel in line with the swinging arm) and a rubber mallet. What I would also need in the future was two complete sets of wheels, both with discs and a set of cush drive rubbers so I didn't have to swap them. It's possible to cut some corners, of course but having what you need, ready to hand makes for a much easier life. Like everything, preparation and readiness were the keys.

Getting the rear wheel off was so much easier after it had all been sorted by Jim and Doug, to whom I shall remain forever grateful. I removed the rear wheel and fitted the rubber cush drive pieces to the wet one.

Getting the rear back in is a delicate balancing operation without a support block under the wheel; something I would have to make for future use. It would also be worth having captive spacers, rather than the loose ones that come with the bike. Still; the wheels were on and the bike was now ready for a wet race.

The sun came out. I couldn't believe it but left the wets on for the moment, as there were still lots of black cloud on the horizon.

A wet track would offer me the opportunity to try out wet tyres for the first time, so I looked at my watch to work out if I had enough time to get to the race office for a practice pass. The wind was getting stronger, so the race office announced a delay in proceedings, pending a track test by the officials.

It would be tight but I went to see Tracey (club secretary) anyway. She told me I'd not signed on, nor had I handed my tech card in. When Kevin had taken my bike to scrutineering, I had my gear checked and got the final signature but had not have taken the card to the office, which is why I never received a programme. I had technically raced illegally yesterday. Tracey was very good about it, telling me that I wasn't the first rookie to have done this and certainly wouldn't be the last. I went back to my pit space, grabbed the card and Kevin's bike to cycle back to the office, where I exchanged my tech card for a programme.

I didn't bother with a practice card now; there wasn't enough time. Once I'd returned, the sun was out in force and so the dry tyres would have to go back on. However, I had returned Barry's 12mm hex tool so had nothing to get the front wheel off. I put out a request, asking if anyone had a tool I could borrow or buy. Fellow rookie Vanessa Gillam's husband Mark was spannering for her and offered me one, telling me to keep it until the last race, in case I needed to do another swap. Yet more evidence of the friendliness that is the paddock. I refitted the dry wheels. If it did rain, I would simply sit it out.

Race 3
(Row 13, Grid 38)

The weather-imposed delay meant that all races were to be reduced from 12 to 10 laps, to give everyone a chance to race.

The bike was fuelled and we were ready to go. The first call went out and, as I got ready, a man offered to remove the tyre warmers and stands for me. I accepted gladly and apologise for not remembering your name, sir. I left the gazebo at second call and I was guided to row 13, grid position 38 in the collecting area.

It was windy but not so much that it affected the bikes. Our warm up completed, we waited for the red lights to go out. Once we set off, those fast crashers behind me on the grid charged past before I even got to Paddock Hill. There was only Vanessa (Gillam) behind me now but she got under me at Druids, gradually creating a gap through Graham Hill and Surtees. I plugged away, keeping (hopefully) better lines and, when I was inevitably lapped (after only two laps), I just tried to keep up, in the hope of at least bringing down some lap times.

On lap 3, I realised I had no transponder fitted. I was gutted and angry but thought there was no point in continuing as nothing will be recorded. Getting back to the paddock in a very dejected mood, Carl Bell approached me to ask if it went all right. I told him what I'd done and he said, "No, you'd have been all right. When they realise you've not got a transponder, they do a manual time. It might not be as accurate but at least you'll have got some times in."

I was gutted on track but I was devastated now. I didn't know what my lap times were but it had all felt so much better this time. Still; there was no point in worrying about it now. So long as the weather held, there was still Race 4. I fitted the transponder and left the bike to rest with its tyre warmers on.

By the end of the race, the wind had really got up. I looked across to Kevin's pit space to see him, Jo and a bunch of people desperately holding on to their gazebo as Kevin tried to dismantle it, while fighting its attempt to impersonate a kite. I went over and about eight of us held it down, unclipped the storm ties and gently tried to close the framework.

We failed because, as another gust caught the roof fabric, it ripped a gash the full length of one side. In our haste to close it up, one of the legs buckled. Kevin was remarkably relaxed about it and dumped the whole unit into a skip.

My gazebo had fared better. Perhaps not having the sidewalls had been an advantage. However, the frame was moving around a lot so, while Kevin's friends were still about, we repeated the exercise. Aside from a minor twist to one of the connecting pieces (which was simple to remove, straighten and refit once I got home), it came off mostly unscathed.

The weekend had been more educational than I could ever have imagined. I was impressed not just with the way that Bemsee runs an event but also the way in which everyone chipped in to help or to provide gear, advice or encouragement. My gazebo event had been one such example. The paddock atmosphere is brilliant and, despite the intense rivalry on the track, in the paddock or in the Kentagon restaurant, it's back-slapping, drink buying and piss-taking all round.

As far as rivalry on track is concerned, even at my humble "dead last but finished" position, I hadn't made it easy for people to pass. OK, so ultimately I had failed but I would look up the track to see where people were (exiting Druids was normally the best place, as I saw them approaching Paddock Hill), prepared myself for the inevitable but held my line.

Of course, that wouldn't always be the racing line; I was still missing apexes but even that was improving, as I took on the advice of one of the Bemsee instructors; "Keep talking to yourself. Out loud. If you're talking, you're breathing, which is also important. It takes about a minute to do a lap of the Indy. You could hold your breath for that long, so talk. Tell yourself where the line is and talk your way through it. If the guys pass you, tell yourself to follow them for at least corner to drag you through. But keep talking."

I learned early on that, when a group comes up and rider A passes you on the left, it was likely that rider B would pass on the right, simply because rider A already had the other line. You also learn that, with perhaps the exception of the top riders, everyone has their own line and no one line works for everybody.

The Brands Hatch Indy circuit is short (just over one mile) but is perfect for learning to race. From the start line, getting over to the left as soon as possible lets you swing to the right side of the track where the solid white pit lane line ends, into Paddock Hill bend. Clipping the kerb almost three-quarters of the way round the corner, you drop down the stomach-lifting Hailwood Hill, then up to the tight, right-hand Druids Corner hairpin.

If you're good, you can hug the inside of the corner, forcing everyone to take the long way round. Many riders (yours truly included) go out to the left two-thirds of the track, cut the right side of the corner (so long as there's not another rider there) and lift the bike to swing out to the left as they start down the hill.

About halfway down, you need to cross over to the right, to hit the outer apex on Graham Hill/Bottom Bend, the first of only two left-hand corners. It looks easy but Brands is great at biting unwary riders. If you don't get it right (and you'll be going VERY fast at this point), you'll be riding along the kerbstones on the right side of the Cooper straight or worse, on the grass. If that happens, stay on it and stay upright until the kerb ends before getting back on the track, especially if it's wet.

Assuming you've made it safely onto the Cooper Straight, you will next encounter the Surtees/McLaren chicane. Surtees is a left-hand but you need to straighten the line into the right-hand McLaren bend, allowing the reverse camber of Clearways (horrifically scary as the bike slides sideways if you get the power on too early) to make you drift over to the left, leaning further over as you cut back across Clarke Curve to get back over to the right side of the track just at the marshal hut, lifting the bike, changing up the gears and wringing the neck of the bike onto the Brabham Straight towards the finish line. All I needed to do was follow my own advice but it was getting there.

Back in the paddock, I fuelled the bike (word of advice: buy a 5 litre measuring jug) and gave the bike a once-over to make sure nothing had come loose. All seemed in order, so I went into the caravan to get something to eat.

How hungry and thirsty does adrenaline make you? Very, it would seem. I heated up one of the ready meals that Andy and Cheryl had brought over and drank what felt like half a gallon of elderflower cordial. Sitting in the caravan, contemplating the disaster of the morning and reminding myself to forget it, move on and concentrate on the last race, I heard a tapping on the roof of the caravan. Looking out of the window, I saw... hail. Fantastic.

Race 4
(Row 11, Grid 31)

The announcement came over the Tannoy. "Attention paddock. We're going to give the weather a little while to see what it wants to do, so if everyone can hold station for the moment, we'll announce the next race when we feel it's safe."

I heard Barry fire his bike up behind my caravan and saw him get his gear on. He was riding in Thunderbike Extreme and Minitwins (so he must have been absolutely drained by the end of the weekend). I checked the tyre warmers. They weren't doing much other than fighting a losing battle against the cold, biting wind. Starting my bike, I got the crash helmet and gloves from the caravan and looked across to Kevin's space. His bikes (he'd got one bike for dry and another for wet conditions) were still sitting silently across the way. I looked back at Barry to see him ride off on his Honda Fireblade.

I had got a bit ahead of myself. As Barry rode up the paddock for race 11, his friends had come over to do the last-minute preparation on his Minitwin, which he would then use in race 12; my race. That time came very quickly and the first call came. I put my helmet and gloves on and waited for the second call, whipped the warmers off, took the front stand away and balanced the bike as I pulled the rear stand away. It's times like this that the benefit of having someone with you really counts. I'm used to getting the bike on and off the rear stand now but if I can offer one piece of advice, having someone with you that you can trust is invaluable and allows you to just concentrate on racing.

I made my way to the collecting area, behind Doug, riding Barry's SV. He stopped at the start of the garage lane, waiting for Barry to come back to the collecting area. As I approached the collecting area marshal, she said, "20? Row 11, grid 31."

Bloody hell. How had that happened? Yesterday, I had started at the back of the grid in position 39 but as the weekend had passed and the attrition rate had risen, other people's misfortunes had done me a favour. For this last race, there were actually eight riders behind me. EIGHT! I couldn't believe it and kept having to look behind me to confirm it. I was at the front of the second collection area group, which felt like being in pole position.

We took our places on the grid and went out on the warm up. Filing back into our grid positions, I could hear the revs building up in anticipation. The marshal lifted his flag again, pointing at the lights. For what seemed an eternity (seconds fly by on the start line) the bank was black and then on went the lights.

Two rows ahead of me, bike 415, ridden by Alan Hensby, leapt forward and then stopped. Too late, Alan - the officials will have seen that.

The lights went out and we shot off. I was amazed at how fast even my poor old wheezer went from the start line and actually felt myself struggling to hold on. I soon snapped back into reality as everyone except the last two riders hurtled past me at Paddock Hill.

I thought I'd got used to that but this was scary stuff. There was no time to think about it, though, as I first stamped on the gear lever and then back down through the gears as we approached Druids at a stupid pace en masse.

Around Druids, I took up the honours of tail-end Charlie again, as the remaining riders (I only recognised Vanessa) passed me in to Graham Hill. I kept up with Vanessa as far as McLarens but felt the bike stiffen as I leant over. I lost my bottle briefly, wound off a little, berated myself and, as I lifted the bike onto the Brabham Straight, dropped a gear and thrashed my way towards Paddock Hill.

I got into sixth gear for the first time all weekend but then realised I needed to go back down quickly as the 300m marker shot by. Grabbing a handful of brake, I took the corner way too wide and bounced along the kerbs down Hailwood Hill. Damn; those things are uncomfortable. I took the tight line around Druids (easy to do, as I was now by myself), moved left then swung back right to get round Graham Hill. I could still see Vanessa ahead of me but by the time I was on the Cooper straight, she was already tipping into Surtees.

It was time to just enjoy the ride and put some decent laps together. Remembering the advice of "talk, talk, talk", I kept going, looking across to Paddock Hill as I came to Graham Hill again. I saw the first rider emerging from behind the pit wall, so I knew it wouldn't be long before the thunder was upon me again. Sure enough, by the time I was leaning into Clark Curve, they all swarmed around me and disappeared once more.

For my first race, I had been scared of everything; stalling, being hit, being overtaken, crashing. Sure, everything was pretty intense but it only took a couple of laps to get used to most of it and, after I'd been overtaken by a mob one time, I knew it was going to happen again and didn't even think about it. I can't say I didn't care because having other people overtake you sucks but it's all part of the learning. For this weekend, I knew that being overtaken would be inevitable. I just had to concentrate on keeping on track, getting my head down (something that Kevin pointed out to me. I must work on my body position) and pointing the bike down the track, with the throttle fully open or the brakes fully on. There is no in between. Unless you're Steve Male, who still needed to switch the "coasting" setting off.

Everything seemed to click in this last race. My lines felt better, although I did screw up on the approach to Paddock Hill, as the bike had a tendency to find a false neutral coming down from 5th gear. Doing so made me change back up so I cruised down the hill before finding a suitable gear (they're all in there somewhere) and getting back into the swing of it.

The ten laps were over all too quickly and as the chequered flag was waved, I could hear myself actually laughing. How did that happen? I'd gone from abject terror to all-out fun.

I looked across at the sea of orange-clad marshals and waved acknowledgement to the seemingly hundreds of them all around the track. As I passed and they applauded, I realised I was grinning like a loon. Even little old last finisher me was being congratulated as I turned into the garage lane.

I parked up and a passer-by set the bike on its stand. More kindness of strangers but it all helps. Getting my helmet and gloves off, I went over to Kevin to thank him for his support and let him know how I got on. I told him how I kept missing gears and he took a look at the bike. The root of that problem looked to be the relative angle of the gear selector rod and its connection to the gear shaft. The splined joint was too far forward, making it more difficult to make clean gear changes. If I rotated the joint and reduced the angle to 90 degrees, gear changes should be easier and give me one thing less to worry about.

The weekend was over all too fast (see what I did there?) and, although I hadn't been fast, I had achieved an ambition that had been forty years in the making. I had emulated many of my childhood heroes, albeit it at a much lower level and had enjoyed every minute of it.

I walked up to the garages to return Mark Gillam's hex spindle tool and to congratulate new friends Dan (a seriously fast rookie - three third places, one second place) and Vanessa, my fellow back backmarker (but still faster than me). I also met Alan Hensby, jump start supremo and Matt Wetherell who frankly put us all to shame (three second places and a win). As Matt came up, he cried, "Steve!" and I knew my reputation was sealed. Everyone knew who I was; the wobbly pensioner on the black and yellow crock making everyone else look great. I didn't care though.

I didn't know how well I would perform. I had ridden the Indy circuit before at a track day but racing was completely different to any track day. The circuit is 1.2 miles long and the goal is always to get a sub-60 second lap. I was nowhere near that but my posted times were:

Race 1 - 1:15.14
Race 2 - 1:12.74
Race 3 - 1:13.98
Race 4 - 1:15.78

I put the last result down to concentrating too hard on getting lines right, three false neutral moments and lack of nerve. That will all come eventually and it didn't matter. I went out and did it.

"Today, I was a racer".

Chapter 3:
"Homework On The Bus".

It had been a while since the bike and I had seen any action. Brands was seven weeks ago and, because I had missed the Oulton Park round, the bike hadn't been out of the garage since then. I had learnt a lot at Brands but knew there would be more lessons as the season progressed. Financial considerations/poverty meant that I couldn't attend every race, so would have to make the most of the opportunities I'd get at the rounds I planned to attend. I live on the south coast, so Round 2 at Oulton Park, nearly 300 miles north in Cheshire, was always going to be a stretch. Cadwell Park would be my next outing.

Cadwell Park; I have been a BSB spectator at this circuit number of times before with friends on what became an annual pilgrimage. As marriages and other commitments came along, those pilgrimages tailed off and I'd not been to the Lincolnshire circuit since 2007.

The last time I had actually been on the track was in 2005. Back then, I owned a brand-new Yamaha R6, to compete with my friend Mark's 2004 GSX-R750. We both fancied ourselves as useful, if not fast, riders and attended our first track day that year, followed by a day at the Ron Haslam Race School at Donington Park.

We had gone to Cadwell for the August Bank Holiday BSB round and stayed for a track day on the following Tuesday. At only £89, we couldn't pass up the chance to try our new rocket ships over The Mountain. Once the racing carnival had left, we set our tents up in the top paddock, ready for the track early the next day.

There was a light drizzle when we woke; never a good start but by the time we had set up in the paddock, the rain had stopped, although it would come and go all day.

We rolled our bikes off the trailer and onto their paddock stands. We had no tyre warmers but knew to drop the tyre pressures as they were going to get hot and harder as the air expanded within. Over-inflated tyres on a race track make for a very flighty bike.

I removed the valve cap and pressed the pressure gauge onto the front wheel valve. The gauge read 36 PSI, so I released some air until it read about 28. Repeating the exercise for the back wheel, the gauge read 4 PSI. Thinking that I must have not pushed the gauge on properly, I tried again. This time, it read 3 PSI. I pressed the tyre, which collapsed under my thumb. Turning the wheel, I found a screw sticking out of the sidewall. Bugger.

I went to the on-site tyre fitter, who didn't have a Michelin to match my front, naturally. He told me that my only option was to buy a full set of Pirelli Supercorsas from him which, at £250 for the pair, meant that my cheap track day had instantly become less of a bargain.

I had to wait until the fitter had sorted the rent bikes before he would fit some for me, so I missed the sighting laps and consequently my first track session (you're not allowed on track without the bike displaying a "sighting lap completed" sticker). It had started raining again, so at least I avoided that problem. I approached the head instructor who said that one of his team would take me out at the back of the next novice session to show me the lines, after which I'd be left to my own devices.

When the novice group was called again, I lined up at the back with the instructor. We went out after the last group of riders left the collecting area. We joined the circuit at the Hall bends and, almost immediately, I became aware that there were not just novices in this group.

As I tipped left into the first left-hander, a rider cut through to pass me on the inside. I lifted the bike only to have another pass me on the right. I freaked out and struggled to catch up with the instructor. I was being passed by riders all over the place and could not get into any rhythm at all so, when the instructor peeled off (thanks for nothing), I simply wobbled round the circuit, wishing for the fifteen minutes to end.

The next session wasn't much better, although I felt a little less uncomfortable. On returning to the paddock, the talk was mostly of the guys using the rental bikes. Despite being in the novice group, they were clearly far more experienced, based on the pace they were maintaining and the overtakes they were making. The concern was not just that they were in the wrong group but that the organisers weren't doing anything about it.

It all came to a head for me on my final session. I was getting more confident (no jumping the Mountain, of course) and beginning to enjoy myself. I came out of Barn to join the start/finish straight and could see a rental bike rolling slowly ahead of me on the left of the track. The next corner, Coppice, is a lovely left-hand, uphill corner so, as long as he stayed where he was as I passed, I would keep right and tip the bike nicely into the bend.

As I finally reached the tipping point, the other rider picked up speed and swerved to the right of the track, directly in front of me. I was going full tilt and had nowhere to go but onto the damp grass. I looked down at my instruments. I was in sixth gear, doing 10,500 rpm. I had no idea how fast that was (I was later to find it was 95 mph), because I had taped over my speedo. I had brand new tyres that were not scrubbed in, on a bike that was barely five months old.

I lifted my feet off the pegs and kept my hands off the brake and clutch, my mind thinking, "Six grand! Six grand!" I flew up the hill, past the oak tree (now gone, thankfully) and returned to the tarmac along the Park Straight. A marshal was talking animatedly into his walkie-talkie, probably suggesting a recovery van and a large broom. The rider who had forced me off had by now also got to the Park straight, where he had stopped (yes, really) to watch me struggle to regain some level of control. I was fuming and just wanted to go home. However, giving up at that point would mean I may never want to go on a track again. I pressed on, a dose of red mist over me and I caned the bike for what turned out to be the final lap of my final session. So ended my only experience of Cadwell to date.

Anyway; back to this year's preparation. At Brands, I had been granted a temporary amnesty concerning engine protectors. My SV didn't have them but Scrutineering said I could race, on the understanding that protectors would be fitted before my next round, which would be here. Procrastinators will always think they have more time than they do. It was as well that there was the long Easter weekend leading up to Cadwell, so I had the luxury of two extra days off work to sort my shit out.

At Brands, Kevin had introduced me to his friend Mark Hazelbrook. A former Minitwinner, Mark was now retired but had a lot of SV spares that he needed to get rid of. He lived in Surrey, which I could get to on the way home from work, so we agreed a date and I collected a pair of front discs, some pads, a set of clutch plates and an offside Gen 2 engine cover. It seems that all racers accumulate a hoard of spare parts, either through auctions, or by way of inadvertently destroying a bike at a meeting. Mark was now concentrating on off-roading and no longer needed any of his SV stuff. Agreeing a price, I loaded up the van and made my way home.

Now I had the parts, I needed to get them fitted. I also needed to get the bike prepared for its next outing. I got to work on the Saturday afternoon, the weekend before the Cadwell round. The first job was to apply the recently purchased yellow vinyl to the bodywork. I reasoned that vinyl would be cleaner and give a more consistent colour finish.

Applying vinyl over anything other than a flat surface is, well, problematic and a very skilled job, i.e. out of my capability. The adhesive side will stick to everything, including itself and me, or the vinyl starts to roll back up if not properly secured. It also creases easily but gentle application of heat with a hairdryer helped keep that to a minimum.

Having laminated the bodywork, I then took on the rather simpler task of fitting cush drive rubbers to the wet rear and disc rotors to the front wheels. Even then, there was a minor issue. I had a Gen 2 front end and had bought a set of ten bolts to fix the discs in place. The bolt shoulders, however, looked to be about 1 mm too long, so when they bottomed out, the discs still floated rather than being clamped in place.

I found a set of washers to bridge the gap on each bolt, applied thread lock and tightened everything up. I now had a complete set of dry and wet wheels which, given the forecast for Louth at the weekend, was probably a good thing. Although I had been able to change wheels at Brands, not having them as complete assemblies had been a real issue and just added to my anxiety at Brands. I was beginning to get organised. Kevin would be impressed.

The next job was sorting the gear change to stop getting false neutrals. This was irritating on a track day but in the heat of a race, being able to successfully select a gear at the right time is fundamentally important. Having a screaming engine and no forward motion makes you forget what gear you may have been in, leading to all manner of other panics. While it may have helped me build up my canon of excuses, I really needed to sort this problem now the bike was being raced.

At the end of that last race weekend, Kevin had noticed something that, because I'd been looking at it all the time, I had completely missed. The problem was that, due to the relative orientation of the connection to the splined shaft and the gear linkage, changing up involved pulling the mechanism through an awkward angle. So, while the fairing was off, I rotated the connection a little more to make the included angle between it and the linkage about ninety degrees. That way, changing up or down should prove less of an issue. We would see at the race meeting.

My SV has a racing gear change set up; one up, five down, rather than the other way round. The reasoning is that it's easier (and faster) to stamp your foot down on the gear lever on acceleration than it is to hook your foot under the lever to lift it. Even at my pedestrian pace, every second really does count.

I kept the biggest job until last, though; fitting engine protectors. I had bought a pair of bolt-on covers from GB Racing to fit. The alternator side engine casing is the same for Gen 1 and Gen 2 bikes but the clutch cover for the Gen 1 bike has a separate, plastic cover that goes over the clutch. This is a known weak point as, when the engine gets hot, it can warp, resulting in oil leaks.

The good news is that the Gen 2 cover bolts directly in place of the Gen 1 version and is a one-piece unit, with no plastic cover. The better news was that Mark had sold me the casing, a clutch and a pair of front discs for £50. I had to order a replacement gasket but that only took two days to arrive.

Fitting the alternator protector was a breeze. I simply removed three bolts, positioned the protector and fixed it with the extended bolts supplied. It took less than ten minutes. That left the clutch side to do, which would be a bit more involved, as it involved a degree of dismantling.

You can change the clutch cover without draining the oil. By leaning the bike right over on its left side, the oil flows to that side of the engine. This leaves the joint line between the clutch cover and the main engine casing above the oil level. I positioned a pair of tyres against the retaining wall in front of my garage and rested the bike against the tyres and wall. Before fitting, I looked at the new casing to see how it was fixed to the main engine casing. Fourteen M5 bolts clamped the castings together around the periphery, including two that went through the water pump housing. I decided to remove the water pump first, so I could access the other bolts, only to find it wouldn't budge.

After a few unsuccessful attempts, pulling and twisting the pump housing, I took drastic action and consulted the workshop manual. There I learned that the pump had to come off with the side casing because it was also fixed inside the cover. "No problem", I thought.

"I'll simply disconnect the water hoses and that will give me better access to the front bolts."

Getting to most of the bolts wasn't too much of a problem but, because the engine was still in the frame, some of the bolts were awkward to access. I finally got them all out and placed them in a magnetic bowl for safekeeping.

I looked at the workshop manual again to check the best way to remove the casing, as it didn't simply pull away. In addition to the bolts, there are two dowelled points that align the cover and main engine casting, which prevented easy removal. It was likely that the cover had never been removed and that everything was gunked up. I consulted a YouTube video where the author used a blade screwdriver to tap the joint outwards and watched as the engine simply fell away.

The reality was of course completely different. I found a wide blade screwdriver and tapped gently at the joint but the case didn't budge. I tried again, striking more firmly but still the case remained stubbornly solid. I didn't want to cause any damage (putting a hole through an engine casting would be a serious job-stopper), so was reluctant to hit too hard, too often.

It took me over an hour to get that cover off, using longer and longer screwdrivers to prise the faces apart. I was worried that I would damage the joint faces but the main casing at least came off unscathed. The old side cover was destined for the bin, so I didn't care about that. I removed all traces of the originsl gasket from the joint surfaces, ready for the replacement cover.

Before they could be fitted, I had to address the water pump removal. The internal pump spur gear is retained using a circlip, so a trip to the local motor factors got me a set of circlip pliers. Twenty minutes later, I was back at the bike and had assembled the pump into the new casing. I fitted the new gasket over the dowels in the cover before carefully reassembling everything. Refitting was completely straightforward, other than the suspicion that I may have stripped one casing thread. I fitted the engine protector over the top and the reassembly was complete.

I reconnected the radiator pipes, filled the system with distilled water, flicked the "engine on" switch, pulled up the choke and pressed the starter. To my delight (and relief), the SV started on the first attempt. I let it run for a few minutes to make sure there were no oil or water leaks (there weren't) before hitting the kill switch.

Having satisfied myself that nothing was loose, I set about refitting the fairing. I had taped the Dzus fasteners (two per side) to the inside walls of the fairing upper section when I'd repainted the bodywork but when I removed the fasteners that I'd taped to the fairing, I found only three. A quick online enquiry confirmed that I'd be able to buy some spares at the circuit, so I fitted three out of four fasteners to retain the fairing before bolting the rest of the lower to the frame.

All in all, it had been an education. I'd learned how awkward replacing a simple casing was if you didn't have the tools. I also learned to do things methodically, having first double-checked everything before wading in. That meant checking how it all went together and came apart before committing myself. I didn't want to start taking things apart only to discover that I'd need a specialist tool or part and couldn't put the bike back together until I had those things. Seeing the reassembled bike was very satisfying. Having completed the work, it went back in the garage, ready to load on Wednesday.

The last item I had to address was fitting replacement numbers. I had been given a pair of numbers at the last Brands track day by Rod Harwin and now used up the last of those two numbers on the fairing's new yellow nose. I had to make a new set of side numbers, though, as I had ruined the previous ones when I removed the old yellow Gaffer tape background.

I made new numbers using my vinyl cutter, so the bike now sported five new number 20s; one on the front, one on each side of the fairing and a pair on the seat unit. It was as ready as it was going to be. All that was left to do was wait for Wednesday to get packed.

Wednesday morning dawned considerably colder than the previous few days and I was glad that I'd done all the work while the sun had shone. Today, there was a feeling of impending rain, so I loaded the van. I seemed to be getting better at packing as there was a lot of space when I'd finished, even after double-checking my list. To make sure I'd not left anything behind, I had a list of the things I'd need to take taped to the inside wall of the van. There was a bike list, a paddock list, an ancillaries list, a riding gear list, a caravan list and finally a food and clothing list. The food and clothing would be dealt with on Thursday, just before I set off but everything else on the checklist was crossed through as it was loaded. I was very pleased to have actually been organised this time around. Using such a checklist simply eliminates one worry. With everything packed, I just needed to get a good night's sleep ahead of the journey.

Chapter 4:
Round 3: Cadwell Park (Louth, Lincolnshire)

Thursday: Arrival

Thursday arrived quickly and, despite getting to bed early, I had almost no sleep. The anticipation of a race meeting at the scariest race track in the UK had my mind racing. I was up at 6:30 and showered and dressed before 7:00. Having been properly organised yesterday, I had packed, closely following a list taped to the van wall. I had a new van which, unlike the previous one, didn't have built-in storage, which meant a lot more cargo space; enough to even include my mountain bike. Cadwell Park is very hilly, so if I couldn't set up near the race office, I didn't want to end up walking for miles. With the van packed, all I had to do was buy food for the weekend, which I had sorted just before heading off.

The first job was to get the van fuelled; a scary prospect, as a complete fill takes just shy of £100. I also needed petrol for the bike, which gets the highest octane fuel I can find. With it being so underpowered, I needed any potential advantage I can get, even if that's only rich fuel.

Despite the welcome assistance offered by Kevin at Brands Hatch, I had mostly been left to my own devices. This isn't a criticism; ultimately, you need to do your own stuff but I would not have got through without Kevin's unwavering support. The thing is, however you set up at a race meeting, each racer needs to concentrate on his or her weekend. Everyone helps where they can, of course but most are single rider teams, touring the country in their vans and caravans (mostly). Some bring tents, some have motorhomes or even race trucks and others sleep in their van or awning with the bike. Those racers in particular are a very hardy breed but then bike racers are hard.

Kevin had taught me a lot but still I was delinquent in many areas so, for Cadwell Park, I enlisted the help of an old school friend, Mark Lucas, to be my spanner man/paddock buddy. Mark and I have known each other since we were fifteen and we're both bike obsessives.

Racing is hard enough so even having someone there to just refuel, fit tyre warmers, get the bike on its paddock stand or simply talk with can make a world of difference. Mark and I have been friends for so long that he was the obvious choice to bring as teammate and mechanic. Neither of us had been to Cadwell for years, so this would be quite the experience.

I phoned Mark to tell him that we weren't allowed on circuit until late, so he suggested meeting at Peterborough services around 3:00 pm. Cadwell would be about two hours further north and, if there were enough racers, surely we'd be able to get on site? I told him that we might also meet Carl, Dan and Vanessa, the other rookie racers I'd contacted. As it turned out, Carl was already well on the way but Dan and Vanessa had been massively delayed, so we all agreed to meet up on site.

Carl phoned just as I peeled off the M25 to join the M11 north; an interesting junction if you're in a van pulling a caravan. Two hundred and seventy degrees of ever-tightening bend requires a lot of concentration. Carl and his wife Lin were approaching Cambridge where they would stop for a coffee. I knew it would be at least an hour before I would arrive so told them to carry on and I'd meet them at the circuit.

I pulled in to Peterborough Services at 3:00, just ahead of Mark and phoned Dan but he was still an hour behind us. Vanessa hadn't even left Sussex yet so was unlikely to arrive until after dark. Mark and I pressed on, him following me to the circuit.

We arrived at about 6:00 and I phoned Carl, who had bagged a spot near the track entrance. The club was insistent that no one could set up until 8:00. There was a track day in full swing and, until they had left the site, the Bemsee riders would have to hold station. In the meantime, all we could do was hang around until the inevitable crush that was fifty-plus vans and caravans trying to get a spot.

As it turned out, we were able to set up next to Carl and started pitching up before anyone had the chance to tell us not to. It was beginning to get dark, so I connected the leisure battery to enable us to have some light from the caravan. We set up the gazebo while there was enough daylight, after which we could get the generator running to power up the caravan so we could make dinner.

Ah; the generator. I had bought this new, unused unit from a "bloke in Hastings" and up until now, hadn't fired it up. I'd taken it to Brands but hadn't needed it then, as I was able to connect to the on-site mains power. Cadwell has no hook-up points, so a generator is essential.

A generator must be powerful enough to run everything you're going to use. In my case, that was a caravan, gazebo lights and, most importantly, tyre warmers, which each ran at 650 W.

My generator was rated at 3000 W and was good for 2700 W constant running. Mark checked the oil level, topped up the fuel, switched it on and yanked the cord. Nothing. I hadn't expected it to fire up on the first pull, so he tried again but still nothing. However, a few tugs later, with both of us sharing starting duty, it roared into 96dB of life. I connected the generator to the caravan, flicked a switch and the caravan ceiling light came on.

"We have power!"

As it turned out, we didn't. Well, not 240 volts of power, anyway. What I had actually done was switch on one of the 12V lights, which was drawing power from the leisure battery, not the generator. We only realised this when plugging in the mains charger to top up our phones. Suspicion was aroused when there was no light on the charger. We walked to the generator, chuffing away behind the caravan but there was no power light and the voltmeter needle wasn't moving.

Knowing my record/reputation, I had at least anticipated this and had asked Mark to bring his little (650W) generator along, just in case. It wouldn't power up both tyre warmers but would at least be enough to have one going. I would heat one tyre up and leave the warmer on while the second got its heat. It wasn't ideal but was better than nothing.

Carl and Lin were staying in a Louth B&B, rather than on circuit. Carl's friend Wayne was sleeping in the team van, so he let us use the second output from his generator, so we'd have light for the evening. He'd need it himself for Carl's warmers during the weekend but we'd be all right for the first night. Mark would check out my generator in the morning. I would also invest in a splitter junction for potential later use.

By now, we were really hungry. At Brands, I had been so busy that I had forgotten to eat and drink properly. This is another good reason for having someone with you; they're going to get hungry and thirsty too, so you always have a reminder to eat and drink.

We drove into Louth, where we found a Morrison's supermarket. It was now 9:20 and, although we were hungry, neither of us felt up to having anything heavy, so we grabbed a couple of sandwiches, along with some general provisions. We paid up and, as we left the shop, a staff member locked the door behind us. We clearly couldn't have left it any later.

We were challenged at the circuit entrance. There had been no security when we went out but now we weren't being allowed back in without tickets. They were in the van, in the paddock. Despite pleading, he refused us entry, saying we should have someone bring tickets up to us. The only other rider I had contact with was Carl who was by now in his B&B. I offered to surrender my phone as security and then Mark would drive back with the tickets.

We left everything in the van for now, had our meagre meal and coffee before settling down for the night. The forecast for Friday was good, I had instruction booked in the afternoon and would be able to start familiarising myself with the circuit in plenty of time for race 1 on Saturday.

Friday: Practice Day

The day opened bright and sunny and I felt pretty good. Cadwell Park is long, narrow and technically challenging with a lot of elevation changes but I wasn't going to be fazed if at all possible. Everybody who knows Cadwell knows about the dreaded Mountain; a short but very steep incline with a blind crest that leads to the Hall bends. The circuit is more than that though and, other than the start/finish straight, the rest of the circuit is either steeply uphill or down. This was going to be interesting.

Of course, at nearly 57, I didn't really need "interesting". I needed safe, I needed comfortable; pipe and slippers. Still; I was here now and the whole point was to be a racer. Racers may do safe but comfortable? Not a chance.

I signed in at the race office and got my helmet and bike stickers that would allow me onto the track. The Minitwin practice sessions were at a quarter past the hour, so I had time before I needed to be out. I gave the bike a couple of cursory checks and waited for the call.

My generator still wasn't putting out any power, so we had to rely on Mark's little 650-watt unit. That was fine for lighting in the caravan (until 11:00, when all generators had to be shut down. We had to use the leisure battery after then) but it wouldn't run both tyre warmers.

Fellow rookies Dan Thomas and Simon Wilkinson were set up across the way. Dan took pity on me, letting let me run my tyre warmers off his generator. There's the joy of club racing; everyone pitching in to help one another.

The call came out for the Minitwin practice. Mark and I peeled the warmers off the tyres and I set off along the paddock road in the wrong direction, heading for the front of the collecting area, rather than the entrance point. I swung the bike into the next tier down and got myself to the collecting point.

I handed my yellow practice card to the marshal who checked the stickers were in place, numbers were attached to the bike and that the transponder was fitted and working. All good and approved, I rolled forward to the pit lane entrance. For us mere mortal club racers, getting onto the circuit is via the upper paddock entrance which brings you straight on to the Hall bends; a series of gentle, undulating bends through the wooded section of the track.

Did I say "gentle"? As soon as we were allowed on track, the fast boys shot past me, flicking right - left - right - left - right into the hairpin and down towards Barn corner and boy, they were quick. By the time I had rounded Barn, they were already approaching turn 1, Coppice, having blasted down the start-finish straight. This was going to be a baptism of fire.

My lines and body position were, of course, appalling. It had been such a long time since I'd even been to Cadwell, let alone actually ridden on it so I took my time to see where others were going and did my best to follow suit. I still had that mental image of being punted off at Coppice at the track day, all those years ago. That recollection of bouncing along the grass and re-joining at Park straight meant I was probably being a little over-cautious.

One thing had occurred to me from the off, though. The riders were way faster than those I'd encountered at track days but I felt much safer here. Everyone wants to win but no one is prepared to do it at all costs and there is definitely a greater sense of respect between racers compared to track day riders. There are no Rossi wannabes here; we are almost all entirely self-funded and have no desire to bin our pride and joy, not even those with scabby bikes like mine.

That's a bit disingenuous, really. The official photos that had been taken at Brands showed a clearly unfinished #20 bike tootling around the Kentish circuit but before I had left for Cadwell, I'd repainted the fairing (a heavy dose of Hammerite (sticks to anything) in smooth finish black) and applied yellow vinyl to the nose, belly and tail as background for the numbers, so the bike now looked considerably more presentable.

Practice had us out for 15 minutes at a time but I was struggling to sort out the racing line. Sometimes it felt all right but then I'd get drafted by a very fast rider. I just felt like I was getting in the way. After a few laps, Dan Singleton, a fellow Minitwinner and one of the instructors, passed me before tapping his seat unit, indicating that I should follow him. We rounded Charlies 1 and 2 then dropped into Park straight, where he looked back to signal, "Pin it!" I twisted the throttle to its stop and felt my stomach being left behind as the bike shot off down the incline and back up towards Park corner. He nodded his head and then pointed to the piece of track I needed to aim for at Park. I hit the apex well enough, only to overshoot and fly along the thankfully dry grass before getting back on track at the Gooseneck. Calming myself down, I dropped down to Mansfield and leant hard left towards the chicane. Dan pointed to the apex points and I followed him through and up towards the Mountain.

Shit; the Mountain. Dan simply flew up, his front wheel lifting heroically as he made the crest. Me? That'll have been about 30 mph, my bike meekly bobbling over the crest, both wheels firmly fixed to the tarmac.

Back into the Hall bends, round the hairpin and Barn and Dan was off. Looking behind, he once again indicated me to give it the beans. I was in third gear and opened the bike up, seeing the rev limiter light come on as I changed up, up and up again into sixth gear.

Bloody hell; I was rolling into Coppice in top gear. Holy shit, that was fast! I bottled it and dropped the bike into fourth as I went round Charlies 1, where Dan was now leaving me behind. He slowed a little and gave me the "Pin it!" sign again and I duly obliged. I charged up the hill towards Park corner but this time got myself further to the left so I could make both Park corner and

Chris Curve cleanly before heading down to the Gooseneck without scaring myself to death.

I continued round Mansfield, the Chicane and up the Mountain (less fear and more speed this time), through the woods and back towards the finish line where the chequered flag was out.

Holy cow! My heart was pounding and I was grinning like a loon. I caught up with Dan and we exited the track together. He rode to his pit space before walking back to where I was rolling the bike onto the stand with Mark.

After some detailed explanation from Dan, I began to understand how I should approach Cadwell Park. Sure, it's scary at first but, taking it one section at a time, it becomes less daunting. Dan suggested that in addition to my booked instruction, it might be worth getting out with the 300s to increase my track exposure. "Get your lines sorted, which you were starting to do, then everything will start to fall into place. As your confidence grows, your speed will increase." I was feeling better already and looked forward to the next session in 45 minutes' time.

10:15 came, along with our call out. I mounted the bike and Mark rolled the paddock stand back. Firing the engine up, I went into the collecting area and joined the others onto the track. Feeling a little less reticent, I was happier to thrash the bike a little more. I missed apexes here and there but was generally feeling more confident as the session progressed.

Rising up and round into Charlies 1 and 2 for my fourth lap, I felt the rear wheel lose grip. Thinking I had over-reached my ability, I lifted the bike up. Going down the straight, the back end felt awful, snaking left and right. I felt like I was riding on marbles and was convinced that I had a flat rear tyre when, tipping into Park corner, the rear gave completely and slid sideways. I pulled up again, raised my left hand in case anyone was coming up behind and coasted along the grass towards the beckoning marshals.

"You all right, son?" a grey-bearded marshal asked.

"It felt like the rear tyre was going down," I replied. "The back was all over the place."

Checking the rear wheel, the marshal said, "The tyre looks fine. Do you want us to take you back in the van, or can you ride it?"

I tried the bike on the rough tarmac. It felt all right, so I elected to ride slowly back. The marshal pointed out where the road went and I gingerly rode back to the paddock, where Mark got the bike back on to the stand.

"What happened?" He asked.

"Back end gave way."

We looked at the tyre, which was still fully inflated, so I couldn't understand what had happened. Then we looked at the wheel hub.

The bearing cap had belled outwards and had ejected all but five of its ball bearings. The other ones would probably be rolling around somewhere at Charlies 1 at the moment. It was no good; the rear wheel had to come out, so we set about loosening the chain adjusters and undoing the spindle nut.

Getting the spindle out, however, was another matter entirely. With no wheel bearing to support the wheel properly, everything had over-heated and the assembly was firmly jammed together. The spacer and brake hanger had all but welded to the spindle, which refused to move. Any attempt to turn it had the brake hanger turning with it until it stopped against the swinging arm, meaning we could only rotate everything about 45 degrees.

I'd had that problem removing the spindle at Brands, which was down to general cleanliness at the back; something that I had since addressed. There, we had got the spindle out, cleaned it up with emery cloth, re-greased and cleaned all the faces, after which everything assembled and dismantled with ease. This time, there was no getting the rear wheel assembly apart. It looked like the weekend was over before it had even begun.

I located a motorcycle repair shop, Quickshift Motorcycles, in Louth that was open. I phoned up, speaking to the owner, Paul; an affable lad who was keen to look at the bike and would stop what he was working on in order to see if he could get my errant rear wheel out.

The shop was a fifteen-minute drive and tucked away in a small industrial estate on the edge of town. There was a black Kawasaki parked out front and a Honda replica racer on a ramp. Paul beckoned us in and we wheeled my poorly bike onto the second ramp, where he locked it into place. Thirty minutes judicious application of heat eventually got the component parts separated and Paul was finally able to pull the spindle out

It was a mess; the bearing was completely destroyed, dislodging the spacer and brake hanger in the process. These in turn had cut new grooves into the spindle. Paul removed what was left of the bearing housing, which would never see action again.

He didn't have suitable bearings but I was grateful he'd been able to save the wheel. The spindle was polished up again and finished off with some emery cloth. While scarred, it was still perfectly serviceable but I'd look for a spare one as soon as possible. We refitted the wet wheel, spinning it on the refurbished spindle. Satisfied all was well, we loaded the bike back into the van.

I was gushing with praise. Up until that point, I had fully expected to be packing up and going home. At the very least, I could now swap tyres on the rear wheel which, while a pain, was better than not being able to ride any more. Finding a replacement bearing was unlikely at such short notice, so I asked the race office to put out a request for a spare curvy rear wheel.

For all that 'drop everything' hard graft, Paul only wanted twenty pounds. I gave him forty, saying that he had saved my weekend and even that felt like I was robbing him. Sadly, he would be working all weekend, so he couldn't even my offer of free tickets.

We arrived at the circuit in good spirits but I still needed to sort out the back wheel, in case it dried out. Rain was forecast for Saturday, so I would be good as long as it remained wet. I couldn't believe that I was hoping for rain but there it was.

I had a call put out but there were no spare wheels available at the circuit. As we passed Vanessa's race truck, she and husband Mark beckoned us over for an update. I told them that we'd been able to get the bike sorted but that I now had a new issue getting another bearing set or a borrowed wheel.

"Take our spare." Mark offered. "We've got two wet sets; the full wets and these ones, which have mild wet/intermediate tyres on. Looking at the forecast, we're going to need the full wets tomorrow but, in case it dries out, borrow this wheel and you're sorted."

I was very grateful and took the wheel down to Rod Harwin's service tent where, for a fiver, he did a quick tyre swap and wheel balance. Taking the wheels back to my pit space, Mark and I decided that fitting the borrowed wheel now would be a good idea, if only to see how quickly we could do it.

Unfortunately, Vanessa's bike was a Generation 2, "pointy" SV, whereas I had a Gen 1, "carby/curvy" model. While the two bikes share some components, the wheels are not interchangeable. The spindle sizes are different, so Vanessa's wheel was not going into my swinging arm.

I took the wheel back to Rod Harwin, where he relieved me of another fiver to swap the tyres again. Another salutary lesson had been learned. I was grateful to Mark and Vanessa but would keep a better eye out next time.

Without a suitably shod rear wheel, any further practise was out of the question. This was a disappointment as I had booked instruction with head instructor, Jeremy Hill. Had there been time to swap the tyres, I may have been in with a chance for the last session but that time had run out, so I went to find Jeremy. It was cooling down now and, in the shelter of the scrutineering bay, we chatted about the bike, me, the circuit and bike riding in general.

"What goes through your head when you go out on track? Excitement, fear, nervousness? Anything at all?" he asked me.

"I'm not sure that I worry too much," I ventured, which was partly true. "Sure, when I'm on any track for the first time, I'm nervous, especially here, as I've not ridden Cadwell for so long. I'm aware of being a green beginner and that I'm really slow, which is a worry for me. The other thing I realised was that:

a) Brands Indy is easy by comparison and
b) Cadwell is so long! It's like it's never going to end!"

Jeremy nodded in agreement. "Anything else?"

"Well, I knew my times were slow at Brands and I had an idea as to when the lapping would start. I guess I was especially nervous in the first race but knew that, if I saw the leaders going down Paddock Hill as I approached Graham Hill, then they'd probably catch me by Clearways. I was at least prepared for that, come race two."

"Okay, let's talk about that, as there's a few points that your comment raises. First, remember that this is YOUR ride. OK, so it's on a race track but at the end of the day, it's just you riding your bike. Don't worry about the others out there. You certainly don't want to be thinking about who may or may not be approaching."

"Second, remember the first rule of racing - it is the responsibility of the rider behind to pass safely, not for the rider up front to get out of the way. Keep your line and they'll pass when they can. Don't worry that others are coming. Your responsibility is to ride, not to worry about the others coming up behind. Have you got a name for your bike?"

"A name? Blimey; I don't think I've ever named a bike."

"What? No! You've got to name your bike, Steve. How else are you going to bond with it properly? My last three bikes have all been Bruce. Whenever I get something right, I'll tap the tank and say, 'Well done, Bruce' and get on enjoying the ride. As I'm going around, I'm constantly saying, 'Come ON, Bruce. Go get 'em!' or similar. You'll be surprised how much of a difference it makes. Your bike is your friend and you're both out for a great ride. You must get a name sorted."

I thought about it. "In that case, I'll introduce you to Sylvie later," came the reply.

"Sylvie? Sylvie the SV? That's wicked. Perfect. Now, when you next go out, you can coax her as you're going. When things go well, celebrate with her. If they're not so good, then it's, 'That's OK, Sylvie, we've got more time yet. Let's pick it up and go'. "Sylvie"; I love it."

Jeremy's enthusiasm was infectious and I liked him immensely. Sure, I was nervous but how could I not be motivated after that pep talk? Every race club needs a Jezza.

He continued. "Right; you ARE coming to the track walk, aren't you?" I was but the question was clearly rhetorical. I'd missed the Brands track walk but I had no intention of missing out this time. The walk would be at six o'clock, starting at the collection area and would take about an hour.

Walking The Walk

Mark and I wandered down to the collecting area just before six o'clock. It was already heaving. We all listened to Jeremy's opening comments and then Mark elected to go back to the caravan so he could phone his wife. I joined Dan Thomas and Simon Wilkinson, to hear what pearls Jeremy would come up with.

Jeremy's enthusiasm seemed to have no bounds, describing each piece of track in minute detail, how to approach each section and how to compensate for poor weather conditions. He showed us not only where the apexes were but also where to ignore one, such as in Charlies 1 (because it's a double apex, cutting in too early at the right-hand Charlies 1 will screw you for its continuation at Charlies 2, the next right-hand bend.)

Starting at the Hall bends, Jeremy led us through woods up to the hairpin, highlighting the risk of leaves if it got very wet on Saturday, before moving on to Barn corner. Once onto the start/finish straight, we were warned not to get too enthusiastic for the first couple of laps but at the same time not to hold back if the bike felt right.

Jeremy led us to the next point, turn 1, Coppice.

"Now, boys and girls. This is Coppice. Coppice is a LOVELY corner, which you can take nearly any way you like as it sweeps up towards Charlies. However, what have you got to remember, especially at the beginning?"

We looked at him, enraptured but clueless.

"Come on! It's a left-hander. Nearly every corner at Cadwell is a right-hander, so that side of your tyre's going to get well warm and sticky. The left side is not going to get such a good workout, though, so be careful at the start. You should give it at least a couple of laps before going all hero. Right; let's look at Charlie 1 and 2."

We followed him up like a bunch of young Hamlyn residents, Jeremy occasionally swigging from his energy drink rather than tooting on a pipe, as we walked up the hill towards Charlies.

"Cadwell is a lovely track. Yeah, it's technical and everyone's scared of the Mountain (which they don't need to be) but I mean; LOOK at it! I love it. Right; Charlies. As you come up out of Coppice, you'll be sweeping over to the left of the track, looking for that apex. However, we're going uphill now and most of you will need to drop a gear as you approach, especially those of you on those diddy two-strokes.

"As we come to Charlies 1, you'll need to be on the left but you're looking for that first apex. See that dark line running along the centre of the track? You want to keep just left of that to start and then cross it up there, where you can see another line making a cross in the tarmac. You're now aiming for the right side of the track but don't think this is the apex, because Charlies is a… DOUBLE apex. If you go in too tight here, you'll get all squirelly before Charlies 2 and you'll be having a chat with the Marshals along the Park straight. They're lovely people but you don't want that. You wanna be racing, right?"

His delivery was sublime and he had full control of his audience. There was so much to take in and I'm sure I wasn't the only one suffering from information overload.

"Onto Park straight, then," he continued. "Thrash it here. Hard against the stop and change up as quickly as you can before you get to those countdown markers. You need to be in top well before the 300 metre countdown sign, right? Find yourself a decent braking marker, knock it down a couple of gears and sweep round Park, heading towards Chris Curve. Here, you want to be staying near the centre of the track as you approach Gooseneck, which will be our next challenge."

We walked round Park, Chris and Gooseneck and down towards Mansfield. The walk illustrated just how hilly Cadwell Park is. Much of Lincolnshire is flat but here, Mother Nature appears to have gathered all the hills and vales in one five-square mile area. Jeremy stopped just before the corner at the bottom of the hill.

"Mansfield has the perfect braking marker and target point. This diamond (he pointed to a diamond-shaped repair in the track surface) provides a great visual aid. If it's dry, aim for the right-hand corner. If it's wet, get yourself roughly halfway between the edge of the diamond and the kerb. Don't touch the kerb if it's wet, though, else you and your bike are gonna be TOAST! You need to knock it down a gear here to give you the drive as you exit Mansfield towards the chicane. Don't forget that it's another left-hander, though so keep it sensible for the first lap or two."

We walked on. A number of people were comparing notes, looking back towards the Gooseneck before turning back to face the direction of race, their hands out flat, making the classic replication of a bike leaning over. My head was swimming as I tried to keep abreast of Jeremy's commentary. It was like no school lesson I remembered.

As we started walking through Mansfield, he got us to stop and pose for a mass photo for the Bemsee Facebook page; 50-odd nervous rookies on the embankment and Jeremy in the foreground grinning like a Cheshire Cat. Having sorted that, we made our way to the chicane.

The chicane isn't popular, as it spoils the tempo of an otherwise beautifully flowing track. It was put in place following a disastrous crash by Yukio Kagayama in the 2003 BSB Championship that ended his season and nearly cost him his life. Jeremy was another non-fan and related a discussion he'd had with former BSB champion John Reynolds.

"I told him, 'That chicane? I hate it – completely screws you for the Mountain approach.' John wasn't impressed, 'cause he told me, 'I designed that.'"

"'It's shit', I told him. Probably not nice but none of us like it, even now."

"However, you can make the best of it, so long as you approach it correctly. When you exit Mansfield, keep in a lower gear and swing out to the left. As you go into the chicane, you're aiming for both kerbs to make a straight line. As you lift out of that left-hand exit, you can see the track widens, so you can briefly pin it for the Mountain approach. Let's go!

"OK; the Mountain. This left-right bit at the bottom is a bit tight and you've not really got many options because you need to be in the right place as you crest the top. So; out of the chicane, keep over to the right. Find a braking marker near the kerb, tip left then right so you're coming up the hill just right of centre. At the top of the Mountain, running along the centre of the track, there's a joint line. Use that as your marker and try to stay right. Not too far, mind. Too far right and you're on the grass and into the Armco. There ain't much room and if you hit the grass, you will definitely be off. We don't want that, do we? Course we don't.

"You also REALLY don't want to go too far left. Too far left means catching the kerb and bouncing onto the grass. If you're lucky. More likely is that you'll do an end over end and that really WILL hurt. As a rule, when it's wet, painted kerbs are a big 'no-no' and that's especially true at Cadwell.

"You can't see it as you come up, of course, like most of the circuit but you'll be hitting a slight left on the crest, then right as you get back to Hall. So; get yourself a little right of centre and give it as many beans as you think you're hard enough for. Taking off is great but remember; it'll lose you seconds and, if you're one of the quicker riders, every second counts.

"There you go, guys. Cadwell in a nutshell. Don't be afraid of the Mountain. The track might feel skinnier than some but it's a beautiful circuit. Just go out and enjoy yourself. I mean; that's the whole point, isn't it - having fun? Go on, then. Thanks for coming. See you all in the morning."

A ripple of applause went around the crowd. Jeremy was hugely entertaining. He really knew his stuff and the circuit. I for one was pleased to have made the walk and, information overload or not, Dan, Simon and I discussed what we'd been shown as we walked back to the paddock.

Back in the gazebo, I caught up with Mark. We swapped the front wheel, to have the bike set up for a wet session tomorrow. The forecast had a 90% probability for rain, so not having a dry rear wasn't such a big deal, even if the thought of doing my first race at Cadwell on a soaked track wasn't high on any wish list. Still;

nothing could be done about that now. We were as ready as we were going to be. "Sylvie" was fuelled and Mark and I had done a few last-minute checks, including fitting replacement Dzus fasteners (quick-release clips) for the fairing that I'd lost last week. All that was left was to get something to eat.

With limited facilities, we decided to get something in town We found a busy chippie, where I ordered cod and chips for us both; perfect, healthy food for racers. With two unfeasibly large boxes of hot food on my lap, Mark drove us back to the circuit.

As we approached, we were once again stopped at the gate but Mark was ready with our tickets this time. The tickets were scanned and we drove back to the caravan.

After the very welcome fish supper and a cold bottle of Peroni each, we washed up before settling in for the night. Tomorrow would be qualifying and racing day, so I needed to get some sleep.

Saturday: Qualifying/Race Day 1

Practice day had been scorching but race day dawned wet. Very wet. Still; that was all right as we had already fitted the wet wheels last night. Despite my concerns about the circuit and the weather, I was looking forward to my first wet race. Everyone would be slower and smoother, plus Cadwell is twice as long as the Brands Indy track, so it would be a while before I faced the inevitable lapping moments.

Due to the weather, all classes would be given a quick practice session before qualifying, which was as well, given the track conditions. I got changed and Mark asked if I had a waterproof suit cover. I didn't so he suggested a bin bag. That would at least act as a windbreak under the leathers.

Getting a pair of scissors, I cut out holes for my head and arms, then slipped the bag over my t-shirt before putting the base layer on, followed by the back protector and leathers.

If I'm honest, when I bought those leathers, they had just fitted. Over a year had passed since then and my sedentary lifestyle meant the inevitable middle-age spread was in full evidence, so putting the suit on, while a challenge, was at least possible. Back protectors had become mandatory for 2019 and getting suited up was more than a squeeze now. Note to self: DIET.

The call came for the Minitwins. As I rode out from the gazebo, it started raining. Following advice from Rod (Harwin) yesterday, I had put some heat into the rain tyres for about ten minutes; just long enough to open the blocks up but not so much to start degrading the rubber. As I approached the collecting area, Carl Bell called me over. He'd just completed his practise session and was keen to pass on some advice.

"It's very slippery out there, Steve. There are loads of leaves on the inside line between the Hairpin and Barn. It's also really windy up at Park and Chris, so watch out for the cross wind."

With Carl's warnings ringing in my head, I rode down into the collecting area. Vanessa pulled up next to me and I leant across to pass the advice before we were signalled to join the track.

It was good advice. The whole inside line was coated with leaves, with maybe a metre-wide strip between the edge of the leaves and the outside white line to ride through. As we made our way to the start-finish line, a narrow dry line was being formed as everyone rode line astern. Once onto the straight, many riders left their inhibitions behind and caned it up to Coppice, leaving me for dead. I did notice, however, on my first return to Barn that there were two bikes parked up against the Armco already, having not even completed the first lap. Being slower had given me a temporary advantage.

I was concerned that vision in the wet would be an issue but during practise at least, where we were more spread out, riding fast allowed the rain to run off the visor quickly. Tilting the head left and right got rid of any persistent droplets, so all was good. I left a small gap at the bottom of the visor to prevent it misting up.

Having survived practice, we came in to wait for the qualifying call. I went to see how Dan was getting on. The rain and wind had not been kind to his gazebo frame, which had buckled in the wind. It was now being held together with a variety of cable ties and oddments of timber he had found in his van. Unfortunately, all the repairs were doing were creating breaks further along the frame. Simon and I held it all up while Mark and Dan liberated some timber from a nearby skip enclosure to reinforce the frame. Dan had the only mock Tudor gazebo on site.

I had found it difficult to get my base layer on earlier but Rob Cameron, owner of 151s, the undersuit of choice, was not only on site but was set up a few metres along from me. I popped in to see if he had a top in large. He did, so I bought a suitably lairy yellow one.

I looked at the bike in his awning; a Kawasaki Ninja 300, which he was part-sponsoring for Lewis Jones, another up-and-coming talent *(Lewis ended the season as the Ninja series runner up)*. We chatted about the bike, the weather and then I got to tell him how my rear wheel had destroyed its bearing.

"Do you know what part number it is?" he asked. "It's just that I might have some here."

Really? That would be a stroke of luck but I wasn't going to build my hopes up. I had no idea what the part number was but, although one rear bearing was gone, the other one was still in place. I could check.

"Have a look," said Rob. "If I've got a pair, you can take them. Don't pay me; just bring a replacement set to your next round."

Not daring to hope, I ran back to my gazebo and picked up the damaged rear wheel. Getting it back to Rob's truck, we looked for the part number. He went into the back of the truck and pulled out a bag full of boxed bearings. In that bag was a pair of matching bearings. "There you go. Just bring me the same when you come to Snett."

I was gobsmacked. Having put out an unsuccessful request earlier, I hadn't expected to find anything now. I was elated. If I could get the bearing fitted, I'd be back to having a dry and wet set up again.

I phoned Paul at Quickshift to tell him I had a pair of replacement bearings. "Get that wheel down here now," he said. Mark loaded the car and set off, as I got ready for qualifying.

Feeling much happier, I joined the Minitwins in the collecting area and we set off for our qualifying session. I'd missed qualifying completely at Brands, thanks to another rear wheel incident (let's hope there wasn't a pattern developing here) and didn't know what to expect. As it turned out, it was simply a case of getting the tyres warmed over a couple of laps and then, well, thrashing the bike as much as I dared to get the best time possible.

Once again, Sylvie's lack of power showed its card. While the pole sitter managed a 1:51.424 lap, despite the continuing rain, I could only come up with a best time of 2:32.225. This was appalling; 41 seconds behind the leader but at least I got a qualifying time. Unlike professional racing, even slowpokes like me are allowed to race and aren't bound by the 95% time of the fastest rider, probably because we're paying for it. I was at the back of the grid but had got there on my own merits this time.

2:32 is a poor time but I could now set some realistic goals, based on my Brands experience. Not wanting to be too ambitious, my initial target would be 2:30 for my first race, thinking even I should be able to take two seconds off that terrible qualifier. What I really wanted to do was get at least ten seconds off but I needed to be realistic. At Brands, I was consistent and there had been little difference between each race. I didn't expect anything to change much for Cadwell.

Mark returned with the wheel, now wearing shiny new bearings. Paul had worked his magic again and, an hour and £25 later, we were ready to roll. Happy days.

Dan Thomas was preparing for the Thunderbike race. It wouldn't earn him any more signatures but would get him would get more track time and experience. With his current form, he might also bag another trophy.

Dan was the complete antithesis to me; confident, skilled and bloody fast. After that first Brands race, I knew I was going to be a tail-ender who would have to get used to being lapped but Dan was something else. He'd won second and third place trophies at every race so far and was only disappointed that he'd not yet achieved that elusive first rookie place. For that, he would have to get the better of Matt Wetherell who, as a police bike instructor, was going to be hard to beat.

I was happy to circulate but wanted to get better and definitely needed to go faster. At 56, I was painfully aware of my limitations and my mortality. I wasn't a fearless young gun who had no responsibilities but I still wanted to make realistic improvements. Thus my "Let's take two seconds off" target.

Dan checked his fuel. "I've been getting through about four litres each time, so I'm going to put six and a half in. That way, I'll still have the two litres required if I get called in to scrutineering.

I hadn't even thought about how much fuel to put in. Not wanting to run out, even taking the two-litre minimum requirement into account, I had simply been filling the tank; another basic rookie error. An SV650 fuel tank holds nearly 14 litres, which is about 10.5 kilos. Six litres would come in at 4.5 kilos. I was therefore carrying an additional and unnecessary 6 kilos of fuel, sloshing around in the tank. I needed every assistance that I could get and six kilos of excess weight was not going to help my cause.

Mark Gillam had calculated that Vanessa had been getting through 0.23 litres per lap. For six laps, we would theoretically need 1.5 litres to complete the race, another 0.25 litres for the warm up lap, plus the two-litre minimum at the end of the race, so four litres should be more than enough for a race.

Another trip to Rod Harwin got me a syphon and a five-litre jug. We extracted all the fuel and found that, even after qualifying, I still had nine litres in there, which wasn't doing me any favours. Having removed it all, we replenished the tank with six litres. At my pace, there would be plenty of fuel left. I knew I'd get lapped so would only cover a maximum of five out of the six laps. Four litres would have been more than enough but I was taking no chances. Besides, if there was a restart, there'd be no chance to go back for more fuel.

Before changing, we checked the track condition. It had stopped raining but from the Mountain, we could see the start/finish straight. The track was still soaked, with a river running across the finish line. We were definitely using wets.

We went back to the paddock, to find Dan in final Thunderbike preparation. He looked a little tense, so we helped by removing his tyre warmers. I took out the front paddock stand and, as Dan got on the bike, Mark took away the rear. Dan made his way to the collecting area, while we walked to the clubhouse to watch from the start of the Hall bends.

The bikes set off and we watched Dan set up to his grid position; row 5, 15th slot. I was still trying to get the idea of someone with one meeting under his belt being so far up the grid. The lights went out and the bike flew off in a foggy cloud of spray towards Coppice. As they disappeared from view, we craned over to look to the foot of the Mountain, waiting for them to reappear.

The first few charged up the Mountain and into Hall Bends. We couldn't see Dan but it's not easy to keep up with riders. At the start, you remember bike numbers and colours, along with what the rider is wearing. Once you get that sorted, next you're finding yourself counting places until the lapping starts, after which you give up working out who's where and just check that your rider is still riding. We'd missed Dan first time but would watch as they went along the finish straight to catch up again.

Only we didn't see him, nor did we catch him on the next couple of laps. We finished watching the race (where I regretted not entering, as there was a very pedestrian Ducati that even I could have passed) before walking back up to the paddock.

Dan's bike was already there, mounted on its paddock stands and covered in grass. He had been punted off at Chris Curve and had to lay his bike down. He'd snapped a crash bung and bent the gear and clutch levers but the bike was otherwise intact, albeit looking a little second-hand. A few delicate taps with his club hammer got the levers straight and he cut a length off the crash bung without affecting its fit. Dan and his bike were good to go again.

There was still a while before we were due out, so I returned to the caravan for a drink. I hadn't drunk anywhere near enough at Brands so I wasn't going to repeat the mistake. I had made a bacon and egg sandwich for Mark and myself this morning, so had at least eaten. Another mental diary note would be to plan what and when to eat in future; plenty of fruit and snacks, pasta and a decent (but not heavy) breakfast. Oh; and plenty of loo breaks and a good night's sleep would help.

Wear had made my leathers more pliable and less restricting, although they were still a bit tight. I would have to get that sorted, especially if I was going to get a chest protector. Only back protectors were mandatory but many riders wore chest protectors too. Others had airbag suits or airbag vests that fitted over their suits. The level of protection afforded to a bike racer today has improved vastly but the risks remain high.

Race 1
(Row 13, Grid 37)

The first call for Minitwins went out as Mark and I tidied up. It was important that we kept the working space under control and that we knew where everything was. Racing is stressful enough without adding the worry of mislaid tools. I only wished my garage at home was as tidy.

I removed the front tyre warmer and stand, then put on my helmet and gloves while Mark sorted the back end. With him holding the paddock stand, I found it easier to get on the bike and roll it forward, starting it as it rolled off.

Dan, Simon and I rode to the collecting area line astern. As we approached, a little boy held up a sign that read "Wet race - rain lights on". Next to him, his mum, the marshal called me over, checked my number and said, "Grid 37, row 13."

I pushed Sylvie to our lowly last grid place and waited for the rest of the grid to roll up. It seemed an age until we got the green flag telling us to go on the grid for warm up.

As we made our way through the woods, I could see that the leaves had been swept up and there was now dry space through the woodland section. It was still slippery though and everyone was being cautious.

I wasn't the last rider to arrive, despite my grid position. One of the higher-ranking riders threaded his way to a point nearer the front as the marshals guided him to his spot. The lights seemed a long, long way off but that didn't matter; all I had to do was make sure I got away cleanly with everyone else.

The marshal stepped off the track. He waved his flag and we shot off towards Coppice; a heaving mass of noise and spray. Everyone got back to the grid without incident, lining up again for the start. The start marshal waited for a green flag at the back to wave the all-clear before stepping away from the track, pointing to the lights. The revs went up.

The lights lit up, we waited, they went out and we were off! Being at the back didn't have me any slower off the line; the one thing I had been able to do so far was make good starts. I'd get the revs up to about 3,000 and hold the bike on the clutch, slipping it out as the lights changed. I managed to hold on to the tail of fellow rookies Alan and Vanessa but they started to pull away from me once we'd gone through the first corner and entered Charlies 1 and 2. I had remembered from last night's track walk not to peel in too early. As Charlies is a double apex (hence Charlies 1 and 2), the apex is not where you'd expect it to be. The problem for me was that I was thinking too much about this and, by the time I'd cleared Charlies 2, the rest of the pack had cleared off.

I tucked in and stamped through the gears, only getting up to fourth by the time I'd reached Park corner. Alan had managed to pick up a place but I was catching Vanessa up rapidly.

Too rapidly, as it turned out. I saw her bike's nose dive as she braked really early, so much so that I nearly rear-ended her. I changed my line, putting me to her left side as we leaned right into Park towards Chris Curve. Unfortunately, I made the mistake of not changing back down, so couldn't make a clean effort through Gooseneck.

Coming down to Mansfield, I aimed for the diamond-shaped repair near the corner. Jeremy had advised clipping the right-hand corner of that diamond if the track is dry but going further right if it was wet. It was and I did, happy with how I'd got round. I swung left to line up the chicane (another non-favourite) but hadn't changed out of fourth and Sylvie struggled to pick up. I dropped back into third but that lost me more time. Vanessa had made better progress and was already tilting left for the Mountain approach.

I followed her in, first left then immediate right to get onto the Mountain for the first time where again I heard Jeremy's advice. "There's a dark line running up the hill, right along the centre. Approach it from the left but hit the crest just to the right of it. Don't go too far left or right as there's no escape from the grass." I crested the hill way too meekly but got over safely enough to approach the Hall bends.

Hall bends are lovely, rising and turning gently right - left - right - left before reaching the first proper test; the Hairpin, a sharp right-hander that drops you steeply towards Barn Corner. As I came out of the hairpin, I could see Vanessa tipping into Barn. She was still reachable. If my bike had the grunt, that was.

Back onto the start/finish straight, I remembered to change up as the rev limiter light came on. I got Sylvie up to fifth by the time I reached Coppice. Vanessa was still in sight.

Round Charlies 1 and 2, I clicked into fourth to make the rise, selecting fifth once I'd straightened up onto the Park straight. I didn't get into top before the 300-metre marker but again, Vanessa was braking hard as she approached Park corner and I had caught her once more. Park Corner looked like my best chance at passing, so I followed her through to Chris Curve and on towards the Gooseneck.

Dropping into Mansfield, I was so intent on following her line that I forgot to change down again, so didn't change to third until after exiting Mansfield, which was way too late and allowed Vanessa to leave me standing again.

So it was for the rest of the race; me catching Vanessa at Park, only to see her shoot off after Mansfield until the race was over. I was passed by the leaders on the fourth lap; something I was happier with than Brands but it meant I didn't complete the full race distance. I remembered to be in third gear before turning at Mansfield by the end of the race and, although I had come in honourable last place again, I had learned an awful lot about the track in that short time.

I may have been last finisher but I did at least finish. The race had been very wet, with water running off the track everywhere. The attrition rate was high, with six non-finishers. Most had come to grief at Barn Corner, where there were a number of bikes against the Armco, their riders looking glumly back onto the track.

I rode past, over to the exit at the base of the Mountain and on to my pit space. Seeing Mark waiting with the rear paddock stand in hand, I broke out into laughter.

"That was AWESOME! I want another go!" I shouted. I had come last but really didn't care. Cadwell was the one track I had been worried about but if that race was any indicator, I had no reason to be. So long as I looked out for myself and respected the track, everything would be fine.

We wouldn't be out for a while, so I had a chance to relax. Mark syphoned the fuel and refilled with six litres but we left the tyres for the moment. The high clouds were moving by pretty quickly, so the track may well have dried by the afternoon but I wasn't going to change anything just yet.

Mark and I took a stroll to the clubhouse to grab some lunch. I wanted to call my other half Cheryl to let her know how I'd got on but I had left my phone in the caravan. Not wanting to keep her in the dark, I borrowed Mark's phone to speak to her.

There was no answer on her private number, so I immediately dialled her work mobile. She answered, saying simply, "Can I call you back?" She was probably in a meeting, so I said that was fine and hung up.

Unbeknownst to me, the reason that she couldn't speak to me at that point was because she needed to compose herself. I had called both her phones in quick succession, using my mate's phone number. She saw that as, "Mark is trying to get in touch because Steve has crashed/is injured/is dead." A little while later, I got a text from her pointing out exactly those scenarios. I felt awful and phoned up immediately to apologise.

In hindsight, I should have known. Cheryl was incandescent and justifiably so. I was eventually forgiven but I knew from then on to not call unless it was from my phone. She would rather have a go at me for not contacting her, than have a call from someone with bad news. So, that was today's big lesson; if my phone wasn't immediately available, wait. Sometimes, we blokes can get it very, very wrong.

Having settled that particular issue, Mark and I sat down to eat; filling our stomachs and some of the time before my next outing. The meal was bland but I didn't care; I was famished and would have eaten a cardboard box had it been on offer. That first mouthful made me realise how hungry I was.

While eating, Mark offered some feedback. "You don't look very confident out there," he said. "Don't get me wrong. It's easy to sound critical when I'm just spectating but you were much quicker on your R6, so I know you can go quicker now.

"You're not leaning into Hall, either. I mean, the bike's almost upright going in and you're sitting right up, looking really tense."

He was right and I knew it. I'd been overthinking everything; I remember berating myself at Charlies, Mansfield and the chicane in particular. If I'm honest, I was grateful for the comments, as they confirmed what I suspected. I would try to relax more in the next race.

I walked to the race office to see if the result sheets were out. They were and, despite coming 30th/last, I was pleased to see that I had indeed achieved a 2:30 lap. Well, 2:30.556 but it was a step in the right direction, so that was good. Mindful that I'd improved but then lost it a bit at the opening Brands Hatch meeting, I wasn't going to allow myself any premature celebrations. I'd gone a bit quicker and was fine with that.

The next couple of hours were spent catching up with my fellow rookies Dan, Simon, Vanessa, Alan and Matt. We'd all had good races, Matt and Dan in particular. Matt had got his umpteenth rookie winner's trophy and Dan had come a creditable fourth. He was really disappointed but had struggled to pass a backmarker (not me this time) whose lines he couldn't figure out through Hall Bends. By the time he eventually got past, he'd lost too much time. Still; it was more points in the bag, so he wasn't too worried.

Race 2
(Row 12, Grid 34)

The call came for Race 15, our second outing. Although there were fallers from this morning's race, most had still done enough to qualify above me. I had moved up one place, though, so would give it my best shot to get further up. The rain had stopped some time ago but the track was still wet pretty much everywhere. I noticed about half a dozen bikes with dry rear tyres on, though and wondered if the riders knew something the rest of us didn't.

Like many UK circuits, Cadwell Park has its own microclimate; there could be blistering sunshine in Louth four miles away but teeming down here, or vice versa. The same applied to the track and the Hall bends to Barn corner section will invariably be the last place to dry. It's all under trees and is reliant on bikes lifting the wet through the tyres. The park section is higher and more open, so get both sun and wind to speed up the drying process.

There was bright blue sky in the distance but still a rivulet of water running across the flag line. We made our way through the woods onto the start line, waiting for the warm up lap. The marshal waved his green flag and we were off.

Despite that wet patch on the start line, as we rose out of Coppice and into Charlies, the track was almost dry. I was concerned about my tyre choice but I wasn't the only one using wets. Besides, at my pace, the tyres wouldn't be getting a lot of wear. I'd be fine.

It played on my mind though and, as we returned to the start line, I was more nervous than I had been for race 1. Wary about doing my first wet race, all I could do was wait for the lights to change.

The lights went out and I got (for me) a phenomenal start, passing three riders immediately. So much for the nerves. A rider at the back followed me, before muscling his way through the pack to disappear from my view as everyone leaned left into Coppice.

Through the first, then the second and third bends, I was still ahead before Sylvie's 59 asthmatic horses started showing their colours as all but one of the riders I'd passed returned the favour down the Park straight. I caught up with them on the top corner but my nerves were not as steady as theirs and they left me behind at Chris Curve, going into the Gooseneck. Vanessa was still behind me though, which was good. For now, I was not last.

By lap two, Vanessa had got her act together, passing me easily as I approached Park corner; ironically, her weakest point last time around and where I had been planning to pass her all race. Again, Sylvie's lack of grunt made keeping up with her difficult at best. Passing? Well, that was impossible, although much of that was also down to me braking too early and my unwillingness to lean, which would allow me to go through corners a lot quicker.

My inexperience brought up a couple of issues. Firstly, I learned quickly that racing lines are very important; sticking to your line especially so. I could hear the fast riders coming as I approached the chicane on lap four and braced myself. The anticipation of being passed was as frightening as the passes themselves because, as I was passed by Keith Povah and Dan Singleton to my right, my instinct was to get out of their way, so I lifted the bike and moved left, putting me directly in the path of Glyn Davies. How he kept it upright, I never knew but I made a point of finding him in the paddock to apologise as soon as the race was done.

The second incident was at Park Corner. Once again, my fear and lack of experience had me try to get out of a rider's way by lifting Sylvie up. What I didn't realise was that I was being passed on both sides and the second rider literally took paint off my fairing. There was no time to be frightened or to think about it; I just had to get on with getting around the track, so gritted my teeth and carried on. It all happened so fast that I didn't even get the chance to see who it was and, with wanting to stay on board and finish, I never had the opportunity to talk to the other rider afterwards.

Aside from my two "racing incidents", the race was otherwise uneventful for me. On the way down to Mansfield on the last lap, however, I saw Sam Kent's bike on the grass, with Sam standing forlornly on the hill with a marshal. "Aw, Sam! Not again!" I thought, remembering his huge off at Paddock last time out. Sam was fast, way faster than me but man, he was a heroic crasher. As it was, his beautifully turned out SV now looked more like a battered bobber than a race bike. Still; he'd got it repaired after Brands and was at least here. Whether he'd be racing any more this weekend was another matter.

I slowed down, intending to offer Sam a lift before remembering that this was an amateur club race, not a MotoGP event. Sam would go back with his bike in the recovery van; the marshals were a rescue, not a delivery service. I carried on back to the paddock, amused at my naivety.

Mark was helping Dan get his bike on to its stand when I returned to the paddock. He came over to do me the same service and said, "That looked better. How did it feel?"

I'd taken his comments on board and hoped that I had looked less awkward going into Hall. Mark thought that it looked smoother and that I was shutting off later. I was still too timid on the Mountain, though. We'd see if there were genuine improvements when we read the result sheets.

I went to the office and got result sheets for Dan, Simon and me. I scrolled down the list; there was Dan in 17th place (third rookie), so he was back to his trophy-winning ways. Simon had got 27th and I had once again got last place, albeit 30th this time.

I looked at my best time: 1:26.981. Bloody hell; that was more like it. It was still slow but that was a good three seconds off my previous time and five seconds faster than my qualifier. I could report back home to Cheryl that Steve was racing rather better this time around. We packed the tools away again and re-fuelled Sylvie, ready for tomorrow's shenanigans.

Everyone was heading to the Clubhouse for the awards. I wanted to acknowledge the results of my fellow Minitwin rookies, so Mark and I joined them in the bar. Or at least tried to. The place was heaving and very loud. So much so that, although we heard the Minitwin class being called, we didn't hear any of the names. Deciding to quit while we were ahead, we returned to the caravan.

All that nervous energy had made me ravenous again, so Mark and I went into town, where we found a great Italian restaurant, Via Italia. Although we hadn't booked, the waitress smiled and led us to a table. A Steak Stroganoff for me, Steak Gorgonzola for Mark and a large Peroni each went down very well. Frankly, I could have eaten it all again but allowed temperance to guide me. Suitably sated, we went back to the circuit, flashed our tickets at the gate and settled in for the night. Sunday's forecast was unclear so we had kept the wet set up. Tyre choice could wait until morning.

Sunday: Race Day 2

Race 1
(Row 11, Grid 33)

Just as the previous two days, I was wide awake by 6:00, so walked down to the shower block while it was still quiet. Although it wasn't. Only three of the four showers were working and there was a scrum for the remaining places. Still; people were getting in and out quickly enough, so I didn't have much of a wait.

Suitably scrubbed, I walked back to the caravan. It was still wet underfoot but the forecast was for sunshine today. Huzzah!

Back in the caravan, Mark was up and dressed, so I asked if he'd like an egg and bacon sandwich. He declined and, not wanting to create too much washing up, I grabbed a bowl of Weetabix instead. Oh, the glamorous life of the motorcycle racer.

We ate in contemplative quiet, washing the cereal down with a cup of tea each. Carl and Lin were on their way to the Clubhouse to grab breakfast with Wayne, so it was just Mark and me for the moment. We walked to the Mountain to check the track. It was still wet but the breeze was picking up, so there was a chance it would be dry for the Minitwins.

It would be a while before the Minitwins would be called. There was another disruption due to a faller having to be taken to hospital by air ambulance, following a nasty tumble. Word got back that the rider, Bob Couchman, was making good progress and had remained conscious throughout. The helicopter had, however, landed on the track, so the Blue Haze two-strokes were sent back to the paddock until the area had been cleared.

The track was still damp, so we were looking at wet tyres. Bob's crash had put everything back and it looked like we'd not be racing until after lunch. I joined Carl who, following his own tumble on Saturday, felt unable to ride for the rest of the weekend. He'd had gone out in practise to see how he felt but had too much pain in his leg, after he had been pinned down under the bike, the footrest having dug hard into his calf.

I joined Carl and Wayne at the Mountain grandstand, watching the Rookie 600 race, trying to judge the conditions. Everywhere was drying; everywhere except the start/finish straight, which still had that river running across it just after the flag.

The 600 race progressed and the track got drier. I decided to change my tyres as there was more than just a thin dry line on circuit now. Everything had been delayed, so there should be time. By way of confirmation, the Tannoy announced that an early lunch was being called so the Minitwins would be first out after lunch.

The weather was improving by the minute, so Mark and I got the dry tyres back on. We worked together on the front first before sorting the rear. In hindsight, it would have been better to have each concentrated on a wheel. We were halfway through refitting the back wheel when Mike Dommett announced that, "Minitwins would be out in eight minutes' time".

Time was short and we still hadn't got the wheel assembled. It took a few fumbling attempts to line the brake hanger, spacer and hub before Mark could finally push the spindle into place. After a quick check of the chain tension, I got my helmet and gloves on to make my way onto the track. Mark cleared up the gazebo and then made his way back to watch from outside the club house.

The track was almost completely dry now, so changing tyres had been the right decision. I was happier knowing having the right set up but was unhappy about running on cold tyres. Later, Dan and I agreed that a wheel tree would be in order, along with a second set of tyre warmers so that the right, warmed tyres could be fitted quickly for any occasion. That would be an expense for another day, though.

We did our warm up lap (there was no surface water to speak of, so no issues) and I made my way to my allotted grid point. There were another five riders behind me for the start and I was keen to lose as few of those places as possible. I was getting more used to the expectations and had the engine revving at a constant 3000 RPM, holding it on the clutch, ready for the lights.

The lights went on and then out in short order. Even so, a rider ahead of me made the most spectacular of jump starts, getting himself a good bike length forward before the rest of the pack flew off the line. I made a good start again, getting past the jumper, closely followed by the other tail-enders. I lost a couple of places and then saw a raised hand ahead of me. This was the first time I'd seen a stalled bike and had to take immediate evasive action to get around the rider. We all cut a path either side of him and then peeled right into Coppice for the third time.

I wasn't going to worry about being gentle with Sylvie this time and practically caned her out of Coppice. I knocked down a couple of gears as I entered Charlies; a bit too many, as it turned out and the rev limiter kicked in, allowing everyone to get past. Cursing loudly, I changed into fifth to make chase. It was already too late but I recall getting into top gear far more frequently and keeping up with Vanessa for much of the race. However, by lap four, I was being lapped by almost everyone, which unsettled my rhythm. As I peeled out of Barn on lap five, I saw Vanessa reach Coppice; another lost opportunity.

Desperate to make up some of the deficit, I had Sylvie pinned, going into Coppice full tilt in top gear, dropping to fifth as I exited the corner and rose up the hill. Charlies 1 and 2 were taken beautifully and I felt a huge grin coming across my face.

"Come ON, Sylvie!", I heard myself saying. Jeremy would be proud. I pushed hard, overcooking it a little into the Gooseneck, which had me pulling up a little early and screwing Mansfield up as a result. I settled down for the chicane and could see Vanessa was just tipping left to the foot of the Mountain. I was definitely catching her. A quick left, then right had me opening the throttle a little too early as I crested the Mountain; enough to make me realise that the front wheel was up.

Holy shit; a wheelie! The front went light as I wound the throttle open. The bars wobbled but the front was pointing the right way as the wheel landed again.

I made chase into the Hall bends, with no riders behind me now. As I rounded the hairpin, Vanessa was entering Barn. I was too late. That wheelie had slowed me down (and unnerved me a little) but I didn't care. It had felt fantastic. Rounding Barn, I dropped a gear, tucked under the screen and charged up the start/finish straight. I was gutted to see the chequered flag being waved; I was convinced I could have caught Vanessa for a spring to the line had I got one more lap in.

It didn't matter, though. That, for me, had been the race of the weekend. Almost everything had gone right. The lap times felt better but I'd not know that until I got the results sheet. I didn't slow down much on that warm down lap and once again used the chicane rather than ride through the cones, simply to get as much use of the track as possible. It also allowed me to acknowledge the marshals, who were applauding every contestant, even slowpokes like me. I slowed down from the chicane and swept left at the Mountain for the track exit point. As I rode up the pathway, a marshal beckoned me to the collecting area.

I had been selected for a random dyno check. I laughed out loud, much to the bemusement of the marshal. This should be interesting. Vanessa and Nick, two other rookies had also been selected, so I pulled up alongside them. I couldn't believe that I was going to get a free dyno check but then learned that they don't tell you what power your bike is making. All they do is tell you whether it's within the power limit. "Dyno" Dan Beighton came over to take my bike.

"Race shift? Road shift?" he asked.

"Race shift", I told him. "Oh and the kill switch 'off' position is actually 'on'."

"Of course it is," came the reply.

"If you get more than 59, I'll be very happy," I ventured.

"You know we're not allowed to tell you the result, right?"

"Yep. Just saying."

With that, he wheeled Sylvie into the back of the truck, strapping her in and thrashing her within an inch. Reversing back out, Dan pushed the bike back to me.

"You didn't get more than 59, did you?" I asked.

He looked at me and, after a dramatic pause, said, "No." Now he knew why I had laughed at being selected for the dyno test. I rode back to the paddock, where Mark was waiting with the paddock stands. He, too, knew the futility of trying to test the bike so we took shared amusement at the notion.

Vanessa had been told that there was "room for improvement", whereas Nick's report was that his bike "was fine". I knew I needed to do stuff to give Sylvie more poke but that would have to wait at least until Snetterton. In the meantime, Mark and I checked that everything was clean and/or tight, put fuel in the tank and chilled until the next call.

Race 2
(Row 12, Grid 35)

Despite my fears of this circuit, things seemed to be going well. Of course, I was still too slow but my lap times were coming down. While we had been waiting for the dyno check, I'd looked with envy at Vanessa's bike dash. She had a datalogger fitted which recorded her lap times. I had to wait until later in the day to see what I'd achieved and even then it would only list the best time. Full data information wouldn't be available for a while. What I did know was that each time I had gone out, my best lap time had reduced. Slowly, slowly, catchee everyone else. Sort of.

I wheeled Sylvie up to Dan's gazebo and fitted the tyre warmers. It was now sunny, so the last race should be good. In the meantime, Mark and I started packing. The gazebo roof and sides had dried out, so this would be the best time to pack it away. Mark would load the van while I was out on track.

As had been the case at Brands, there was always something to do, even when I wasn't racing. There was some maintenance task or cleaning activity in the gazebo, sorting something to eat or drink, getting result sheets or other official stuff. Rarely did we find ourselves with nothing to do, other than in the evening. Once the bike was prepped for the next day, we could then relax.

I strolled down to the race office, where the results sheets were now available. At the bottom of the sheet was a note: "No 20 - please make sure you have a working transponder fitted."

Bugger. I had made sure the transponder had been fully charged before I left home on Thursday. It had been flashing in waves of four, indicating four days' worth of charge. When I had checked on Saturday, it was flashing twice, indicating two days' worth of charge. It would appear, however, that the last remnants of charge had ended during my last race, as the result sheet only showed two laps worth of data.

So, with Sylvie fuelled and the tyres cooking, I popped over to see Mark and Vanessa, set up nicely in their very professional-looking truck and awning, to ask if I could charge the transponder from their power supply. Mark was more than happy to let me do so and, although I'd only get about an hour's worth of charge in it, it would probably be enough.

While Vanessa was doing the business on track, Mark was always busy in the background, checking the bike out, fettling or poring over the telemetry data. I made a mental note to not only keep copies of the results paperwork but to also start keeping notes on other data; how much fuel I was using, tyre pressures, gearing, etc. There is so much information you can gather at a meeting, much of which will be useful for your own development.

The club result sheets include all qualifying, race and sector times, which is very useful for showing where you are stronger (or weaker). All this information would start to come into its own as my ability and confidence improved. Vanessa was not happy with her results but was being pragmatic. Like me, she was only taking positives and realising that her performance was rising every race. It was the first season for both of us and, although I had really hoped to be doing better, I was still excited at actually being here as a bona fide racer.

Thinking back to my original "low bar" list, I had already made achievements:
1. I'd entered TWO meetings.
2. I'd completed seven out of eight races so far.
3. I'd not crashed yet, although I'd already seen lots other riders go down.
4. I'd not killed myself yet, either. Always a bonus.

The only item I'd failed on was to not finish last. However, the way I saw it was that, at both rounds, I may have come in last but other than the first race of the weekend, both at Brands and Cadwell, I was never at the back of the grid. I had been last finisher but every race had had a minimum of two non-finishers, so I kept moving up the grid as the weekend progressed. Slow? Sure but I was finishing. I was learning a lot about each track and felt that, with more application on my part (and maybe some work on Sylvie's engine), I could improve on any return visit.

I reminded myself that it had taken me 40 years to get here. I was older, a little wiser, far more aware of my mortality (and lack of flexibility), definitely more cautious yet I was still having a ball. As I got faster, especially if I got an overtake that I didn't relinquish, there'd be no stopping me, albeit at a lower level to the racing gods I was up against.

The timetable was still behind schedule, even after a shortened lunch break, so I wandered back to the Mountain grandstand, where Carl and Wayne were watching the second Rookie 600 race. It's no fun watching the race you're supposed to have been in but Carl wanted to gauge how many championship places he may have lost.

I walked back to the paddock, as the Minitwins would be due out soon. I hadn't reached my space when the first call went out. Mark was there, looking out for me.

"I wasn't sure if you were coming back," he said. He had fired the bike up already and was pulling the rear warmer off in readiness. I ran across to get my helmet and gloves while he finished getting the bike ready. Suitably togged up, I got to the collecting area, where I was sent to grid position 35, just behind Vanessa. She rolled up next to me and leant over.

"You never came back for your transponder," she told me.

I looked down. Bugger; I'd done it again. Knowing that I didn't have time to get it now, I put my hand up and a marshal stepped over.

"I've left the transponder behind," I said.

Sighing, he took a note of my number. "OK. I'll radio the office to let them know." I now knew that I'd have another "No 20 - please fit a working transponder" on my race report when I went to pick it up later. There was no point in worrying about it now. All I had to do was get on with the race.

We were waved through then set off on our warm up lap. I was beginning to like this circuit. Cadwell Park is narrow but it is beautiful and I couldn't wait to return. Back to the start line, I held the engine revs at 3000 RPM, holding the clutch to just below its biting point. The lights went out and we were off.

Immediately to my right, Vanessa's front wheel went skywards, popping an almost vertical wheelie. I flew past her but got passed almost instantly myself by Matt Wetherell, who'd not finished the previous race and had gridded behind me. Damn but he was fast. I watched in awe as he scythed his way through the pack ahead of me before getting my head down and lining up for Coppice.

We peeled left and the pack stretched out. By the time I had exited Charlies 2, the leaders were already leaning right into Park corner and smaller, mid-pack groups were forming. I remembered Jeremy's comment about ignoring everyone else, so got my head down (I also remembered to tuck in a bit more now) and reeled in the corners, if not the other riders.

Once again, it was only another lap before I resumed tail end Charlie duties thanks to a lovely overtake from Vanessa, who was making a bit too much of a habit of this. My aim of using Park as the ideal place to pass her was now becoming her favoured "overtake Steve here" spot. Still; it didn't matter. All I was concerned with now was making my lines, hitting the apexes, relaxing and improving my race craft.

I was lapped by probably half of the grid once again but the race seemed to be over too quickly. Sunday races are usually longer but, as a result of the unscheduled air ambulance visit, all races had been reduced. Both Minitwin races had gone from eleven to eight laps. I didn't even get that many, as I was lapped by the fifth circuit in each race. Despite that, I was really warming to the place. By race 4, I had finally started to relax; something that was reflected in my improved lap times.

The chequered flag came out and, all too soon, racing was over for another weekend. I made my way back to the gazebo.

Best laps this weekend:

Qualifying: 2:32.225
Race 1: 2:30.556
Race 2: 2:26.981
Race 3: 2:20.083
Race 4: 2:18.729

While still appalling (the weekend's best Minitwin time was 1:39.227), I took comfort in getting 13.5 seconds off my lap times over the weekend. This from someone who had come in with little confidence and an inherent fear of this particular circuit. So; not a bad weekend. All that remained was the five-hour drive home, a welcome from Cheryl and the dogs and a long night's sleep. Next up for me would be Snetterton in June. Until then, I had time to repaint the fairing and, if time and funds allowed, getting the carbs checked.

Chapter 5:
More To Do, More To Spend, More To Worry About.

Back home, it would be six weeks before I was out on track again. Much as I had wanted to enter the next round at Donington, funds were already tight, I had commitments and it clashed with Cheryl's birthday. She has been very supportive of this mid-life crisis ambition but I wasn't going to push my luck. Or my bank balance. I'd only entered two rounds so far and I was already haemorrhaging cash.

In previous years, I had provided a little financial sponsorship to some of the racers I knew, mostly youngsters in national support classes. This year, I had to apologise to anyone I had helped and tell them that any funds I had this year were likely to be spent on my own forlorn ambitions. Little did I know how expensive even my modest aims were going to be. Unless there really was no money at all, I still hoped to be able to attend at least four race meetings. I would then assess things to see if there would be a follow-up year. That, of course would be a discussion for another day, especially with Cheryl.

The long break allowed me to consider my options. I still had to work on my courage but Sylvie's (I was already used to using the name) lack of performance was a major issue. A 59-horsepower bike among a pack of ones putting out high 60s or low 70s was never going to be anything other than an inconvenience to everyone else and a frustration to me.

I was skint, so I wouldn't be able to get a decent bike, even if I sold Sylvie. Even finding money for the Snetterton entry fee was looking doubtful. Being self-employed means that, if you don't work, you don't get paid and I'd already had time off for a short break, as well as the time taken to attend the Cadwell Park round.

Finding a race-ready bike mid-race season was highly unlikely and even if one was available, I'd have to sell Sylvie first. My only option therefore was to try and improve on what I had and get the old girl up to scratch, or at least a bit closer to being so.

I made enquiries through the Minitwin social media groups but without funds, there was nowhere to go. The things I would need would involve money, potentially lots of it.

There was another option; my Gen 2 SV road bike, which hadn't been run since November last year. I considered stripping and converting it to a race bike but knew that wasn't realistic, at least not as a short-term, quick-fix solution. That had been the idea back in 2015 and I decided against it then, due to having neither the time, space nor skills for such a project.

When I first looked into the idea of racing, before buying Sylvie, I had contacted SDC Racing in Stevenage. They bought cheap SVs to convert into Minitwin-spec racers. At the time, the SDC option was too expensive, which is why I had looked at building my own. In the end, I had bought Sylvie, as she was almost Minitwin ready. I had to acknowledge her shortcomings now though, so contacted SDC to ask what budget I would need for them to convert my road bike (or to sort Sylvie). Some or all of the following seemed to be in order:

1. Replacement race-spec exhaust.
2. Hi Flow air filter.
3. Carb tune. To do this may require the wrecked air screws to be drilled out. It may be easier to source a new set of carburettors.
4. Re-lap the valves.
5. New piston rings (as I can't guarantee the engine's mileage).

It wouldn't be cheap but even if I had to have all that work done, it would be less drastic than cannibalising my road bike, based on the feedback I got. With an empty bank balance and pay day not due for a couple of weeks, everything was put on the back burner.

The financial life of the unsponsored racer is not easy. Wanting to pursue this obsession but knowing you also need to cover luxuries like, say, food and a mortgage tend to take the shine off things. Add to that the fact that, in hindsight (and based on how long the bike had sat in my garage before actually seeing a track), it would have been far more sensible to have waited and saved more money to buy a race-ready bike in the first place. I was now spending too much just trying to catch up. I might have to admit defeat, sell the bike, get a half-decent one and start again.

I sought advice from the guys in the Minitwins group. Many offers were made for exhausts, with prices ranging from reasonable to eye-watering but among those who, as one put it, would happily take my money, came the voice of reason.

"Steve, get your brakes serviced and running well. Strip the calipers and have everything moving smoothly. Put some high-spec brake pads in and get the system bled. The carb air screws may not be an issue but make sure the carbs themselves are free-running and that they open up fully. You may be surprised at what a simple bit of servicing will achieve and, if your brakes are improved, even if the bike doesn't have the power you'd like it to have, being able to brake later than the rider in front of you will give you some advantage."

This was sound advice and, with no money available, cleaning the brake calipers and carburettors was an obvious first step. I could look at the bigger engine servicing items in the winter. If I had the engine serviced, the bike could then be run on a dyno to see if it was any better. If I could at least get the power up to say, 62 HP, I'd be happier. I still needed to work on my nerve but that was something only I could do. I had to get my fear level down and remember that Sylvie was capable of far more than I was subjecting her to. That would come with practice and experience.

The advice brought a couple of things home to me. Firstly, my self-belief still needed much work and secondly, the level of support from everyone in the Minitwin class was humbling. Everyone in club racing wants you to do well. So do the people who are involved but not actually racing; wives, husbands, family members and friends. There is support from everyone. Well, almost everyone. A conversation with Mark Gillam, my main rival/tail-ender Vanessa's husband, reminded me about that support. Mark had been watching the Cadwell races by Hall bends. In front of him, another spectator was tutting.

"Bloody back markers. What are they doing? If they're not quick enough to be out there, they shouldn't be racing."

Mark challenged the man. "Oi! My wife is one of those back markers. Do you race?"

"No," came the reply.

"Well, unless you have the balls to do it yourself and get out amongst them, I'd shut up. She is at least racing. What are you doing, apart from criticising what you don't know about?"

I love our supporters.

Back to my current issue. Another recommendation from everyone was that I should do more track days. Alternatively, Bemsee test days, even if I wasn't actually racing, were available at about £90. Test days came with 1:1 instruction if requested and were free; something you needed to pay for at private days. I certainly needed more track time. The only way to learn a track was to ride it. The only way to learn to brake later was to ride the bike and practice. The only way to get my knee down (no, I still haven't) was to corner faster, brake later and lean over further. None of this could be done unless I rode the bike more. So; more track days, then. The money pit was rapidly becoming an abyss.

When we look at professional racers, we see them doing that 30-45 minute race and think, "That's a good life." Of course it is. It's glamorous, exciting and high-energy. What we don't see is the years of intense training, constant testing, data interrogation, on-board footage, track walks and the like that goes on throughout the career of that successful racer. If anything, it's worse for the privateer racer who not only has to do all that but also has to hold down a 9-5 job.

Not even the greatest riders in the world simply rock up, mount the bike and go out and win without first having done their homework. Today, we look at the likes of Marquez, Rossi, Rea, Bautista, Byrne, Haslam et al and forget that, while they are brilliantly talented, none of them achieved overnight success. Of course, some will have had privileged backgrounds or generous sponsors but they all started at the same level. A lot of them may also have had an inherent ability but every one of them will have built on his (or her) craft. They have all increased their speed, developed their skills and ended up having countless crashes and breaking their bodies to be able to regularly lift that shiny token at the end of a race.

As I say, most of the riders at world-class level also have an inbuilt skill set that the rest of us can only dream of but even when watching the leaders in my racing class, from the start line and as they inevitably lapped me, I was amazed at how fluid and confident they are. Being in such company, even at club racing level, was truly humbling, if you'll pardon the cliché. Those leaders are national-level racers who, with some decent backing, were more than able to give the professionals a run for their money. The track is by far the best (and the most intense) classroom you can get. Being amongst these fantastic racers allowed me the perfect opportunity to learn from them close up. Very close up, in some instances but learn I did.

Looking at those two overtakes at Cadwell; the first where I lost paint on the fairing at Park Corner and the second where guys passed me on both sides over the Mountain. The paint swapping incident was, well, focussing but I was surprised it hadn't scare me as much as I had expected. It made me jump, of course but, before I had entered my first race, I really was expecting to be permanently terrified. Of course, I was nervous, especially at the very first grid at the very first round at Brands but adrenaline kept much of that fear in check. This was a hitherto unknown character trait and quite a revelation. Racing was teaching me so much about myself as well as the bike and I wasn't quite the wimp I thought I was. When that close pass was made, all I allowed myself was a quick, sharp intake of breath before getting on with trying to catch the rider and follow him around the next corner.

The Mountain overtake was a little less clear-cut. I heard the pack coming and, based on my track position, knew they'd probably pass on my right. I realise now that I had over-compensated for this, which is why Glyn Davies ended up mounting the kerb as he passed me. At least he didn't hit the grass but I had also learned from that incident. Every time I went over the Mountain from that point on, I knew where I was aiming for (the dark line just right of centre) and, if anyone was coming up behind me, it would be their responsibility to find a safe way past, not mine to get out of their way; standard racer rules. I would aim to hold my line at every race, especially over the Mountain. Of course, I didn't get passed on every lap but maintaining that concentration and sticking to my lines clearly demonstrated the value of consistency; something that would later be reflected in my lap and sector times.

Having fellow racers provide advice and encouragement was another factor. As I have alluded to before, no one wants you to fail. Of course, everyone wants to beat you but you're not just making up the numbers, even if you're at the back. Matt Wetherell had put it well. "No matter where you are on the grid, just being there is what makes it a race for us all."

Chapter 6
Prepping For Snetterton

My next round, funds permitting, was at Snetterton, a fortnight away. There had been too many things for me to organise, so the bike had been left in the garage and not been looked at since Cadwell. I had ordered replacement wheel bearings: two sets of fronts to replace my bike's ones, plus a set for my second rear wheel and a pair to replace those that Rob Cameron had lent me at Cadwell.

I now had a new list of things to sort. I contacted my friend Steve Shrubshall, asking if I could use his workshop to replace the bearings as a priority. If we had time, it would be good to replace the chain and sprockets, too. Those on the bike were the same set that had come with the bike back in 2016. They looked all right but were probably due for replacement. If Steve could accommodate me, that was going to be a great help.

I had another, indirect request for Steve. My headstock paddock stand didn't fit into the yoke mounting hole but I knew Steve's own stand had fitted well. He had offered to make a new pin for me and I was keen to take his offer up now. The interim stand I'd bought was all right but the bike was always precariously balanced and I was never confident it wouldn't fall off, especially at Cadwell, where there were no level surfaces.

The final area to check was the carburettor operation. There wasn't time to strip them (I couldn't risk not having a bike for Snetterton) but I wanted to know that they were at least operating properly and able to open fully. So long as there was time, Steve was happy to get stuck in.

I didn't know if I'd have the money for Snetterton. I checked my bank balance but things were not looking positive. I needed about £400 for racing and testing and there was £15 in the bank. I was due to be paid on the day that Bemsee would take the entry fee but the salary might get paid in in until after Bemsee's withdrawal attempt. This was evidently playing on my mind as it came up in a dream that week. I was in the collecting area, ready to pull away to join the grid with everyone else. I was too far up the grid, somewhere around P12, so I knew it was a dream but when I went to get going, the bike stalled, only starting after most of the grid had got on to the track. When I did finally get the bike running, a marshal came over to tell me I hadn't qualified, so wouldn't be allowed to race.

That was it; all a bit bizarre but I could do without such dreams, thanks all the same. Racing was already seriously burrowing into my subconscious. For so long, it had been a dream and now here was I, actually having dreams because of it. Weird.

Steve kept his shop open late on Wednesdays so his mates could make use of the facilities. I met him through a Minitwins group and he had extended the same offer to me. As it turned out, Steve had done 95% of the work on my bike whenever I had taken it over. He and his friends were always keen to see my bike.

We carried out a cursory check. The chain and sprockets looked fine. There was a little wear but until this year, it didn't look as though the drive gear had taken much punishment. Breaking the chain, cutting the new one to length and riveting it together was going to take more time than we were likely to have so I put the unopened box of bits back in the van.

Wheel bearings were another matter. We looked at the set in the dry rear wheel. One side looked reasonable but the other bearing had bulges where the balls had been trying to get out. In addition, the inner race was cracked. I was really fortunate to have got away with it at Cadwell but I was not going to risk using that wheel at Snetterton; not with a bearing in that state.

Steve got to work, removing the old and fitting new bearings. I now had two sets of wheels that shouldn't give me any issues for the rest of the season. Advice from other riders was to replace the bearings at the end of the season, ready to start for the next one.

They were only £6 each; a small price to pay for such a vital element. I had considered cheaper bearings, some of which were only £3 but these were high-spec SKF units and I thought my life was worth the extra few quid. I'd had a close call at Charlies and had no intention of pushing my luck. Racing is dangerous enough without taking unnecessary risks.

The next job was getting the paddock stand sorted. I bought a headstock stand but none of the pins fitted my bike so, at Brands, I had to buy a stand that supported the forks from underneath. This type of stand is always hit and miss and there is always a risk of the bike falling off. A headstock stand is more secure and is the choice of professional racers.

Steve turned up a pin on his lathe and offered the revised stand to the bike. It was a perfect fit and lifted the bike about three inches off the ground, ideal for getting the wheel in and out. I thanked him for his continued support, loaded up the van and drove home.

I had no spare money to get anything else done, so Sylvie would have to go to Snetterton as she was. That was all right, as I'd already decided to accept the bike's limitations and would now look at simply improving my own skills and confidence.

As it happened, I sold my car recently and the money came in just at the right time. True to form, the payment for the Snetterton round went out 24 hours later. I also received a text from my instructor, for the test day. My next move would be to get in contact ahead of Friday.

The payment had gone and then Simon Wilkinson sent a message confirming that he, Dan Thomas and I had got a garage together for the weekend. That was great, as it meant I wouldn't have to pack the gazebo. All I had to do was pay my share of the garage money but that wouldn't be due until the Sunday before we left.

Everything seemed to be in place. All that was left was wait for the next race weekend and I was already impatient.

Chapter 7:
Round 5: Snetterton 300 (Norwich, Norfolk)

Thursday: arrival and set up.

Round 5 for everyone else was Round 3 for me, as I'd missed the Oulton Park and Donington Park rounds. Oulton was a good seven-hour drive and was only a one race day event which, for a rookie of my limited means, seemed pointless. Donington Park, a round I would have loved to have attended, clashed with a wedding and Cheryl's birthday, so I really couldn't attend. Missing two meetings had allowed me time to juggle funds at least and so my third round would see me returning to the Norwich circuit for the first time since last year's track day.

The fortnight leading up to Snetterton had been fraught again, mostly down to a lack of money. The van insurance and road tax had just been paid out and the Tax Man was chasing me for non-existing funds. Still; I could forget that for the next three and a half days.

When I had caused that phone call induced anxiety attack for my other half at Cadwell, I was taken with a comment she'd made on her Facebook page; that about me living my dream. At my time of life, such a phrase never really occurred to me but she was right and, sitting in my caravan in a contemplative moment made me realise how easy it is to forget troubles when you're racing a motorcycle.

I arrived at the circuit at about 7:00 to find the race office locked, so getting a key to our garage was going to be an issue. Or not, as Rob Davie, one of the four riders who had pitched in for the garage hire, had arrived ahead of me, set up, closed the door (having first left the key in the lock) and gone to his hotel. I thus spent the next hour unloading the van and setting myself up next to Rob's bike.

I phoned my instructor, Ben Rowswell to see if I could come over for a chat. As it turned out, he was standing just in front of me, so we walked back to garage 17 for him to look Sylvie over, ahead of Friday's practice sessions.

"Have you been to Snetterton before?" he asked.

I told him that I had but "only once, last year."

"OK. How do you feel?"

I told him that while I wasn't as nervous as I had been at the start, I was very aware of my limitations and I wasn't very confident. Additionally, I told him about the bike's lack of power but that my goal was to simply improve my ability and times.

Seemingly pleased with that last comment, the next question was, "Have you got your knee down?"

I laughed (which probably told him all he needed to know). "No. No, I haven't."

"Why not?"

"That will be the fear factor again"

"OK. Well, there's nothing to worry about but we'll see how we get on. We just need to get you out there. The confidence will come in its own time. So will the speed. Can I sit on your bike?"

He mounted the bike and immediately frowned.

"Blimey, how do you get on with the bars being that far back?"

I hadn't really thought about it but asked his opinion.

"Personally, I prefer them almost flat because it keeps my arms in a natural position. With them set like this, you're forcing your arms against your body. It must really make turning the throttle uncomfortable. The other thing is that, as you brake, rather than having nice straight arms to take the pressure evenly, you're twisting your wrists, which will make you really tired."

There was a lot to consider. Ben said that, for the first session, where I'd need to concentrate on relearning the track, I should leave the bars alone but then move them forward before the second session to see how it felt.

With a bucket-load of new information to process, I thanked Ben and went to get some dinner. Having eaten, I just put my head down and was asleep before I knew it.

Friday: practice.

I was awake by 6:00 and, while it was breezy, the sun was up already, so it was quite warm. I got dressed and stepped out of the caravan to go for a shower. It was as well that I had gone so early, as there were only three male shower cubicles. I may have to use the caravan's unit during the weekend but at least I had power, thanks to a hook up lead connected into the garage. I was the only one of our group with a caravan, so it wouldn't be an issue to anyone else.

The garage only had one double socket, so we needed to get creative with hook ups and extension leads in order to power eight tyre warmers, chargers, kettles and so on. If rain came as per the forecast, we may need to warm up more than four pairs of tyres.

Ben came over to say that my session had been moved to the afternoon session, so wouldn't be out until about two o'clock. Rob, Dan and Simon had booked full-day practice, so I could help get their bikes on and off the stands. I also took the opportunity to record some rough lap times for Dan and Simon, both of who were getting around in about 2:25. I had no idea what I would be doing but had estimated around three minutes per lap, based on my Brands and Cadwell speeds. Unfortunately, I'd not know until race day, unless Dan ran a couple of rough time checks for me. He had been moved to the faster, non-Rookie Minitwin group for practice, so was going out at different times to Simon and me. As a comparison, I thought I'd check out Matt Wetherell's times. I assumed the rookie series leader could put in better times but was still surprised as to just how much faster he was. By my rough, mobile phone lap timer reckoning, Matt was putting in 2:15 laps. Alan Hensby later told me that Matt had posted a 2:10 lap in one of the morning sessions. As a police motorcycle instructor, Matt was obviously handy on two wheels.

About thirty minutes before we were due out, Ben came into our garage to give me final instructions as to where to meet him. The plan was for me to go ahead of him and then he would bring me back to pit lane for feedback before going out again. I realised that, at only fifteen minutes per session, we'd be lucky to get five laps in, especially at my pace.

I waited for Ben at the pit lane exit point and the first group of riders set off. Once the final group had gone, Ben rolled up to pit lane and we set off.

I had been prepared to be scared at Cadwell Park, as it has a fearsome reputation. Snetterton, on the other hand, took me completely by surprise. At first glance, it looks unassuming; two long straights with ordinary corners at each end, plus a tighter infield section that made up the "300" part. I had watched a number of on-board videos, particularly of Minitwins but until you actually get on to the track, you really don't realise what you are going to put yourself through.

At three miles, Snetterton 300 is the longest track on the calendar. What makes it particularly scary is the complete absence of any elevation or contours. It is flat as a pancake with next to no camber, no rise or fall and no undulations. Even the Bomb Hole is barely more than a dip. This makes reading the circuit more difficult because you are unaware of any of the corners until you come to them. It's easy to find yourself off-line due to the lack of camber, making it easy for the bike to swing out unless you keep your nerve. I was to learn this to my cost on the first lap.

You join the circuit from pit lane about two-thirds of the way along the Senna Straight, followed by the sweeping right-hand Riches corner which leads up to the first of two hairpins, Wilson, another right-hander. After a short straight, you come to the first left-hand bend: Palmer.

I went in way too fast and, not having the confidence to lean the bike enough I flew off the track at Palmer, straight onto the grass. Fortunately, it was dry and I got back onto the track before Agostini, the next hairpin. We completed the lap and at the final corner, Ben guided me back to the collecting area.

"You could have made that corner," he assured me. "You had lots of lean left. Trust the bike and it will work in your favour. Right; let's get back out."

We set off down pit lane again, back on to the track. The next lap was uneventful, if slow but by lap three, I was once again getting over-confident and went off at Palmer for a second time. I went in much faster this time but realised earlier that I wasn't going to make the corner, so sat the bike up before rattling across the rumble strip kerb. By the time I had re-joined the track, I needed to brake much harder, as Agostini arrived at an alarming rate. I went round that hairpin way faster than was good for me and then screwed up my exit by changing up too quickly, which had me making all the wrong shapes round Hamilton. By the time I turned into the Bentley back straight, I had composed myself again and thrashed the bike hard towards Brundle, Nelson and the Bomb Hole.

The Bomb Hole leads to my favourite corner in Snetterton, Coram Curve; a wide, sweeping right-hander that is, thankfully, very forgiving. It can catch out the unwary (i.e. me), as it leads directly onto Murrays, a tight, right-angled left corner that takes you back to the start/finish straight. While I never went off track at Murrays (a lot of riders did, some of whom returned to the paddock with seriously second-hand bikes), it is a very focussing point in the track.

The chequered flag signalled the end of the session and we made our way back to the paddock. I rode down the fire lane and back to the garage. Ben rode on into pit lane and pulled up in front of our garage.

My lines hadn't been bad, apparently but there was always room for improvement. My biggest issue was body position; that term much beloved by track day regulars. I needed to spend more time with my arse hanging out on one side or the other of the bike, Ben told me. If I moved the handlebars, I'd find my arms would be more comfortable when pushing the bar and the bike would drop further as the countersteer manoeuvre was made. Having only one bum cheek on the saddle would allow everything else to be in balance.

I still had a long way to go but had at least survived another on-track session and so got on with refuelling the bike. My next session was not for another 45 minutes, so Dan, Simon and I checked out one another's bikes.

Simon had bought a large pump to drain the fuel tank. The rest of us had cheap syphons, which made getting unused petrol out easier but could never quite get to the very bottom of a tank. When I checked mine, I was convinced there was nothing left and was amazed that I had been able to complete a lap. Using Simon's pump showed that there was in fact another six litres left. Once we had drained the tank fully with Simon's pump, I put in a fresh five litres.

I reckoned we were using fuel at a rate of 0.15 litres per mile. Saturday's races were five laps, so 15 miles. We'd also need a warm up lap and the final warm down lap (which would finish half way round, at Agostini). That meant about 20 miles, which would be three litres used. The rules state that there must be two litres of fuel left at the end of the race, so we agreed on five litres being a sensible payload. Saturday's weather forecast was heavy rain, so it was likely that we'd use less anyway, as the speeds would be down.

While we deliberated, the rain started. Light at first, it was soon coming down hard and, with a strong wind, it was quite squally out on track. Ben returned and asked if I still wanted to go out. I would need to race, whatever the weather but our next session was only fifteen minutes away and we hadn't fitted wets yet, so I suggested missing the next session but doing the last one. I needed to try the bars in their new position and wanted to see how Snetterton changed as a wet track. Ben went to change his wheels and said he'd see me in an hour.

Rob came in from the blue session with a badly beaten up bike. Covered in mud, its already dented body had a number of new battle scars, including a brake lever that was hanging off and a missing footrest. The bodywork had remained mostly intact but Rob was going to have a lot of work to have it ready for Saturday.

The call for our group went out. Helmet and gloves on, tyre warmers off, I rolled Sylvie of the paddock stands. I wasn't going to wait in the rain any longer than I needed to, so didn't venture out until the second call. Dan and Simon followed me, waiting at the track entry point while I looked for Ben. The first group went out and Ben waved me through behind them.

Snetterton in the dry is daunting but in the wet it took on a completely different nature. While it was easier to see the track due to the glistening surface, that also meant grip was down. I thought about what I'd been told regarding wet weather tyre performance and knew I had to trust them. I had been surprised at the grip my Bridgestones had afforded me at Cadwell, so knew the only limiting factor would be my nerve.

I rode steadily for the first lap, taking care not to overdo it at Palmer (I was beginning to remember the corner names by now) and, within a couple of laps, I was going round at what I hoped was a sensible pace. Ben passed me a few times to point out those points of the track that I needed to aim for so by our fifth and final lap, I was feeling pretty good about my performance. I was conscious that I had also not been breaking any records, as I really didn't want to drop the bike. Unlike Rob, I didn't have any spares if I had a tumble. The chequered flag came out and we rounded the Wilson chicane, where Ben pulled over to have me try a race start.

"If it's this wet tomorrow, you'll need to put down power under control," was the advice. He shot off and I revved the engine but slipped the clutch so as to take off without the rear wheel coming around. Feeling the bike, even with its lack of horses, fly off the line in those conditions was particularly satisfying. We were directed off the track, Ben pulled over and removed his helmet.

"I thought you said you didn't like the wet."

"I don't."

"Well, you were much faster than you had been in the dry and you were really hanging off the bike. That was a massive improvement. How did you find the new handlebar position?"

"Much better. I could feel my entire palms against the bars this time, so turning the throttle was more comfortable. Braking felt better as a result, too."

"There you go. You did look a lot more confident this time. What I'd like to hear is you telling me you didn't get lapped at some point this weekend. Snetterton is the longest circuit in the series, so even the fastest riders will take a while to get back round to you. Even if you're thirty seconds a lap down, they'd only just be catching you on the final lap, so go out and enjoy it."

Back at the garage, I couldn't help but grin like a loon. Buoyed by Ben's encouraging comments, even the prospect of rain for the racing wasn't going to get me down. How brilliant is racing?

With practice day complete, Dan and I took our bikes to scrutineering. Aside from not having any dust covers on the tyre valves, Sylvie passed with no issues, as did my riding gear. Tech card signed, I rode back to the garage. Dan and I went to the race office to sign in, get our practice cards and programmes.

Back in the garage, Simon was having electrical issues, which had forced him to peel off the track during the final session. Fortunately, a replacement fuse had him sorted and he, too, was able to get his bike and gear signed off.

I cracked out a fistful of beers, passing one each to Dan, Simon and Rob. Dan asked if anyone was up for a track walk. Rob was still busy sorting out his bike and, as he was already a seasoned racer, elected not to join us. Simon and I were more than happy to tag along, just to get more of a feel for the place. There was no official walk this weekend, so we'd have to make it up as we went along. A casual saunter allowed us to check out various aspects of the track that we might have missed while tearing round on the bikes. At three miles, it was a long saunter. We were out for the best part of an hour but even without Jeremy Hill's professional guidance, it was still a useful exercise.

Even walking round the track, we could see no real evidence of elevation changes. Brands Hatch and Cadwell are hard, up-and-downhill walks, with little in the way of any level surface. There was no such concern at Snetterton. Looking around, you can see for miles; everything is just so flat. Snetterton is the fastest track in the series but go offline and it will bite errant riders badly.

The forecast was still pessimistic for Saturday, so we settled in for the evening. By 10:00, I was out like a light.

Saturday: Qualifying/Race Day 1

What is it about race weekends? During a working week, it's all I can do to get up by 6:30 yet at any given race meeting, I am awake and up well before that. I opened my eyes and reached across for my watch. 5:00. Bloody hell.

Now wide awake, I strolled over to the shower block. They were all free but, as I got out, there was a queue to get in. Clearly, I wasn't the only one with an "early bird" mind set come race day.

I made breakfast and coffee before sitting down to update my race diary. There was plenty of cloud cover but no rain yet. I wasn't holding my breath, though. Dan had read that Storm Miguel was going to visit, which would make for interesting racing conditions.

I invited Dan in for a coffee. While the water heated up, Rob opened the garage and we went in to do our initial checks. By 8:00, Simon joined us and the whole paddock was beginning to wake up.

I went to garage 23 to see Alan and Matt. Vanessa was missing this round, so I was hoping to make Alan my wingman. It's useful to have someone else to act as a target, wherever you may be on the grid. Today, it would be Alan.

Racing was starting to take my life over completely. Even a racer at my level soon gets hooked in. I had promised only to do one season of racing but it was going to be very hard to give this up now. Even if I could afford to enter every event, I knew it was likely that I'd want more. Riding with Bemsee was fantastic. The Minitwin class was brilliant, the riders were friendly and supportive and, by racing standards, it was almost affordable. Despite my ability and the bike's shortcomings, I felt there was unfinished business. Some minor improvements to the bike, more tuition and experience for me might even find me somewhere other than at the back. I may have been racing as "ATB ('At The Back') Racing" but I didn't want to remain there. I wasn't last in the championship but I was still the last finisher. The fact that the only people behind me in the results table were the DNFs (did not finish) still grated and I wanted to see a result sheet where I wasn't the last rider to pass the flag. I didn't care if I came in 29th out of 30. Not finishing dead last had never been so important. I really was getting a race head on.

The first job of the day would be noise testing. Knowing Sylvie's propensity for backfiring when cold, I decided to start the engine and make sure it was fully warmed up before going out.

True to form, while she started on the first press, it wasn't without her now trademark belching of flame, accompanied by a massive bang. Simon was knelt down fitting a tyre warmer and got the full experience, making him jump back suddenly. Sorry, Simon.

Once the engine had settled (and its associated pyrotechnics display abated), I joined a line of about thirty riders waiting to test. The testers were getting through the bikes at a rapid rate and I was soon called up for my turn.

"Set it at five and a half thousand", the man with the microphone stick shouted. I duly wound the engine up as requested.

"That's 101, plus a bonus 110 for the backfire." Oops. He applied a "noise test - passed" sticker and waved me off.

The rain started just as qualifying got underway. It wasn't long before the tarmac was drenched, so wet tyres would definitely be the order of the day. Dan was out first, for Thunderbike Sports qualifying. Racing is expensive but when you're paying £400 for a weekend, an additional £50-60 to enter a second series seems almost like a bargain. While you double your risk of crashing, you also double your track time. It won't get you any more signatures, however, as you can only get one signature per meeting per day. Dan was, however, collecting trophies wherever he went. I was inordinately envious.

We turned the tyre warmers on about 15 minutes before we were due to go out. Wet weather tyres benefit from a little warming but only enough to allow the tread to flex when riding. Putting warmers on for too long or letting them get too hot will rapidly degrade wet tyres.

The call went out and we donned gear, peeled off the warmers and went out into the light rain to go to the assembly area, me following Rob, Simon and Dan. We were soon joined by Matt, Alan and Sam.

Practice pass cards were handed over, rain lights turned on and we lined up. Transponders and lights were checked and then we were let loose.

Some of the more proficient/impatient riders barged past before even getting out of the gate. I was happy to let them get on with it; at three miles long, it would be a while before I'd see them again anyway. The track was awash with standing water and, once on the circuit, everyone took it steadily. We set off, turning right into Riches and then up to the dreaded Wilson hairpin. Sam passed me on the approach but tucked his bike as he went round, sliding less than gracefully over the kerb towards the marshals. Another meeting and poor old Sam had crashed again. This time, he'd got no further than two corners.

The sight of Sam skating rapidly in the direction of the marshal was sobering. Although I wasn't going fast, I could feel myself slowing further. Realising this would do me no favours, I picked up the pace to make up some lost time. Getting a bit too ambitious heading towards Agostini hairpin. I felt the back wheel slide under me, so rolled the throttle off a little.

I almost managed to copy Sam's manoeuvre the next time I exited Wilson. I was looking to see if he was all right but knew that "where you look is where you go". A few seconds bouncing across the rumble strip had me focussing again and chasing Alan. I did make up time in some sectors but each time I did, he outgunned me around the corners and I never quite reached him. Finally, at Coram, I got within spitting distance of him. Now I would surely bag an overtake but as we exited Murrays, the final corner, Alan's left arm went up and he peeled off into the pits. I was gutted but crouched down to give Sylvie one last caning for the final lap. I had only managed four but I had at least got a qualifying time in.

Of course, that qualifying time was embarrassing. The pole setter, Glyn Davies, posted a best time of 2:20.771. As Tail End Charlie, I crept in at 3:10.667; a full 50 seconds behind. This was not good but three riders, including poor old Sam, hadn't qualified, so I would start the first race on the last row but one.

Back into the garage, we checked our fuel usage. Based on what we had each managed to get out of our tanks, we agreed that a five-litre load would be more than enough for the race and still leave the required two litres left at the end.

We were sorted and ready to race, just needing to double-check for fuel, make sure everything was tightened up and that the tyre warmers were fitted (not turned on yet, as wets were still fitted). We sat and waited for the call for Race 4.

Word had gone around that Storm Miguel's arrival was imminent. Bad weather is one thing but when it comes with a name, you know you're in for a challenge. Sure enough, come 10:00, we were in the middle of a biblical rain storm, with a deep, wide river running in front of the garages and sharp, horizontal rain teeming down. I didn't have waterproofs for my leathers., which were perforated too. I was going to get wet and very cold. I didn't relish going out but Vanessa was 55 points ahead of me and I needed all the points I could get. At my current rate, I was coming home in eighth in my class, which was netting me eight points. On current form, that would be 32 points for the weekend. If I could get a seventh place, that would be another point but with the weather as it was, simply getting out should earn everyone 25 merit points.

Race 1
(Row 12, Grid 36)

The rain was still pelting down and fighting a high wind when we rolled up in the collecting area. The marshal shouted our grid position above the lashing wind and rain and told us we'd need our rain light on. You don't say…

I took my place on the grid and waited for what seemed an age before the marshal waved his flag for us to set off on the warm up lap. The pace, while not frenetic, was still fast and I watched as the riders disappeared in a cloud of spray ahead of me. We turned into Riches but even the leaders seemed not to be leaning at all. Everyone was "threepenny-bitting" the corner, unsure as to how much grip there was. Wet weather tyres are amazing but standing water was everywhere and the risk of aquaplaning was high. Additionally, with such heavy rain, any grease on the track would be being lifted, further increasing the risk of a fall.

Into the Wilson hairpin, I was still in touch with everybody as we straightened up towards my nemesis, Palmer. I was particularly wary today but got round with no issues. Up to Agostini and Sam Kent, just ahead of me, stuck his right leg out and peeled off back to the paddock. He had at least made it further round this time, albeit only one more corner but he was later to tell us that his bike was mis-firing and he didn't want to risk it.

Wet weather is the Achilles heel for the SV650. An almost horizontal front cylinder means that, in heavy rain, water finds its way straight to the front spark plug/injector. A lot of Minitwins have a shield fitted under the radiator to deflect water away; something that I would later wish I had got.

We worked our way around the circuit, nobody really pushing until the Bentley back straight when, once again, the front-runners disappeared into a thick fog of tyre spray. Around Brundle, Nelson and the infamous Bomb Hole we went, on towards Coram and finally into Murrays to line up on the grid.

I slotted Sylvie into grid position 36, next to Alan Hensby. We gave each other the obligatory knuckle touch and then waited for the lights. They glowed red in the mist, then they were out and off we flew.

Any caution by the front runners was cast aside as they charged up to Riches. All I could see was spray; making out the shapes of other bikes was next to impossible. This was terrifying. All that went through my head was, "What the hell am I doing here?"

I had looked at the circuit map before coming up and thought that, at three miles long, a three-minute lap should be a reasonable target for my novice ability. Out here in the wet, I wanted nothing more than to finish the race. Times were irrelevant to me just then; I'd have been happy with anything. This was now just about staying on the bike and surviving the race.

I made Riches and continued up to Wilson. Knocking down a gear, I went round too slowly, so dropped down another gear as I was exiting, which is terrible race craft. I approached Palmers where the first of what would be many yellow flags appeared. We weren't even a third of the way round the first lap and already there were fallers. I got through Palmers and stamped the lever up another gear towards Agostini. Again, I was too tight and heading towards the painted rumble strip; not what you should do in the rain. I leaned over a little more, clipping the very edge of that kerb, berating myself for looking at it, rather than towards the next corner, Hamilton. I negotiated the Hamilton-Oggies-Williams left-right-right complex and got on to the Bentley Straight.

I could still just see the pack, or at least the spray cloud it had created, so tucked in and crashed through the gears. My visor was steaming up so, as I dropped into fourth (I'd not been going fast enough to get into top gear) through Brundle, I had to hold my breath as I went down into third for Nelson.

I had just enough time to crack the visor open as I leant into the Bomb Hole and then almost immediately dropped it shut again. Lifting the visor up just that couple of millimetres was enough to allow some very fast-moving air in to clear my vision. It also allowed very painful, needle-sharp raindrops through, so I had to close it again.

Barely lifting Sylvie out of the Bomb Hole, I dropped her back down to take the lovely right-handed Coram Curve. This had been my favourite corner but in the sodden race conditions, it took on a whole new look. The racing line I'd taken yesterday wasn't even visible but under a raging torrent of water. There was so much water and it was flowing so quickly that it was difficult to differentiate between track, kerb and grass. I stuck to what I assumed was a safe area that left tarmac all around. That made turning left into Murrays difficult but, as I was going so slowly, I simply paddled around before caning the bike back along the Senna start/finish straight.

"One lap down, four to go, Sylvie," I said. Actually, at this pace, even if I completed a race, I couldn't see me completing any more than four laps. I was petrified but needed all the points I could get, so I had to finish, wherever that may be.

The rest of the race was mostly a lonely, cold, wet and windy trawl until around lap three when the world and his wife flew past. As I went round, I became aware (mostly because of how slow I was going) that the circuit was littered with bikes at every sector. The attrition rate was huge and I would be intrigued to see how many made it to the end.

When the yellow and black "Last Lap" came out, I nearly cried. I had never wanted to get back to the garage this much. Seeing the chequered flag was a huge relief. I patted the tank and sat up just after the finish line. By now, I was soaked through and, as I looked across towards the Armco, those wonderful marshals were applauding us all as we returned to the paddock; such a simple gesture but it puts you on top of the world. Besides, those poor men and women had been standing out in the same horrific conditions as me. Where I had only had to endure twenty minutes, they'd be out in it all day. Who'd be a marshal? Such an amazing thing to do and all the riders acknowledge their support.

As it happened, the crash rate was massive. Of the 36 starters, only 23 completed the race, with me making up position 23 (which would be my best result of the season). I didn't care, though. All I had wanted from the start of that race was to finish. I was last again but I had finished. Three rookies had retired but ten experienced riders had also gone down, so I considered myself fortunate. Both Sylvie and I had made it through, although on the last couple of laps, that "water in the front cylinder" gremlin paid a visit. I had to keep revving the engine simply to keep it running but run it did and we saw the chequered flag.

My time? Well, while not the four minutes I had anticipated, it was still a woeful 3:22.296. That was an average of 52 mph. The next slowest rider, Alan Hensby, had lapped twelve seconds faster than me and winner Dan Singleton had got in a 2:31.067 lap. In the rain. There were a number of sub-2:50 laps; a huge, heroic achievement, given the appalling conditions. I really hoped that our next race would not be a repeat.

Back in the shelter of the garage, I checked the tyre damage. As I had been so cautious, there was next to no wear and it would certainly last at least another race. This was just as well because I had no money left. We all hoped that the weather would clear up a little before we were out next.

It was all I could do to move around in my leathers. With them this drenched, there was no way I was taking them off, as I'd never get them dry or back on. It was likely that they'd still be wet the following morning so I would have to put up with riding in the wet later on, whatever the weather.

I could do something with the gloves, though and placed them in the caravan's oven. Keeping it on a low heat, I left the gloves to gently steam dry. By the time the second race was called, while they weren't completely dry, they were warm and far more comfortable than they had been.

Back into the garage, Dan was refuelling his bike ready to join the Thunderbike Sport race. Simon and I lent a hand, being careful not to get in Dan's way. When you have a work plan in your head, you don't need somebody trying to "help". Racers know what they want to do, how and when they want to do it so unless asked, it's best to let them get on. Dan only needed fuel, so Simon and I limited the assistance to taking the paddock stands as Dan rode back out into the rain.

I drained Sylvie's tank to see how much fuel I had used. Of the original five litres, I got three back into the pump, meaning for the warm up and the four and a half laps, I had used about two litres.

What concerned me was the amount of detritus that the pump had removed from the tank. For a nineteen-year-old bike, I expected a degree of rubbish but there was loads, which would be another factor in Sylvie's performance. Every time a bit of crap went into the system, it would clog up the fuel filter or get stuck in the carb. A thorough tank clean out once I got the bike home was in order.

Race 2
(Row 10, Grid 28)

The weather eased a little after lunch but there was still water everywhere. In front of the garages, a narrow stream at the top end grew to a wide, fast-flowing river at the end of the garage block. There was the rather surreal site of riders standing in the rain and hosing down their bikes to remove the mud and gravel they'd picked up on their way down. Umbrellas were useless, as the wind simply turned them inside out. As I watched from the relative comfort of my caravan, a gazebo roof flew across the paddock, chased by its owner. Surreal and funny but the rider was at least able to retrieve his parascending equipment.

As our race approached, the rain stopped. Simon and I walked across pit lane to the pit wall to inspect the track surface. While it was nowhere near as wet as it had been a few hours earlier, it was still dark and there was still likely to be standing water at some point of the track. We watched the current race to see how much spray was being thrown up by the bikes as they passed. While there was still water being thrown up, it didn't compare to what we'd experienced in the morning. It would be an hour before we would be called but we didn't know if the rain would return.

Rob wasn't taking any chances. "Pit lane and the paddock are still soaked," he said. "I'm certainly not risking it. I'd rather waste a tyre than wreck my bike. If everyone passes me, so be it."

I went to speak with Alan and Matt. Matt was putting his dry tyres on but Alan was also not going to take any chances. Looking along the paddock, the faster riders were selecting a dry set up, whereas the lower half were sticking with wets. I knew how I would play it; the wets were staying on.

Rob set off to the collecting area. Dan returned to the garage and he, Simon and I followed suit. I was looking forward to this because I would be on row 10, in 28th position; one of my highest so far. Sure, I knew it wouldn't stay that way but I'd be starting from mid-pack!

Only I wouldn't be. Although we had a garage, the Tannoy system wasn't working and we missed our final call to the grid. Rob had just made it but Dan, Simon and I were held in the collecting area. We were going to be allowed on but only after everyone else had assembled, following the warm up lap. This meant only one thing; starting from the back of the grid.

I was gutted. I had finally earned a good grid position, having stayed on board when so many had come off but I was going to be denied the opportunity. We joined the back - Simon, Dan and me - all with the same sense of dejection. I knew Dan was going to be fast so let him take the best grid position. When the lights went out, Dan shot off, making a good ten places before we reached Riches. Without his skill set or his bike's power, I simply followed everyone else but kept up with the back end of the pack.

The pace was faster this time around and, with rain tyres still fitted, I struggled to gain any ground. I had got lapped by the third lap but again didn't care; I had completed the race and nursed Sylvie home without incident. There were more bikes resting against the Armco at various points along the circuit but with the improved conditions, people were able to put in some much better times. Whilst mine was still appalling, I had at least improved on my first race but still hadn't broken that three-minute barrier. My best lap time that afternoon was 3:00.356, which gave me an average of 59.2 mph. I took some comfort in improving my time but still felt a pang of disappointment. Perhaps tomorrow would be better and, with dry tyres on, maybe I'd achieve that elusive 2:59 lap time.

Dan finished as third-placed Rookie but was pulled over for a random scrutineering check. This is unique to Snetterton, as it has full technical facilities available, so bikes can be given a thorough check. Dan told the tech team that he was due to go out in another race, so was allowed to delay the test until after his next race.

Once again, Simon and I helped; Simon changing the back wheel, me refuelling while Dan dealt with the front. The belly pan was full of water, so he unclipped it and tipped out the water. Once done, everything was reassembled and Dan started the engine.

Rob shouted across to him. "Your warmers! Your tyre warmers!" When he had removed the belly pan, Dan had inadvertently caught the gear lever so, when he hit the start button, the back wheel spun round, taking with it the still-fitted (and brand-new) tyre warmer, ripping out the power cable. Dan killed the engine and extracted the torn cable from around the hub before taking the tyre warmer off. He had no time to worry about it. The second call had gone out and he had to go.

On returning to the garage, Dan's day continued to go downhill, because Scrutineering had found a heat shield blanket on top of his cylinders. He was told that it might have allowed his air box to run cooler and therefore theoretically made more power across the bike's rev range. Dan was disqualified from the Minitwin race (and was therefore denied a trophy and grid place next time out). Any advantage from that heat shield would be negligible and his bike only made 68 horsepower, so was under the 72 HP limit but the penalty stayed and Dan had to remove all evidence of the blanket. The upside was that he still had a trophy for the Thunderbike race, which is not as restrictive as Minitwins. He was also allowed to keep his trophy for the first Minitwin race.

We went to Tyrells, the circuit restaurant, to get some dinner ahead of the presentation but it was locked. Undeterred and unfazed by the disqualification, Dan bought pints for Simon and I and we fought our way towards the front, so Dan could collect his (now single) trophy.

As it turned out, Dan wasn't the only winner in our little group, as my name got called out for a spot prize. Properly Protected, the Minitwins title sponsor, gives out £25 cash to a randomly selected participant at each round and today, it was me! To say I was gobsmacked would be putting it mildly. It might not have been a winner's trophy but, after that dire day of racing, I was still over the moon. As I returned to the throng, grinning like a kid with a new toy, a woman walked in with a plate of food. The restaurant was now open, so my winnings were spent on a celebration meal for Dan, Simon and me.

Having drunk, eaten and generally celebrated, we returned to our garage and checked that everything was ready for the morning. The forecast was for good weather, so we put dry wheels back on, refuelled the bikes and carried out some cursory checks to make sure nothing had worked loose. The SV650 makes a great race bike but it is can get quite vibey, so bolts can shake loose. I found three of the four seat bolts and one of the tank fixings had worked loose, so tightened them up. All checks completed, I returned to the caravan to get my head down for the night.

Sunday: Race Day 2

For the first time at a race meeting, I slept in. I should perhaps put that in context; "slept in" meant I woke at 6:15 but that still left plenty of time to prepare for the day. I looked out of the caravan window and was delighted to see blue sky. I didn't want a repeat of the previous morning. With no rain suit and a fully perforated race suit, yesterday had been both cold and wet. The suit had gained a few kilos thanks to the added water content. Dan and I had hung our suits up in the garage overnight but both were still damp so, after opening the garage, we hung them on the pit wall in the sun, to help the drying process.

We'd got the bikes ready on the Saturday. Dry weather tyres were now fitted and five litres of fuel had been loaded. We'd have two seven-lap races today and I'd considered putting in an additional litre, to guarantee having the required two litres remaining by the end but, based on usage so far, knew five would be plenty. After all, I wouldn't get seven laps in at current performance. Which is something I should perhaps touch on.

I recall watching a Bemsee meeting at the Brands Indy circuit many years ago; specifically an MZ race. In that race was a rookie who was markedly slower than the rest of the pack and was being caught within two laps. Being the armchair critics that we were, the group I was with (me included, I'm ashamed to say) were asking why the rider was out there. We all thought that, being so slow, he was a danger to himself and the other racers.

Some fifteen years later, I was now that slow rookie, regularly questioning what on earth I was doing or trying to prove. Ironically, despite my lack of self-belief, which was becoming a broken record even to me by now, every one of the other racers had nothing but encouragement for me. Sure, I was still slow but so far, all my lap times were improving and when I was being passed, I was holding my line, so the overtaking riders had no unpleasant surprises as they shot around me.

This came to a head via a comment in the club's social media site. The gist of the comment was, "There was one rider who was noticeably slower than everyone else. What happened to the 110% ruling? Surely safety has to be the priority."

I knew the comment was referring to me. In my reply, I acknowledged that my speed was down but that, at each stage, from qualifying to the final Sunday race, my times had dropped. Although my first race laps were worse than my qualifying lap (3:22, compared to a 3:10 qualifier), all my times improved as the weekend had progressed. The post thread was later removed.

Race 1
(Row 10, Grid 28)

But I'm getting ahead of myself, spoiler alerts notwithstanding. For the first race of the day, I would join the grid in row 10, grid position 29. I was ahead of only two rookies this morning; Dan (because he'd been disqualified on Saturday) and Sam (because he'd retired in the first race and not participated in the second). There were a number of non-rookies behind me but also a number of empty slots, where fallers from yesterday hadn't been able to get their bikes back together for the second day. As before, my goal was to complete at least one race today, to get another signature. I'd need ten signatures before I could apply for my full Clubman licence and so far, including this weekend, I had gained five of them. I also wanted to get in the top 30 and ideally not get lapped too early.

It occurred to me that, although my ambitions when starting on this journey were deliberately modest, I was already dissatisfied with my performance. I needed more speed and especially more corner speed. I needed to start hanging off the bike a lot more and getting the bike down further. After checking my wet tyres, there was little evidence that I'd achieved any heroic lean angles but I was prepared to let that go, simply because the conditions had been genuinely atrocious.

Today was different, though. It was cloudy but dry. There was no evidence of yesterday's oceanic track surface, either. The track was perfectly dry. The clouds were already dispersing and the sun poking through the remaining light cloud cover. I was determined that I would break that three-minute lap barrier today.

To do so would certainly involve upping my game. Alan Hensby was directly in front of me on row 9 and today, he was my target. I didn't know if I'd be able to keep up with him, let alone pass him but I was going to give it my best shot.

We completed our warm up lap and waited. The lights went out and we were off. If I thought the wet racing was scary, the take-off speed this morning was much, much quicker. I had only got into second gear when Dan flew past, once again scything through the pack on his way towards the sharp end. We approached Riches by which time all but one rider had passed me. Alan was a few bikes ahead and my new target was Sam Kent.

People still went into the Wilson hairpin carefully but, once it was obvious that the grip level had improved, they all barrelled down to Palmer. By the time I arrived, Sam, the next last rider, was already going through Agostini.

I was livid. We weren't even half way round the first lap and I was being left for dead. I crashed the gearbox down to second for the left-hand hairpin, overcooked it and headed towards the offside kerb. Rolling the throttle off, I levelled Sylvie up again and rode on towards Hamilton. Remembering it was another left-hand bend, I drifted across the track to the left-most point, tipping into Oggies. I could still see Sam as he rounded Williams. All was not lost. Not yet.

I lifted Sylvie up at the Williams exit and kept the throttle wide open, going up the gears along the Bentley straight, getting into sixth gear before reaching the Brundle/Nelson switchback section. Having remembered what other rookies had suggested ("fifth for Brundle, then down to fourth before Nelson"), I made the changes but had too much going through my head: "Change gear, brake, tip in, escape lane, escape lane, ESCAPE LANE! Bugger!"

I managed to avoid the escape lane (just) but went round Brundle in fourth and Sylvie bogged down, struggling to keep momentum. I made a real mess of Nelson but knocked the gearbox back into third. The revs picked up and we got around the Bomb Hole in some sort of order.

Next up was Coram and finally the tight left-hander that was Murrays. By the time I was passing the pit wall, Sam had exited Riches and I was once again doing my own track day, all alone.

Still, it gave me the chance to self-assess. I soon learned to get into sixth before the end of each straight, so I knew where I was. I would then could count down to the gear that worked best for me. For Riches, that meant full chat up to the 300-metre mark, where I'd drop to fifth, fourth and third, selecting second just as I reached the Wilson hairpin. Around the back of the circuit, I wanted to be in sixth by the bridge. I'd drop two gears, into fourth before changing back to third as I entered Brundle, where I'd stay on about three-quarter throttle (I really needed to have the throttle wide open here but was still building on my nerve) until exiting Nelson, changing back up to take the Bomb Hole in fourth, keeping it there for Coram, the engine screaming in protest but as I wound the gas off towards the exit, I dropped to third for Murrays and wrung Sylvie's neck again, back up through the gears, into sixth just before the 300m mark for Riches.

The rest of my race was a matter of educational repetition; maintaining lines, changing up at the same place but waiting to change down and braking later and later as the laps passed. It was terrifying and exhilarating in equal measure but still I wasn't laughing.

I wasn't breathing enough, either. Every time I either overcooked a corner or missed my line, I felt a sharp intake of breath. By lap five (my last lap, as by now I was being passed), things had finally got together. When the chequered flag came out, I could properly acknowledge the marshals, having felt that I'd done better than my efforts on Saturday. I was still in a different postcode, of course but it had felt as though more things had slotted together properly, so I was more satisfied with my overall performance.

As I turned into the paddock, I saw that the entire grid was being held back. It looked like another set of random dyno checks were going to be made. I relaxed, as I'd had one at Cadwell, so didn't expect to be called.

"Numbers 0, 20, 40 and 137, please go to the Technical bay for dyno check."

I couldn't believe it but I had been selected, so no choice but to get over there. Simon (#40) led the way. Luke Stanley (#0), Charlie Crawt (#137) and I followed in close formation. Dyno Dan recognised me immediately and smiled when I asked if he could please find more than 59 horses. The truck's ramp raised, taking Sylvie up. She was wheeled inside, strapped in place and Dan got into the saddle.

The sound of a bike undergoing a dyno test is, well, loud. It always sounds like the engine is going to explode as it is revved mercilessly to give out a peak power reading. Soon, it was all over. Dan wheeled her back over and said, "You've lost one."

"Lost one"? That was very bad. Now my wheezy, 59 horsepower bike was now an even wheezier 58 horsepower bike. Any hope of improvements to my times were dashed there and then.

I was devastated. Ever since the opening round, I was undecided as to whether I should spend more money on what I had or cut my losses and get another bike. Learning I now had a potential 14 horsepower deficit was not what I needed.

I rode back to the garage, fitted the warmers and went to look for Dan Singleton, the current championship leader. Dan had offered me a set of injection cams, which he said would add another eight horsepower. I might have to do more, such as fit a race exhaust and get the carburettors serviced but simply fitting the cams should boost the power and help Sylvie to keep up.

I hoped he wasn't in a rush to sell, as I would have to wait until at least Brands before I had the funds. He had a few sets so that would be fine and I agreed to buy a set from him.

I went to the race office to get result sheets for us all. Despite coming last, my times had dropped and I had finally broken that three-minute barrier. My best lap time was now 2:50.193.

Ten seconds off my last time? I was more than happy with that. It was a country mile off the front-runners but it was going in the right direction. I wanted to really give myself a chance to improve for that last race but whatever happened, I saw this as a 32-second improvement on that dreadful Saturday. I grabbed some pasta for lunch before settling in the garage for some downtime.

Going to a race as a spectator means you can see as much racing as you choose. Competitors, however, get to see very little racing because their non-racing time is spent cleaning, checking, fettling or resting. Dan was doing two race classes, so Simon and watched his Thunderbike Sport race from pit lane. Despite being against a number of very quick 600cc in-line fours, Dan and Wil Green, both Minitwins racers, were giving the field a good run for their money. The SV650 is sometime dismissed as a parts bin special but as a club racing machine, it's difficult to find fault. It's not brittle like the two stroke screamers or the highly-tuned 600cc sportsbikes. The SV650 has loads of torque, is cheap to buy and to tune (within the limitations imposed by the class), needs hardly any maintenance, can handle well enough with minor suspension modifications and is generally a hoot to ride. I was very pleased with my choice of series. I just wanted to be faster.

Race 2
(Row 11, Grid 32)

My second race was almost a carbon copy of race one; I gridded row 11, spot 32 (an area I was getting quite used to) and had a similar start, being able to keep up with the pack until reaching Palmers. I noted that a lot of the riders at the bottom half of the pack rounded Wilson's very carefully. A future race here would have me trying to make a tactical start. Knowing lots take the right-hand hairpin really tightly leaves a wide-open space on the left to make more of a sweeping turn and potentially make up a few places. Sadly, this was the last Minitwin race of the meeting, so my theory would have to remain a theory until next season. Assuming I returned, of course.

How much of a carbon copy race was it? Well, my best time was 2:50.445; a mere quarter of a second slower than Race 1. While slower, I was happy to maintain my sub-three-minute target.

For Dan and Simon, however, the weekend had been brilliant, as Simon also earned two trophies on Sunday. I was really pleased for him, despite the envy. It seems odd that getting a small plated plastic cup can give such pleasure. We race for fun but we still want to win. This would be my only year in the rookie class; I knew my chances of getting a trophy were minimal at best but it didn't matter. My ambitions had been low and I had surpassed all of them so far. There were potentially four more rounds to enter, after which I could consider my options. The weekend had not been a disaster at all. I had learned and survived another track and had improved on my times again. From being a racing fan, I had become a fan of racing.

My best lap results for Snetterton:

Qualifying: 3:10.637
Race 1: 3:22.296
Race 2: 3:00.356
Race 3: 2:50.193
Race 4: 2:50.445

Chapter 8:
More Fixes, More Worries

Treating A Symptom

So far, I had been trying to do as much as possible with as little money as possible. Funds were stupidly tight and although I was trying to be sensible, I was still spending cash I didn't have. Since February, each month had been long and drawn out as I kept a daily eye on the bills that had to be paid (but often weren't) to see if I had the money for those wet tyres, entry fees, test days…

After a while, you come to realise that, to make progress, you must have proper gear. That includes a bike that will at least keep up with others. Sylvie wasn't keeping up, even if I discounted my nervy riding. I had considered asking Dan (Singleton) to give her a thrash at Snetterton but decided against it because it wouldn't tell me anything. What would a fast rider getting Sylvie round Snetterton forty seconds faster than me prove, other than confirming that I was a worse rider than even I thought?

I had plenty to think about on the four-hour journey home. At the front of my mind was making Sylvie faster. I rang Dan Singleton to discuss options. He could fit the cams and check the bike over generally, especially the fuelling and carburettors. That should at least get some improvements. We agreed a price and I took Sylvie to Dan the following Friday. Two days later, he gave his opinion.

"It's not as bad as I had thought," he told me. Already, my optimism had risen. "The compression in both cylinders is all right but could be better. I did a leak test and found the front was definitely leaking, which will be costing you horses. It will be worth sourcing a pair of barrels and you should get some piston rings at the same time.

"The cam chain is in perfectly good order with no evidence of stretch. The throttle cable was a bit stiff so I lubed the cable, so it springs back as it should now. There was some crap in the tank but not too much. One of the carb jets had a bit stuck in it, which was difficult to remove but it's gone now.

"Your front brake brackets may have got bent somewhere, which might explain their feel. If you drop an SV, the forks and calipers don't come off well. The forks are made out of cheese, so they bend easily on a lowside. Do a highside and you can scrap the whole front end, so I'd keep an eye out for complete front forks.

"Even taking all that into account, it's really not bad. When you go to Brands, ask for a compliance check. They won't give you a power figure but they will tell you if it's improved. If you tell them the engine has been refreshed and you just want to check it complies with regs, they won't charge."

Dan had done a lot of work and I hoped that I now had a bike that could stay with the pack. I'd need to get used to the new Sylvie but that should not take long and I could now go to Brands with a little more confidence.

As the time for paying to enter Brands approached, I looked at my bank account. It was getting harder to justify the cost for each round and the twenty pounds in my current account wasn't going to cut it. Fortunately, I had just enough in a second account but would not transfer funds until the last minute, in case the bank decided to earmark those funds for something else.

Two days before payment was due, an email from Bemsee announced the opening to book for the last three rounds. Only two of them were open to me, as there was no Minitwin class at the next Snetterton round but I added them to my online basket. Knowing the money wouldn't be taken until a week before each round, I had time to either have it transferred or to cancel the booking if I couldn't get the money together.

This dilemma had me realise just how much of an addiction racing had become, even at my lowly level. I had spent a small fortune getting to events and improving the bike and, three-quarters of the way through the season, I was only just realising how much I still wanted to improve and how much I still needed to spend in order to make that happen.

A bunch of Bemsee riders were attending a track day at the Brands GP circuit a few days before the race meeting but I was skint, so the track day was not an option. I knew my next salary cheque would arrive on the Friday before race day, so I would be able to buy fuel, replacement brake pads and food for the weekend but I was back to worrying about money, just ahead of the biggest race meeting of the season.

I was concerned that I would be at a disadvantage in qualifying, as it would be the first chance to have ridden Sylvie since the new cams had gone in, plus I would be learning yet another new track. I discussed this with Carl Bell, who reminded me that I'd not be the only one not to have experienced the bigger circuit and that, once I'd done a couple of laps, I'd know where I was going anyway. At my last track day, my instructor had told me that my body position was fine and, although I wasn't always taking the best lines, my pace had been improving all day. Perhaps the GP circuit wouldn't be as daunting as I was letting it feel but it would certainly be another test of confidence. We would soon see.

The Bemsee Brands Hatch GP round is always massively oversubscribed. As I had booked three out of the first five meetings, I was eligible for an "early bird" access to book this one. It was the one meeting I had really wanted to attend but I knew that if I was to race again next year, I would need to make a much better job of organising my finances.

To that end, I planned to set up a racing account during the winter months, paying whatever I could afford into it, thus keeping those funds separate from my day-to-day accounts. I didn't need to have money for all rounds immediately but keeping it separate was important and would mean I'd not have to fret about finding money, so long as I paid funds in. Any windfalls I might receive would also go into the fund.

The first big payment that would go in would be the funds raised from selling my road SV. I really hadn't wanted to sell that bike but the pragmatist in me knew that it had sat in front of my garage since December and, although under cover, it would slowly be rotting through lack of use. Before it could be sold, however, I needed to make sure it still worked. True to form, the battery was dead, so I charged it overnight, only to find that it wouldn't take a charge. A replacement was bought, taking the very last of my meagre funds and I took it into the house for its initial charge.

Chapter 9:
"The Big Meet" - Brands Hatch GP

Once the entry money had been taken, Simon Wilkinson, our informal Honorary Social Secretary, sent an email requesting a garage to house him, Dan (Thomas), Vanessa (Gillam) and me. A couple of hours later, he informed our Facebook group that he had secured Garage 7. This would put us next door to Matt Wetherell and Alan Hensby in Garage 8, which was actually the other half of the same garage. While Vanessa, Alan and I were tail-enders, Simon was a mid-pack rider (and now with two trophies) but Dan and Matt were leading the Rookie table, so I anticipated plenty of banter.

I spent the next week watching onboard videos of the GP circuit. From what I could see, the GP section looked fantastic but I was unsure as to how the Indy section would feel once I'd returned to it at Clearways. Still; I'd find out soon enough.

Cheryl and I took the caravan to Wrotham on Thursday evening, where we joined the mass of vans and caravans waiting to get to the garages. Arriving early meant there was plenty of space to manoeuvre the caravan and, with help from Matt Wetherell's father John, it was soon set up. After offloading bike and gear into the garage, we were ready to get back home but, as the first of our group to arrive, I would need to take charge of the garage key. Matt called me over to say that Mike Dommett was handing them out. As I approached, he asked my name.

"Steve Male."

Mike burst out laughing. It seemed that I was now infamous. It comes to something when even the club management know you by reputation, although I was convinced that Matt had had a hand in the amusement this time.

After stowing everything, I locked the garage, stowing the key for Dan, Vanessa and Simon to find when they arrived ahead of me tomorrow.

Friday: practice day

I was at work on Friday but hoped to at least make scrutineering (between 3:30 and 5:30 pm). This being me, of course, I didn't get back to the circuit until 5:15. Saturday it was, then.

I had celebrated my 57th birthday six days previously and it would be Dan's on Saturday, so everyone was bringing food and beers for a party on Saturday evening. Cheryl hoped to get back up and both Dan's wife Lorne and Simon's wife Lyndsay were coming to support us all.

At six o'clock, we walked to the Surtees straight where Jeremy would take us on a track walk of the Grand Prix section. Bemsee is the only racing club that is allowed to use the GP circuit and we were all really fired up for this very special round.

At 1.2 miles, the Indy circuit is short, with only four right-hand and two left-hand bends. There's no time to get much in the way of pace as the two straights, which are themselves slightly curved, are also really short. The grand prix section adds another one and a quarter mile of fast, technical and frankly terrifying track. I had been in awe of Cadwell Park but had found, even at race pace, it was a beautifully flowing circuit. The GP extension at Brands makes it a definite track of two halves. The Indy was short and quick but the parkland GP section was fast and very angular; completely different to Cadwell Park.

As we walked up towards Pilgrim's Drop and Hawthorn Hill, we became aware as to just how hilly the circuit is. Halfway down Pilgrim's, we stopped short of the first of two bridges. Pointing to it, Jeremy told us that, if this was our first visit, we would ALL duck our heads as we flew under the bridge. There were a number of experienced riders nodding and willing to put their opinion in as well, so we had an idea as to what to expect. Walking on to Hawthorn Bend, Jeremy stopped again and smiled.

"You'll all go round Hawthorn way slower than you expect first time but you can always go much faster than you'd imagine."

I couldn't imagine much and thought about how it was going to feel as everyone shot past me as I considered my approach and line. The approach was, however, wide. Jeremy continued.

"As you exit Surtees from the right side of the track, you need to be in the middle for Pilgrim's Drop but there's enough room to make a clear approach from the left of the circuit, which would give the widest field of vision around the curve. Good, innit?"

Next up was the short approach to Westfield; an almost ninety-degree right-hander.

"You can fly around Hawthorn but Westfield should be taken more cautiously, as it's really tight. Right; Dingle Dell."

"As soon as we've got through Westfield, we land straight into Dingle Dell. If you look, you can see how it's a short double right-hand kink that goes straight into Sheene Curve.

"So; Sheene. It may not look it but Sheene Curve is a well tight right-hander. There's a bit of grass but ACRES of gravel with a "come hither" look. Don't go thither, though; it'll take weeks to dig yourself out of that."

At speed, Sheene is a horrifically tight bend with very little grass but a huge amount of gravel. It reminded me of the view a golfer might get when confronted with a hole on an island within a huge lake. The trick for success at the Dingle Dell/Sheene combination was to go in slow, find a late apex into the last right bend before setting up for Stirling's. I would learn just how scary this section would be soon enough.

"Come out of Sheene, you'll swing to the right and then peel left around Stirling's. That'll set you up for the drop to Clearways.

"The GP route needs a different approach for Clarke Curve than when you're on the Indy. There was also that second bridge which, even at a walking pace, looks way too low. They have truck racing here, so there's plenty of room really but when you're approaching it downhill, especially if it's darker, the bridge is below you and you lose all sense of perspective. You will most definitely duck here first time around. OK; we're nearly there. We've just got Clearways and Clark to go. Tired yet?" I was knackered and we'd only walked around half of the track.

We stopped at the entrance to Clearways, where Jeremy got off his bike for the last time.

"Next up is Clearways and Clark. Here, you need to get about halfway across the track, drift right to take it tight as soon as you pass the pit entrance, lift the bike and pin it onto McLarens.

"So that, boys and girls, is the frankly awesome grand prix circuit. There's a lot to take in, I know but you're gonna LOVE it. Now, go on. We'll see you all in the morning."

I had expected a more flowing track; this was going to be a real challenge. With more new information crowding our heads, we returned to the garage to absorb everything we had been shown.

I was worried about how angular the GP section was. Jeremy had been as entertaining as ever, which had helped but it was nothing like I had imagined.

During the walk, Dan, Simon and I had held back from the main group at some points, comparing line options for each section before listening to the Jeremy's advice. There is always so much to learn and, in the garage, we discussed the track again, following the line on a circuit map taped to the wall. There was nothing more we could do now, so we left any further concerns for qualifying. We'd all learn soon enough.

Dan and Lorne returned to their hotel, Simon to his van and I settled down in my caravan. Mark and Vanessa did some last-minute checks on her bike before they too tucked in for the night.

Saturday: Scrutineering & Qualifying.

As I missed scrutineering on Friday, I had to get everything checked first thing. "First thing" was 7:30 but race engines could not be started before 8:15. For Round 1, I had been in the lower paddock and thus close to the tech bay but it's a long way from the garage. I would have to push the bike there, kitted out in my full gear. Getting as far as the end of pit lane was all right but from the entrance to the tunnel under the circuit, it was all uphill.

To get her into racing trim, Sylvie had all unnecessary equipment removed but she was still heavy to push. It was already hot and my leathers were filling with sweat from the exertion. A friendly passer-by helped push me as far as the tunnel entrance, at which point I ignored the "no engine" rule and rode slowly in first gear up the hill through the tunnel, turning the engine off as soon as I exited to coast the last few metres up to Scrutineering.

I rolled up to the inspector who gave Sylvie the once-over. He was happy with everything except the lack of valve caps on the wheels. He was less happy with the warm exhausts but let it go. I leant Sylvie against a wall and got my riding gear checked. It was 7:45 so, rather than push Sylvie back up the hill to the garage, I rolled down to Carl Bell's pit space in the lower paddock to cadge a cup of coffee off his wife, Lin until I could ride Sylvie back. It also gave me a chance to release the steam that had been poaching me under the leathers.

There was a flurry of activity in Garage 7. Vanessa, Dan and Simon had all entered the Thunderbike class for this round, so were busy preparing for first qualifying. Dan had entered both the Minitwin and Thunderbike Sport classes since Oulton Park but this would be the first time Simon and Vanessa had taken the double-dip plunge. Thunderbikes would be first, mixing Minitwin SVs with all manner of 600cc machinery.

Minitwin qualifying followed soon after Thunderbikes. I was quite nervous; a new track meant I would have to be on my toes. We gathered in the collecting area and I presumed we would be sent to the start/finish straight but instead, the marshals pointed us towards Pilgrim's Drop to start our qualifying session from the GP section.

The faster riders barged their way through as we joined the track, riding uphill towards the parkland section. Before I'd even shifted into second gear, they had already crested the hill and were headed down to the bridge. I tagged onto the rearmost riders, desperately trying to remember the lines Jeremy had shown us. I didn't duck under the bridge; I really was going too slowly. I was, however, still too fast (for me) into the Hawthorn Bend entry point. I braked a little, tipping Sylvie in but took it way too wide and slow. Finding myself in the wrong gear, I knocked it down two as I approached Westfield and the revs shot up. My pace was slow enough to get around that one without any issue and I snapped the throttle open to catch up with everyone.

That was a mistake because, as I approached towards Dingle Dell, I went onto the grass. I knew it was going to happen well before as I was completely off-line but was able to straighten up enough to just avoid the gravel.

Swearing to myself, I sorted my head out, went through Sheene and Stirling to head for Clearways. I got a good line onto the McLaren Straights and hurtled towards Paddock Hill. Panicking again, I took it a little wide but Sylvie settled and we shot down Hailwood. I was in fourth gear on the approach to Druids, Sylvie struggling to maintain momentum. Cursing again, I knocked the gearbox down two, paddled around the hairpin, down the hill and around Graham Hill bend.

Back through Surtees, I was again in the wrong gear. The panic around the GP section had knocked my concentration. I headed towards Hawthorn, reminding myself to take it easy this time. I rounded the next two bends satisfactorily before realising it wasn't Westfield where I had the problem before but Dingle Dell. I promptly repeated my error and did a little more grass tracking. And swearing.

I was very slow by this point, so Sheene posed no threat. I took Stirling corner wide and then straightened up towards Clearways. Taking a deep breath, I clipped the white line after the pit entrance, hugging the rightmost part of the track along the pit wall. Tucking myself in, I stamped my foot down through the gears until I reached the flag station, where I drifted left, dropped down two gears and tipped into Paddock in fourth.

Hustling down Hailwood Hill, I got my first real experience of stomach-in-the-mouth at the dip. Grinning, I then realised that I was approaching Druids way too fast, in too high a gear and with nowhere near enough track or time to stop. I didn't even try to lean; I simply let Sylvie charge into the gravel full tilt, coming to a remarkably fast stop. Half a dozen marshals stared at me wide-eyed. I watched their arms raise as I sunk into the welcoming stones. With the wheels buried axle-deep, I lost my balance and keeled over, Sylvie resting on top of me. I flicked the kill switch and it all went quiet.

Two marshals ran over to help extract me, the younger one with a massive grin and his older, presumably more experienced colleague trying his best not to laugh. This was my first crash but wasn't really a proper one. Still; I was happy to have popped that cherry without any damage, other than a beach-load of gravel scooped up in Sylvie's belly pan. As soon she was safely leant behind the fencing, the marshal came over to award me an impromptu "Wrong Way Up" certificate, which I promised to attach to the bike's left flank in the first race.

I had only managed to complete two laps out of a possible six for the fifteen-minute qualifying session but was told that I'd made an appearance in the commentary. More infamy. I stood with the marshals until the session was over, at which point I was told to ride back as quickly as I could, so as not to hold up the next session. Sylvie was fine, if a little dusty and gravel-filled. She started on first press, I waited for the last riders to pass and followed them back to pit lane.

At least I knew where I'd qualify. Or so I thought. As it turned out, I wasn't at the back of the grid, because two riders hadn't made it to qualifying. I knew how that felt but this time I gridded row 13, grid position 39.

Back at the garage, everyone came over to ask what had happened. Sympathy for my error was lacking and immediately I became the target of much good-natured ribbing. I hated being at the back but enjoyed sharing the warmth of my fellow riders' affection. I was teased mercilessly but it was all in good spirits. We were all mates together and besides; someone had to come last. I just wished someone else would take a turn for once.

I had watched a number of riders at the first round and thought, "I'm reckon I could beat them" before soon realising my own shortcomings. My riding wasn't bad but I needed to improve my confidence. Back then, I knew the bike was underpowered but, rather than worry about how I could make it faster, I knew I needed more track time. My times and speeds were improving but there was a long way still to go. With her new cams, Sylvie should at least have more go in her (I would arrange that dyno check during the weekend). I was still the weak link in this chain.

With the newly cleaned Sylvie on her stands, tyre warmers fitted and fuel in the tank, I could relax ahead of race one. That was after lunch, so I went to watch the Thunderbike Sport race.

When the riders were called out, I joined Lorne, her cousin and his girlfriend at the fence along the Surtees straight and asked about Dan's season so far. Lorne was letting him get on with it this year, in exchange for her getting a horse next year. She said that she wasn't a "precious" wife; she knew this was Dan's passion and they wanted each other to do things that made them happy. Lorne rode pillion with Dan but looked forward to getting a horse; something that Dan had actively encouraged her to do.

The race got underway and I spent the next fifteen minutes looking out for my friends. Dan was flying, picking people off from the start. I loved how natural he looked (and not a little envious).

Simon continued his mid-pack pace, with Vanessa bringing up the rear. We all cheered loudly as she passed a Ducati, put space between them and stayed ahead for the rest of the race. I was inordinately jealous but felt like a broody mother; proud of them all while wanting them all to get home safely.

It was difficult to determine where riders were in the standings, as the grid was split into two classes. Dan, Simon and Vanessa were all Thunderbike 'A' but, other than being able to see them as they passed by, I had no idea where they placed. It was only when they rolled into the garage I learned Dan had got his first win. He was not only the first rookie, which would have been good anyway but was the first group 'A' rider past the flag. Finally, after five rounds of chipping away at the competition, Dan had achieved his first genuine win and at his home circuit.

The mood in the garage was euphoric. Dan and I had always got on and, when Simon had his first trophy at Snetterton, leaving me the only trophy-less rider from that round (Vanessa had not gone to Snetterton), Dan had said, "Only a matter of time now, Steve. You are getting quicker, so I look forward to congratulating you." He was genuine in that wish but we both knew it would be some time before I would take a pot home, if ever. I didn't mind, though; I was just happy for my friend.

Race 1
(Row 13, Grid 39)

The timetable meant that we would be out straight after lunch. I grabbed some pasta and water before kitting up for the first race. When the call came, we went to the collecting area and were directed to the start grid. I set Sylvie up to grid spot 39 and knocked her into neutral as the grid began to fill. The last couple of riders threaded their way to somewhere near the front and I clicked up into first gear. The front marshal dropped his flag and stepped onto the grass and we were waved through for the warm up lap. Even that was done at a breakneck pace, with the riders behind me flying past into Paddock Hill. I followed the mass of bikes through the circuit, managing to stay clear of the grass at Dingle Dell this time and returning to the grid with my heart pounding. This was a long track (about 2.4 miles) and I wondered just how scared I was going to be for the next fifteen minutes.

I dropped my visor and held Sylvie in first gear, holding the revs up. The flag marshal stepped onto the grass, his red flag pointing at the lights. Alan Hensby was just head of me. He was rolling back and forth and I was thinking, "Don't jump, Alan." The lights lit up and, once they had gone out, we were off.

Or, at least, everyone else was. Earlier, Vanessa had said to her husband Mark, "Steve always gets off the line better than me, so I always have a job to pass him at the start." Those words must have been still going round my head as I didn't set off cleanly and found myself at the back immediately. Cursing, I swung left to make the drop into Paddock to try and catch Vanessa up. I got close but it was too packed at Druids, so I had to hold station.

As we rounded the hairpin, two riders were standing by the Armco, their bikes on the grass. I went round Graham Hill, where another rider was coming back onto the track. Less than half a mile in and the race was already becoming a war of attrition. I rode through the Cooper Straight towards Surtees but was in the wrong gear for the bend, where I could hear Jeremy saying, "Momentum! Momentum!" Going uphill in fourth gear was awful, so I dropped to third to try and make up some time. I got around the GP section without any major drama, took a deep breath and chased Vanessa around Stirling's, back towards Clearways.

I was happy with my line into McLaren's but still too slow. I could feel the extra power Dan Singleton had managed to inject into Sylvie, though. She was more responsive but I wasn't using the power properly; rolling off too early, not leaning enough and losing corner speed. Everyone was leaving me behind. I knew I was losing time and needed to get my head down and keep going.

The second lap was better but still the times felt poor. Dingle Dell was giving its siren call but I was going too slowly to be sucked in this time. Down towards Clearways, I shouted, "Come ON, Sylvie. We can do this!", laughing at how stupid I sounded.

On to the next lap and, having completed the Indy section, I tipped into Surtees in second gear. The engine screamed in protest but pulled fantastically as I tucked in, pinning it towards the bridge.

There was a red light and lots of waving red flags.

I closed the throttle immediately and saw a white bike in the middle of the track. Ahead of me, Vanessa had swung left to go around it and, as I approached, I saw what no rider wants to see.

Bike number 34 was lying on its right side, at about a forty-five-degree angle to the direction of the track. On the kerb lay the rider with a medic and two marshals crouched down around him. My heart sank. It was Dan Thomas.

We continued round and I thought I saw Vanessa peel off into the pits, so followed. She hadn't but it was too late for me to change direction. I went down pit lane to Garage 7, rode through and back to the collecting area, where the marshal stopped me.

"Sorry," I said. "I thought everyone had come back in."

He looked subdued. "It's OK," he said. "Turn your engine off, though. We may be here for a while." Something in his voice sounded wrong but I didn't ask any more. I hit the kill switch.

There was not a sound to be heard. Radio silence had been instigated; not a good sign, as it means something significant has likely happened. I felt a lump in my throat, hoping that, if it was Dan (I already knew it was), that he'd be OK.

After what seemed an age, an ambulance appeared under the bridge at Clearways, its lights blazing. As it turned into the medical centre, the marshal's radio crackled, "Back to the pits, please."

I was released from the collecting area and rode back. The rest of the gang were a while getting back as they had to follow the Indy circuit section, coming in to pit lane from the Graham Hill exit gate. Sylvie was already on her stands by the time they got back. I helped Simon set his bike up while Mark sorted Vanessa out. The announcement went out advising that the race would be postponed while the area was cleared.

Helmets off, the three of us looked at each other in stunned silence. I knew Vanessa had seen it and assumed Simon had too. Dan was much faster than the three of us, so would have been way ahead of us all. Before long, an air ambulance landed before setting off to Orpington hospital.

The rumour mill started almost immediately but the three of us stuck together, not contributing to anything that others outside our group were saying. Whoever came to ask us, the answer was always the same; we had heard nothing. We were not going to contribute to idle speculation; Dan deserved better. All three of us believed the worst but were collectively praying for the best. Not knowing was messing with our heads and we didn't know what to do for the best.

Lorne and Dan's other friends had left for the hospital. Simon's friend Jackie had befriended Lorne during the season and relayed what little information she had. Whatever his injuries, Dan would not be continuing this weekend.

We needed to get practical. Dan's gear needed sorting and his van returned to Burgess Hill. Between us, we stowed his gear into his van, which Mark and Vanessa would take back later.

The afternoon passed in a fuzzy blur but there was the matter of Vanessa and Simon also being entered in the next Thunderbike race. Neither was sure they wanted to participate. I advised them to miss it, my logic being that the Thunderbike riders didn't know them from Adam. Unlike Minitwins, where we rookies were given a wide berth (because we were recognised), most of the Thunderbike grid was non-Minitwin. Simon and Vanessa didn't know how the other riders would treat them, so I reasoned that it was best for them to sit it out.

The Minitwin race would be another matter. I argued that, despite its competitive nature, racing with Minitwins was like racing with your mates and everyone knew how each other would behave. If we didn't race, there was a chance that we'd never go out again. That would have been understandable but we'd have to face those demons. Besides, we wanted to ride in honour of Dan, who we believed was still fighting in the hospital.

Race 2
(Row 12, Grid 35)

I can remember little of the second race, although I did recall getting a good start, keeping ahead of Vanessa until Surtees, which I messed up. I went in too hot and rode a full bike's length into the Indy section but was able to turn and get back onto the GP circuit. Of course, by then I'd lost momentum, distance, speed, my place and willingness, so simply circulated long enough to get a signature for finishing.

Once our racing was over for the day, we packed the last of Dan's things and Mark and Vanessa took it back. Simon and I went to the Kentagon restaurant to see the prize-giving. We raised a glass to our mate and listened quietly as his name was called for winning the Thunderbike race. We felt awful but ironically, Simon was called up for a spot prize. With his twenty-five pounds winnings, he returned my Snetterton favour and bought me dinner and a drink. Despite our feelings, we were both really hungry. We had our meal on a table away from the building, away from everyone else and lost in our own thoughts.

Once finished, we walked back to the garage. I had some new brake pads to fit for Sunday. Simon offered to help; assistance I was happy to accept, as I wasn't confident on putting them together but Simon and I both wanted to keep busy. We spent a good ninety minutes stripping, cleaning, maintaining and reassembling the front brakes. The existing pads were fine, so I decided to leave them unchanged. The discs looked a little worn, though and I would need to replace them when the season ended.

We had another beer in the garage, tapping our bottles together in salute to Dan and took a deep drink before putting everything away. A few riders had come in, all asking the same question - "Heard anything?" We only ever answered "No" or, "We've heard nothing official."

When Vanessa and Mark returned, we agreed that any official news (rather than gossip) would be kept between the four of us. We would not share anything even with the other side of the garage. We were not going to be the source of hearsay. We just wanted to know our friend was going to be all right. The snippets that Vanessa was able to get from the office were not good, though. When she offered to store the bike for Dan, she was told that it had been wrapped, pending investigation.

With nothing to do and, rather than simply mill about, I returned to the caravan and phoned Cheryl. I told her Dan had been injured but none of us knew how badly and we were still waiting to hear. Nothing had been announced at the prize giving, other than Mike thanking everyone - the medics and marshals for their prompt actions and the riders for their patience and understanding - but that they had no news to give at the time. Sleep was a long time coming. When it did, it was fitful and restless.

We didn't find out what had happened until later. Dan had been closing in on another rider, catching up on the approach to Hawthorn. He was very close and, as he passed on the left, travelling at some 120 mph, his front brake lever had struck the other rider's elbow. Dan's brake had locked on, sending him over the handlebars and putting the bike into a stoppie, where the front wheel locks and the rear wheel lifts, the front wheel acting as a pivot. Both Dan and bike were sent into an area of unprotected Armco before ricocheting back. Dan had come to rest at the kerb but the bike only came to rest once it was back on the track. It's likely that Dan was killed instantly. He was 46 and Saturday had been his birthday.

Sunday: Race Day 2

There was a lot of activity around Garage 7 in the morning, with a constant stream of people coming in, wanting to know if we knew anything more. We all kept to the same story, not wanting anything to get back to Lorne, particularly through social media. We later learned that Lorne had contacted the race office to say that she didn't want the meeting cancelled for her benefit and that people should not be informed until the end of the weekend, when she would release a statement.

Simon and Vanessa decided to enter today's Thunderbike races. I understood but added that, if either of them was unhappy at any point, they should pit early. They had both got their Saturday signature and there were three Minitwin races today, so there should be no issue getting a second one.

Race 2
(Row 12 Grid 35)

The timetable had been altered to include what would have been the last Minitwin race. We would therefore get one race in the morning and two in the afternoon.

We rolled up to the collecting area, still processing yesterday's events. The race had been shortened to six laps, along with a number of other races, to make up for the lost time of yesterday.

I looked across to Simon, Alan and Vanessa. If they were anything like me, their heads were probably not in the right place as we waited to be let on to the track. Personally, I just needed to get the race over with to gain another signature. Once I'd got that, nothing else mattered and I could go home if I wanted to.

On the warm up, I looked over to the right as we approached Hawthorn. In my head, I could still see Dan's bike and that group of people administering to him before the ambulance arrived. My heart was pounding as we went up Hawthorn Hill, through the Minter Straight, around Dingle Dell and back to Clearways.

I had to shake that maudlin feeling out of my head. As I lined up to Grid 35, I heard myself saying, "Stick with it, Dan. We'll do this for you." It seemed such a simplistic thing to say but not pointless. All of us were thinking about our fallen friend and we all felt that he was with us then.

The lights went out and we were away again. Six laps later (five for me), the chequered flag came out. I had completed another race, earning another signature but recalled little of the time between the lights going out and the flag coming out, other than part way through thinking how difficult the GP section of Brands Hatch is to negotiate. I had been in awe of Cadwell but had soon learned how beautifully flowing it is. The Indy section is also flowing, albeit short, whereas the GP section is very technical; fast but angular, requiring some serious bravery if you want to get round quickly. You are on full throttle along the straights but have to brake very hard (and late) if you want to keep any momentum. The corners are almost all right-angles and must be approached with extreme accuracy in order not to be sucked into the huge gravel traps that surround them.

Four riders didn't complete the race, including Dan Singleton, who had bailed out on the second lap. I had managed to get away with not coming off track but that was about it. I had not enjoyed the experience and was very pleased to return to the caravan.

Race 3
(Row 11 Grid 33)

My indifferent mood and performance from the morning race put me on row 11, against the pit wall, next to Vanessa. Thanks to those four fallers, Vanessa and I had been gifted improved grid positions. We sat waiting as the revs rose in unison.

The lights went out and Sylvie shot off the line. I passed Vanessa and tucked down. Up ahead, a rider had stalled his bike and raised his arm. Before I could react, the rider ahead of me slammed into the back of the stranded bike and rider, skittling off to the right towards the pit wall directly in front of me. I saw pieces of bright blue bodywork flying across the track and tensed, bracing for impact. Instinctively, I swerved left then right, barely missing the still-spinning bike but knew Vanessa would was directly behind me. I tensed again, waiting for what I thought would be my first major crash but Vanessa passed by, our bikes missing by millimetres. The red flags came out again.

We coasted round to the Cooper Straight and a marshal told us to switch off our engines. I pulled up next to Vanessa and Alan, both of who looked visibly shaken. I gave Vanessa an encouraging pat on the arm before reaching over to bang knuckles with Alan. This was the big round, the one everyone had been looking forward to most of all and it had turned into a nightmare. All we wanted to do was get it over, get our signatures and go home.

We were held at Cooper for maybe five minutes as the bikes were cleared away and the riders transferred to the medical centre before reforming on the grid. Vanessa looked back at me and I nodded acknowledgment. The marshal retreated and the lights went on.

The lights went out and we were off again. I stuck with the pack around Paddock Hill and down Hailwood, getting into the right gear for Druids, where I took a wide line, cutting across the inside and then back over to the left at the top of the hill, swinging back right as I came down and went round Graham Hill. Tucking down behind the screen along Cooper, Sylvie started coughing. I shut off briefly, then opened up again and she settled as I rode up towards Hawthorn. I looked across to that section of track where I had last seen Dan and then berated myself for not getting on with the job.

Sylvie, however, had other plans and started misfiring badly. I managed to coax her through the GP section, knowing I was well away from everyone else but as I got to Clearways, she shot off again. Thinking I'd risk it one more time (I could pull off the track at any point), we went through McLaren's full tilt, round Paddock, Druids and Graham Hill before the engine cut out on the Cooper Straight.

Enough was enough. I coasted up to the barriers that separated the GP and Indy sections and waited for the bikes to come through. A marshal, seeing what I had done, signalled me to wait until he could see the coast was clear. As Vanessa passed through, he waved me out and I limped back to the garage. Setting Sylvie up on her stands, I watched the rest of the race from behind the fence at Cooper Straight. This was not how I had wanted the weekend to pan out.

At the chequered flag, I returned to the garage, started Sylvie and she roared into life. I was at a loss. The engine sounded beautiful, so I decided to go to the dyno truck and have her checked out. I had only planned to get a compliance check but decided to pay for a full performance test. That should at least show if there were any underlying problems. I spoke to Dyno Dan and told him what had happened, asked if they accepted credit cards and went back to bring Sylvie over.

When I first bought Sylvie, I had been swept away with the notion of owning this cool race bike but, as time passed, I had found endless shortcomings. In hindsight, it would have been better to have bought a properly prepared bike before coming to race. Still, that was academic now. I had spent time and money improving her, although there was still work to be done with my head, especially with Dan's condition weighing on my mind.

I rode to the dyno truck, at the far end of the garages, to talk with Dan Beighton. I described the misfire and said how the bike had finally died altogether (something I'd not experienced since my early track days). With the new cams in, it was time to pay for a proper test and performance chart. Dan had tested her twice and laughed both times. I was hoping for something a bit more positive and told him I'd be delighted if he told me the power figure started with a six.

He strapped Sylvie in and set to work. I couldn't believe the noise and was expecting to see components fly out the back of the truck but it was all fine. The SV650 may be a budget bike but that engine really is bulletproof. After a few minutes of abuse, the revs dropped and Dan emerged from the back of the van.

"Well, you were 58 at Snetterton," he told me. "Whatever Mr Singleton did has done the trick. You've got 68 HP now and the fuelling? Absolutely spot on. That misfiring or cutting out is probably more crap in the fuel lines. I'd get the tank and fuel lines cleaned out again."

I handed over my £30 and got a lovely chart showing a linear rise and plateauing line. I was pleased to see that, once getting to the peak level, the power hardly tailed off at all. Even a bike as old as Sylvie (2000 model year, so nearly twenty years old) still had life in her. I was very happy with that but painfully aware that it showed that I was still the weak link. I needed to sort my head and have more self-belief if I was to improve. We would see what the day's final race would bring.

Everyone was keen to know how we had got on. They were all surprised when I showed how much more power Sylvie was now putting out. The final race couldn't come soon enough.

Race 4
(Row 12, Grid 34)

The call went out and once again, I was the first to roll out of the garage once the second call announcement was made. Once outside, I blipped the throttle a couple of times to see if there was any misfire but all seemed fine, so I stopped at the end of pit lane.

"Row 12, grid 34", came the instruction. I was first out again, but, having screwed that one really good grid position I had been given at Snetterton, I'd rather be first and wait from now on.

I pulled up at the head of the second section of the collecting area. Vanessa was directly in front of me and before long, we were directed to the track.

The marshals checked the track was clear before signalling us off on the warm up lap. Once again, those at the back shot through the grid and flew round to join the other fast boys. I could never understand the logic here, as they'd only have to go to the back of the grid when they returned but hey; they had their race faces on, whereas I was still the middle-aged wannabe.

The pack rounded Paddock Hill and Druids, spreading out once we'd reached Graham Hill bend. All was fine with Sylvie at this point, so I was more confident of getting round this time.

All was fine until Dingle Dell, that was. I had completed the warm up with no issues but, as soon as I lifted Sylvie out of Stirling, she had started coughing again. I wasn't going to risk anything so, as I went under the bridge towards Clearways, I raised my arm and peeled off back into the pits.

I was gutted. Sylvie had been performing so well up to this point. This time it wasn't even a DNF (did not finish) but an even worse DNS (did not start). Still, it was what it was, so I pulled into the garage and popped Sylvie back onto her stand. I walked back into the caravan, got changed and phoned Cheryl to give her the news. She was disappointed for me but pleased to know it was over for another weekend, especially knowing about Dan's crash, even if by that time neither of us knew how bad it was.

I went to the race office to return the garage key and paid the rental charge, telling Sue behind the counter that Vanessa, Simon and I had covered Dan's portion. It was a small gesture but an easy one for us to make. Returning to the garage, I packed my gear into the van by which time everyone else had returned from their final race and started clearing up.

Simon had come third in the morning's race but was not sure about collecting the trophy. I told him that he should; Dan would have been the first to congratulate him and would have been disappointed for Simon not to have collected what he had earned. I understood why winning that particular trophy would have been bitter-sweet but convinced him to go. He agreed and went to the race office to collect it.

Once packed, I made my farewells. Vanessa had let the office know about taking Dan's van back and offered to store Dan's bike when it was released but was told that it had been forensically wrapped, pending the coroner's report, so Bemsee didn't know when it would be released. That was our first confirmation that Dan had indeed gone and it felt terrible.

After giving Vanessa a hug and shaking hands with Mark, I made my way home. I wanted to phone Cheryl but needed thinking time. We had been looking forward to this round more than any other and it had ended disastrously. None of us had ever expected such an outcome. We had finished a round but had lost a friend along the way. I'd lost friends in road accidents but losing Dan felt ten times worse. He had become a close friend and I still had the image of him and his bike on the track, which would take a long time to leave me, if it ever does. My mood on the journey home was very sombre. I took a deep breath and phone Cheryl. "I'm coming home."

In the weeks following Dan's death, we all kept in touch with Lorne. She was keen to talk with his friends and invited us to the celebration of his life later that month.

In the meantime, Bemsee and the Minitwin group had arranged a number of memorial events for the final two Minitwin rounds. Firstly, stickers would be produced in memory of Dan, to be sold at the Cadwell and Brands rounds. The proceeds would pay for a new "Dan Thomas Memorial Trophy" which would replace an existing rookie race at the final. There would also be a tribute parade at Cadwell, ridden by Minitwinners and the Thunderbike Sport racers in honour of Dan. Going to a race meeting never seemed so important. I was definitely going to go, even if I had to beg for the money to get there.

A lot of publicity was given in the racing press and social media, inviting riders to follow the family to Dan's wake, wearing the brightest gear they could, so as to give him a good send off. I met up with Simon, Charlie, Vanessa and Mark so we could all ride off together, as the original "Garage 7" group.

Before going to the funeral, I had a number 34 sown on to each shoulder of my race leathers. John from Mojo Leathers did a fantastic job, taking only a couple of days to complete the work, so I would be riding to the funeral with Dan's number on my leathers. As long as I raced, I would always wear that number.

True to form, the celebration was a lively affair, with a number of lovely anecdotes from family and friends remembering their cool drummer-cum-racer brother. It was the only funeral I've attended that had "We're Not Gonna Take It" by Twisted Sister belting out at the end. A happy occasion to mark a tragically sad moment.

My results:
Qualifying: 2:16.081
Race 1: 2:13.685
Race 2: 2:13.100
Race 3: DNF
Race 4: DNF

(Above) February 2016: how it started. Sylvie, pre-money pit.

(Below) May 2018: ACU test day, Brands Hatch. I've already had to replace the front wheel, due to finding a ding in the original. (Images © copyright Steve Male)

(Above) January 2019: with the first season just around the corner, sorting out the ever-growing list of issues begins in earnest. (Image © copyright Steve Male)

(Below) February: The first proper thrashing at Brands Hatch for the last track day ahead of the season opener. (Image copyright © Jenny Wells)

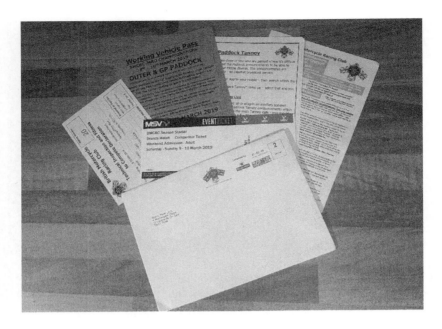

(Above) February: the post tells me that suddenly, it's all very real.

(Below) March - Round 1 (Brands Hatch): A very unprofessionally "prepared" bike (and rider) set up, waiting for the call.
(Images © copyright Steve Male)

"That's me in the programme!" (Image © copyright Cheryl Bishop)

Weather is wet. Top wheel has the brakes but the wrong tyre. Bottom has the tyre but no brakes.
(Image © copyright Steve Male)

(Below) Round 1, race 1. Steve (Suzuki #20) tips in to Druids, closely followed by Martin Tomkins (Ducati #161). (Image © copyright Hilary Hardy)

(Above) Paddock Hill: terrified rookie Steve (#20) about to be lapped by hero rookie Matt (#232). (Image © copyright Jenny Wells)

(Below) Surtees. New leathers, new lid, very scruffy bike. (Image © copyright Jenny Wells)

(Above) With the bike resting against the retaining wall, the job of casing swapping can begin.

(Below) Gen 2 casing and engine protector finally lined up and ready to be bolted in place.
(Images © copyright Steve Male)

(Above) The bike is finally looking presentable, ready for Cadwell Park.
(Image © copyright Steve Male)

(Below) Mansfield, Cadwell Park, during practice. I hate rain. Vanessa (#70) wasn't too keen, either.
(Image © copyright Jenny Wells)

(Above) Round 3 (Cadwell Park): my first wet race. Vanessa Gillam (#70) and I spent all season fighting for last place. I beat her every time.

(Below) The Mountain. I had to wait until the next visit to experience my first Mountain wheelie. Here, Colin Clune (#171) eases past. (Images © copyright Jenny Wells)

(Above) Cadwell Park test day. Apparently, I didn't have a puncture...

(Below) This is what paint-swapping looks like. The result of a very close pass at Park Corner.
(Images © copyright Steve Male)

Best of chums – Vanessa Gillam and Alan Hensby.
(Image © copyright Steve Male)

Mark wonders what the hell his mate has got him into.
(Image © copyright Steve Male)

(Below) Rounding Barn Corner. Nick Cronin (#144) and Tony Parker (#44) are not far behind. (Image © copyright Jenny Wells)

(Above) Round 5 (Snetterton): Feeling more confident with the bike.

(Below) Dan Thomas tucks in properly, showing how it should be done.
(Images © copyright Jenny Wells)

(Above) Round 6 (Brands GP): Steve takes entirely the wrong line out of Clearways during practice. It was sorted by the race, though. (Image © copyright Jenny Wells)

(Below) The Garage 7 line up. Simon and Dan's bikes up front, Vanessa's and mine out back.
(Image © copyright Steve Male)

Round 6 (Brands GP): Sylvie & Vanessa's bike await practice (Image © copyright Steve Male)

Dan as we all remember him. (Image © copyright Jackie Casey)

(Below) My first (sort of) crash earned me this informal certificate. (Image © copyright Steve Male)

(Above) Round 7 (Cadwell Park): Dan Thomas' Memorial ride. Shaun Wallace (#48) leads me, Simon Wilkinson (#40) and Kevin Lilley (#19). (Image © copyright Jenny Wells.)

(Below) Vanessa broke her wrist but still got her final signature. Clubman's licence, here we come!

Sylvie's "In memory of Dan Thomas" badge, which will stay as long as I own her.

(Images © copyright Steve Male)

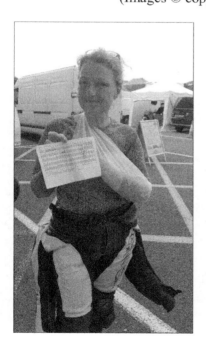

(Above) Round 9 (Brands Indy): Trying to keep up with the fast boys. Minitwin champion Glyn Davies (#26) and Dave Twyford (#184) did at least give me space as they lapped me.
(Image © copyright Jenny Wells)

(Below) This isn't going to end well. Last round, last day, last crash. A proper one, this time but both bike and rider limped away fairly unscathed. (Image © copyright Rod Tietjen)

(Above) The "Garage 7" trophy winners.
l-r: Sam Kent, Simon Wilkinson, Alan Hensby, Matt Wetherell, Mark Gillam, Vanessa Gillam, Lorne Thomas, Yours truly. (Image © copyright Cheryl Bishop)

(Below) Savouring the moment at the awards night.
Back, l-r: Ricardo Branco, Tommy Downes, Morph May, unknown rider, Simon Wilkinson, Kevin Lilley, Alan Hensby, Charlie Downes.
Front, l-r: Vanessa Gillam, Paul Witherington, Dan Singleton, Gavin Davies, Matt Wetherell.
(Image © copyright Jenny Wells)

Chapter 10:
Cadwell Park: The Mountain Beckons Again

Friday: arrival/practice

"IT'S TOO EARLY!"

The plaintive cry was from Cheryl. She was right, of course but a text received from Bemsee a couple of days ago had reminded me that I had booked instruction so couldn't simply roll up mid-afternoon; I needed to be at Cadwell Park before 1:00. I had gone to bed far too late, after sorting some last-minute packing, so that 2:30 am alarm disturbed the deepest of sleeps. It had also woken Cheryl which, at that time isn't the best of plans.

Although I'd been to Cadwell before, for this round, I was taking my own double-dip plunge and had entered the Thunderbike Sport class as well as Minitwins. This would get me more track time and Cadwell was a circuit I was now warming to.

I was on the road by 3:10, pleased that I wasn't dragging the caravan this time, if only because of how much it affects the fuel consumption. Despite being nearly 3 tonnes and 2200cc, my Ford Transit regularly returned 40 mpg but that dropped to about 28 when the caravan was attached.

Why was I not taking the caravan? That was because I had mislaid the keys, so it was stuck in storage for now. My reputation as a disorganized mess remained intact. For this trip, it was back to basics and I'd be sleeping in the back of the van. I'd loaded everything on Tuesday, leaving only the groceries to be packed before I left for Lincolnshire.

Coming to Cadwell Park was important. Aside from needing the signatures (this round should get me the last two needed for my Clubman licence), I wanted the points and I really wanted to take part in the celebration parade lap to honour Dan Thomas. Even if I hadn't raced, I would have wanted to come along for that lap. It was going to be an emotional weekend.

My fellow rookies often had a laugh at my expense, especially where it came to my lack of organization. It was from this gentle ribbing that the idea to award trophies for the group arose. These wouldn't be serious trophies but would have titles such as "Best Binner" (Sam, crasher extraordinaire), "Best Underwear Model" (Alan. Don't ask), "Get Outta My Way, I'm Coming Through!" (Matt, who was by now beyond reach for the Rookie title) and so on. I would organise this once I got home from this meeting.

I loaded the groceries into a cool box, as I wouldn't have a fridge. I had elected to eat a lot of pasta, which could be cooked on a camping stove and eaten straight out of the pan. My daughter Ami had loaned me a sleeping bag and a camp which I'd set up once I'd unloaded the van. It would be fine.

This really was going back to the roots of club racing. Even at an amateur level, there was a wide variety of setups in the paddock. Some slept in a van or gazebo, some didn't even have that and slept in their cars. Those with more wherewithal had racing trucks with fixed awnings, a bike-sized storage space at the back and living accommodation. Most had caravans but there were a lot like me, living in the back of a standard panel van.

Being so early, the roads were clear (and the Dartford crossing free of charge). I stopped at Peterborough services for a thirty-minute sleep before continuing to Cadwell. Vanessa and Mark were already installed, so I set up to the right of Mark's truck to avoid the muddy lake on the other side. Cadwell Park is the only venue on the calendar where we set up on grass and much of the ground is uneven, so it's useful to have a thick sheet of marine ply to set your bike up on. Something for my next season, perhaps. My space wasn't too wet but would still require careful loading of Sylvie onto the stands.

Once I had put the gazebo up, everything was unloaded, Sylvie being the last item out of the van. She was sporting a borrowed red tank on for the weekend (courtesy of Steve Shrubshall), as there was still a suspicion of rust in her original black tank and I'd not had time to clean it out. At Brands, she had stuttered a few times before cutting out completely, so I had her checked on the dyno but was told the fuelling was perfect. Dan Singleton had found rust in the carbs though, so suspicion was still there. Today's test would hopefully prove that the tank was at the root of the issue.

After setting Sylvie up on the stands and fitting the tyre warmers, I put in five litres of fuel. As I poured, I saw what looked like water in the belly pan. I stopped filling and checked. That wasn't water; that was petrol. I checked the rubber fuel line and realised that the retention clip was missing.

A&R had plenty of Jubilee clips, so I bought a small one and set about fitting it. Dismantling the lower half of the fairing to remove the fuel, I filled the tank again.

There was yet more fuel coming out and I found a split in the fuel vacuum pipe where it attached to the tank inlet. I had now lost about seven litres of fuel. I had entered two classes this weekend so would have to buy more in town on Saturday evening.

I removed the tank and the section of fuel line that was attached to the inlet. There was plenty of slack for me, so I trimmed the end and refitted the line. With everything back together (and the belly pan emptied for a second time), I pressed the start button and Sylvie roared into life.

I don't ever expect to tire of that engine's noise. I revved it a few times to sling the oil around before leaving it to settle into a gentle idle to warm up. I then sought out Dan Singleton, who would be my instructor in the afternoon.

Dan was going to be busy. He was instructing a rider in the session immediately before mine. He asked me to wait the collecting area ahead of my session and he'd catch up as soon as he could. His goal for the day was to have me get my knee down; something that every wannabe racer aspires to but something that those of us who join the fray later in life have to think twice about. At 57, I was all too aware of my mortality and had frightened myself plenty of times during the season. Getting my knee down would be very cool if it could be done but I wasn't going to hold my breath. It wasn't on my "must do" list.

Dan asked where my feet were when riding and cornering. I demonstrated, showing how I had the inner balls of my feet on the edge of the foot pegs, so they could rotate freely as I moved around on the bike. While agreeing that was fine for the straights, for cornering, Dan showed how he would place the flat of his foot against the vertical faces of the rear sets. This pushed him off the seat and forced his knee out at almost right angles to the bike. It looked remarkably uncomfortable but I said I'd try it.

I was out on the first session after lunch, so waited in the collecting area for Dan. The mid-size bike group was waved onto the track to start the testing and I waited.

And waited.

Eventually, marshal Jane came over and told me to go, otherwise I'd lose the session. She'd let Dan know I was out on track and he would doubtless find me. I made my way to the entry lane and waited until being waved on to the track by the flag marshal.

It was great to be back on a track. I did a sensibly-paced warm up lap initially, refreshing my memory before really opening the throttle on the approach to Coppice for the second lap. Rising up towards Charlies 1, leaning left but sweeping wide, I dropped Sylvie into third gear to maintain momentum and ready to go up the box to top as I rode down the Park straight.

Almost immediately, the engine misfired.

"Bugger", I thought and rolled off the throttle a little. The engine picked up again and I tried once more but, as soon as the engine was under load, it would lose power, pick up and losing power again. I tried for one more lap but decided it would be safer to pull in. Riders were circulating at considerable speed and I didn't want to get in the way or be the cause of a spill for anyone else. Frustrated that the fuelling still hadn't been sorted, despite the new tank, I coasted round Chris Curve before pulling off by the exit road. The marshal opened the gate and asked if I was all right.

"I'm fine but the bike isn't behaving, so I pulled off."

"Do you need the van?" he asked.

"No, it's OK to ride slowly."

I rode back to the paddock, where I removed the tank to access the carburettors. It looked like I was going to have to bite the bullet and look at them properly. I had eight races this weekend, so I really needed Sylvie to perform but I was extremely reluctant to strip them here, so instead sought advice from Dan Singleton.

Dan had joined the track a few minutes after me but, having not found me, had come back to my gazebo. I explained the issue and, after discounting the fuel tank, he lent me an ignition coil from an injected bike to try. He advised trying the rear cylinder first. That was the one that generally gave trouble, as it always got hotter than the front pot. I took the coil back and delved under the seat to locate the original unit. Both coils were easily accessible and, as I went to disconnect the power cable to the rear coil, it fell off. The spade contact had been sitting very loosely on the coil's male connector, so I crimped the female connector and reconnected the power cable. It was now a much tighter fit and, when I fired the engine up, I jiggled the wire to see if the misfire returned. It didn't but I'd not be able to test it out properly until my next scheduled session, when I could put it under proper load.

When I next went out, the difference was remarkable; no misfire, a much smoother power delivery and suddenly lots of it. Sylvie was now a completely different bike. Had I sought Dan's advice at Brands, I might never have missed those last two races. Still; it was academic now; I was confident that Sylvie would perform better tomorrow. I spent the rest of the session reintroducing myself to this fabulous bike and the track, loving how it all felt now. Every time I had gone out following a tweak, I had been surprised at the improvement in Sylvie's performance. She was twenty years old but had plenty of life in her yet.

After the warm up lap, I gradually opened Sylvie up, feeling the speed rise on each lap. My confidence had grown at each outing and I was really enjoying Cadwell now. First left into Coppice, sweeping wide to run across the white edge line, I aimed for the white line on the left of the track to get round Charlies 1 and 2, setting up for the Park Straight. I needed to know what gear I was in (carby SVs have no gear indicator), so made sure I was in sixth before reaching the 300m countdown marker, dropping down two to sweep round the right-hand Park Bend towards Chris Curve. The two bends are more like one long corner with a bit of straight between them but go quickly enough and you're leaning all the way round. As you get about two-thirds of the way around Chris Curve, you need to be on the left so you can aim for the kerb apex on the right when flicking over into the Gooseneck. Next is the short, steep downhill section to Mansfield. Braking where the tarmac changes colour and dropping into second at the diamond-shaped repair, you cut across the kerb on the left for this ninety-degree, left-corner before heading to the kerb on the right, before swinging left to get a straight aim into the right-left chicane. Up into third, keeping to the right will allow the clearest access to the next left-right combination of bends at the foot of the Mountain.

I was loving this and lined up for the point just right of centre at the brow of the Mountain. Unbeknownst to me, I still had the throttle wide open, which meant the biggest wheelie I have done to date. How big? Well, I felt the front go light and before I knew it, the screen smacked the visor of my helmet. I thought my face was going to split with the grin. The front landed with a heavy thud, Sylvie regained her poise and I charged into Hall bends, around the hairpin and Barn, on to the start-finish straight.

I could hear myself laughing and set up the approach for Coppice once more. As I climbed towards Charlies 1, Sylvie's engine died. Immediately, I raised my hand and bumped the front wheel on to the grass, aiming for the marshal station to my left.

I pulled up by the tyre wall and the marshal came over to check. "Everything all right?" He asked.

"It's good but she just cut out."

I pressed the starter and the engine fired up on first press, before shutting off again. I looked in the tank. It was empty. As I'd only done a couple of laps in the previous session, I had mistakenly believed that there was plenty of fuel still but a combination of not topping up and going around faster on a more powerful bike meant my time on track was over. It didn't matter, though; I had loved this session. The recovery van dropped me off outside my gazebo. I was still grinning. It had been brilliant; my favourite racing moment to date.

I still needed to improve my confidence but the test session had put me in good stead for qualifying. Jeremy would be giving a track walk later, which was always educational. I had time, so prepped Sylvie and went to make dinner.

Or at least I could if I had brought cooking utensils. I had left a shopping bag containing a saucepan, washing up stuff, cutlery, etc. in the kitchen at home. Vanessa offered me a coffee and, as I had no eating or drinking stuff, lent me a mug, saucepan and kettle to tide me over. Generally, riders borrow tools, fuel or bike parts. Me? It could be anything but today, thanks to Vanessa and Mark, I could now prepare my own meals.

Saturday: Qualifying/Race Day 1

I had a comfortable night in the van and was grateful to Ami for the loan of the sleeping gear. The alarm was set for 6:30 but, as had become routine for a race weekend, I was awake before 6:00 and headed to the shower block, returning before the alarm went off.

The forecast was for fine weather on Saturday but a risk of rain on Sunday. I had wets with me but hoped not to need them.

I carried out some last-minute checks and made sure there was plenty of fuel before getting ready for the first of two qualifying sessions. My first qualifying time at Cadwell in April had been 2:32. That was a terrible time but I had at least had the excuse of heavy rain. By the end of that first visit, I had achieved a personal best of 2:18. This was my new target for the weekend. Minitwins were out first this weekend. Thunderbike Sports, my second category, would be the fourth session. Although the slowest rider again, I qualified with a 2:14.352 for Minitwins and a 2:13.037 in Thunderbikes, so was very happy. My next target was now a 2:10 lap. Back in the gazebo, tyre warmers went back on, fuel went in and I joined Simon and Vanessa to review qualifying sheets while we waited for the call for race 1.

For most of the 2019 season, there had been nine or ten rookies in Minitwins. For this Cadwell round, there were fourteen of us so, if I was the last one home, I would only get two points. I was seventh in the rankings and this weekend would be expensive and could cost me championship places.

Race 1: Minitwins
(Row 13, Grid 37)

"Good morning, paddock. This is the first call for race 1 - MRO Minitwins and Rookie Minitwins."

We were up. I got my helmet and gloves on, removed the tyre warmers and dropped Sylvie off her stands. The grass was still wet from Thursday's rain, so I pushed her gingerly onto the tarmac in front of my pit space before pressing the start button. Selecting first gear, I rode to the collecting area. Marshal Jane checked the transponder and gave me my grid position. That would be easy to find, as I was right at the back. The rest of the grid followed in short order and we rolled onto the track. I was directly behind Rob Davie, who I had shared garage space with at Snetterton. Rob was in his fourth year now but was still finding himself mid-pack at best. He was still better than me, though.

I had a clear view ahead and, once everyone was settled, the marshal dropped his green flag and we went out for our warm up lap. Everyone went off Sat almost race pace and I kept up with the pack for about half of the lap. I wasn't concerned, of course; this wasn't the race, after all. We returned to the grid and I took my position. The lights went on and then out and we were away.

I got another good start, passing both Vanessa and two other riders as we passed under the bridge ahead of Coppice. It was at this point I realised I didn't have a proper race head on. The pack condensed tightly as we rounded the bend and I was aware of James Casareto on my left shoulder. Rather than opening the throttle (which is what I should have done), I instead eased off, my self-preservation instinct being stronger than my racing one. Immediately, I cursed and wound the gas back on but it was too late. James took the space and I had to give way.

I was furious. As I went down the Park straight, James shot off, as did Adam Ridgewell. That left only Vanessa behind me. I peeled right into Park Corner and then onto Chris Curve towards the Gooseneck. Vanessa was still behind me as I headed to Mansfield. I found a decent line but didn't change down on the approach. Sylvie bogged down and Vanessa glided past me. More cursing ensued as I tried to keep up but I was so angry that I didn't concentrate on the matter in hand. I wobbled up the Mountain and watched Vanessa disappear into Hall Bends.

The rest of the race was spent having another lonely track day, maintaining lines and hopefully times. I made a point of counting the laps and it occurred to me that I didn't get lapped until the end of lap 3; an improvement on my last outing to Cadwell. The chequered flag went out and I returned to the paddock, last but happy with this outing. The race had been incident-free with no crashes or retirements. I also had my ninth signature and so long as I kept my nose clean, I should get my final signature tomorrow and could send off for a full Clubman licence.

I looked at the results sheet and grinned. I had achieved a 2:09.716 on lap three. I was ecstatic. My target was 2:10 and I had beaten it on my first race. It wasn't enough now, of course and I had a new target to beat but that was very satisfying. There wasn't time to dwell on it now, though. I had to get ready for the Thunderbike Sport race.

Race 2: Thunderbike Sport
(Row 10, grid 29)

The Thunderbike Sport category has so many entries that it is split into three groups and three races:. Rookies were in group A and, in the first race, against Group B. I wasn't at the back this time and had a row of riders behind me. I was a little nervous, as only about a third of the grid were drawn from Minitwins. As a slow back marker, I had found that the Minitwin leaders always gave me a wide berth when they lapped me. Even where it was tight, such as Hall Bends, I never felt threatened by overtakes. In the Thunderbike race, most wouldn't know me, so I would have to keep a weather eye. Warm up complete, we set up for the race. Revs rose, the lights went out and we flew off again.

I was shocked at the aggression. Minitwins provided close, hard racing but these guys stepped it up another level. I was taken aback but got on with the matter in hand. I got a decent start and kept up with the tail-enders but by the end of the first lap, I was already flagging. I had drunk a lot of water before and between these first races but already the energy draining. Entering two classes when I'd done no proper fitness training had been a mistake but I got through the race intact. The aggressive nature of the class paid a price though, with five riders crashing out at various sections. I was last again but I was at least last finisher.

My best time? 2:11.164; a real disappointment but I had been warned that doubling my races would take more out of me and that I shouldn't expect consistently faster times. I now had two results for the day and had time to relax until after the lunch break.

Race 3: Minitwins
(Row 12, Grid 34)

I felt much better, having rested, eaten and taken on water, as we lined up for the final Minitwin race. I had the 2:10 target in my head and waited. The lights went out and the bikes roared off towards Coppice. I was fired up and got myself another good start, getting the better of both Vanessa and James again. This time, I concentrated on what was in front of me, not what might be coming up from behind. The tactic worked and for two laps, I stayed ahead of both riders.

It was never going to stay that way, of course. Vanessa was really finding her mojo and made a beautifully clean pass on me round Park Corner; the corner she had struggled with so much back in April. I was making myself as wide as possible to prevent James doing the same and managed to keep him behind me right up until the foot of the Mountain. Here, I thought it would be a good idea to do a bit of grass-tracking by braking too late. I kept Sylvie upright, though and we crested the Mountain safely, albeit at a rather obtuse angle. Sylvie did another little wheelie as I pinned the throttle to catch James up. He hadn't got as far ahead of me as Vanessa had last time around but still my mortality gene prevented me from pushing harder and I had to settle for my last place again, behind both riders and a best lap time of 2:11.181; almost identical to my previous race.

I wasn't disappointed, though. I had kept two riders behind me for two laps, only allowing them past through a moment's loss of focus. Vanessa came over to tell me she had really struggled to pass but took the chance at Park. It was a great move on her part and for me, the first opportunity to tussle with other riders. I was learning and experiencing more with every race.

As I peeled off the circuit, a marshal pointed to me and told me to go off to the right. Another power test? Surely not. Actually, I was being pulled over for a noise test but, even with her new, growling engine, Sylvie came in at an approved 101 dB. I was waved off and returned to the paddock.

Race 4: Thunderbike Sport
(Row 10, Grid 29)

I had enough time only to refuel Sylvie and grab a Mars bar and drink before the call came for today's final race. This time, my 'A' group would run against the 'C' group. I was prepared for the aggression this time and braced myself for action.

Just as well, really. Once the lights went out, the group shot off at a breakneck pace. I looked ahead and to my right where two riders were almost touching handlebars. As I watched, Matt Hinnells flew up on my right and carved a non-existent gap between the unsuspecting riders. I braced myself for what I assumed would be the impact, as the rider on the left took evasive action and got himself directly in front of me. I then moved to the right, hugging the pit wall and putting myself into a better line for Coppice. I was still in fifth gear but the pace was that hot that I hadn't even let off the throttle or applied brakes. I was convinced that I'd go straight up the grass but Sylvie calmly leant further and further over, taking the full width of the track and sweeping round Coppice and Charlies 1 and 2 in a beautiful, s-shaped wide arc. This felt fantastic. I was still with the pack going down the Park straight and loving it. Around Park, Chris, the Gooseneck and Mansfield and everything was clicking into place.

I took the chicane too quickly and barely avoided going through the escape lane cones. Unnerving myself, I slowed a little over the Mountain and watched as the other back markers disappeared into Hall. Collecting myself, I got through the woods and back onto the start-finish straight, trying to reel the other riders in. Lifting Sylvie up at Charlies 2, I went in too hot again and found myself mowing the lawn for a second time. I was on the grass for almost half the straight but had slowed sufficiently to stay on board. Cursing to myself and apologising to Sylvie, we set off again but the damage had been done. Another screwed-up race through lack of concentration had me finish last with a best time of 2:12.035; my worst result for the weekend.

There had been two fallers, both of them coming off at Charlies. I was grateful that it had happened a few laps after my excursion and that I had not been the cause. Both riders were sat on the tyre wall, their bikes leant against the fence, waiting for the recovery van to take them back.

So ended the first day; four races with every race an improvement on my April visit. Sure, I'd got slower as the day progressed but not dramatically so. I had navigated the circuit far better this time, off-piste moments notwithstanding. I joined Simon and the other rookies in the restaurant to applaud the trophy winners before getting some dinner (I really was famished by this point).

One aspect of the weekend that I hadn't properly accounted for was fuel usage. I was doing twice as many races and going faster, using much more petrol. Add the spillage issues I'd had on test day and, by the end of Saturday, I had used all of the first jerry can and most of the second. A trip into Louth had both cans refilled, ready for the morning. After a quick call home to Cheryl, I hit the sack.

Sunday: Race Day 2

I was awake before 6:00 again. This was my racing life - I would sleep deeply (utterly exhausted) but wake up stupidly early. So it was again today. I was greeted by another blue sky with only a few small clouds dotted about. I grabbed a couple of pastries (I was already starving) and a coffee before sorting Sylvie for the day. We would be first out on track, so I wanted to make sure everything was in place for me to get that final signature.

I was really pleased with how yesterday had gone and especially sorting that electrical fault. Sylvie had run like a charm since then. The season was almost over; I wished I'd checked more thoroughly earlier but it was sorted now. Onwards and upwards.

Race 1: Minitwins
(Row 12, Grid 35)

We were ready to roll. The call went out and we rode to the grid. Once again, I was way out back, with more rookies swelling the ranks. There were also experienced riders behind me as they'd fallen and thus lost grid places. To finish first, first you must finish. (Other unoriginal clichés also available.)

A marshal had raised her yellow flag, about halfway down the grid, next to a rider who was fiddling with his helmet strap. He gave her the thumbs up, so she withdrew onto the grass verge. With all the marshals clear, we waited for the green flag to be dropped and the warm up lap to begin.

It went down and almost immediately, a rider's hand shot up. He'd stalled at the line, leaving the rest of us behind him to look for another path through. A rookie, two rows ahead of me had his head down and pinned it off the line. By the time he looked up, it was already too late.

He slammed into the back of the stranded machine, sending him skywards and into the back of the rider one row ahead. In the meantime, the rearmost bike ricocheted off and was thrown into the side of yet another bike, throwing it and its rider against the pit wall. I looked for a route through the carnage, ducking as shattered bodywork flew back across the track in everyone's path. I slowed Sylvie down and picked my way through the debris.

There were two riders lying on the tarmac and two on the grass. I recognised the furthest rider as Rob Davie. He was conscious but clasping his left leg. The rookie who had instigated this pile up was curled in a ball, writhing on the grass. As I rode cautiously through the mess, I looked over and saw Vanessa following my path. The rider by the pit wall sat up. He was at least all right but I couldn't see the fourth rider any more.

The red flags went out immediately and we rode as far as the chicane, where we were held back by the marshals and told to switch off the engines. Vanessa and I had ridden round in tandem, both looking out for Matt, Alan and Simon, to make sure they hadn't been caught up in the mayhem. All three had got clear; Matt was already well ahead of them before the accident. Simon and Alan had been to one side so, although there when it happened, they were also safe. Of our group, only Vanessa and I had needed to take evasive action.

I looked across to her. "Are you all right?"

"Fuck. FUCK! Yeah, I'm fine. What the hell was that?" She asked.

"I know. This IS the sighting lap, right?"

For both of us, this was worse than the Brands GP start line pile-up, as it had happened right in front of us. I had got away cleanly but this had just been the warm up lap, not the race. We were both shaken by what we'd witnessed and assumed we would be sent back to the paddock. After a couple of minutes, we were told to start our engines… and return to the start line.

I was gobsmacked. Surely they'd not cleared everything already? We made a gentle ride over the Mountain, through the woods and back to the grid. When we got there, there were still two ambulances in view; one was reversing back behind the pit wall but the second was still on the track. Sitting on a race bike, knowing there was a fallen rider up ahead felt wrong on so many levels. The marshals walked through the line of riders and, after a few more minutes, the red flags came out again. We were directed to a break in the track wall and rode back to the paddock.

As I got Sylvie back onto her stand, the announcement came out that Race 1 would be the last race of the day. We understood the decision but it would mean not starting until about five o'clock, which in turn would mean not leaving the circuit until maybe seven. It was a good six-hour drive home, so I decided to skip the final race. I still needed one more signature on my card before I could send off for a Clubman licence, so it was important that I completed at least one more race this time around although, if I missed this one, there would still be three more opportunities. I just needed to keep my wits about me. I put another litre of fuel in the tank and walked over to Simon. There was about forty minutes before the Thunderbike race and, with the bikes ready to race, all we could do was wait.

Race 2: Thunderbike Sport
(Row 9, Grid 26)

Following that harrowing crash, I was a reluctant gridder but also needed that signature. Not quite at the back, I had four riders behind me. With a mix of bikes, anything could happen. The warm up lap passed without incident and we lined up for the off. Vanessa was on the same row as me, to my right in 25th place. We looked across to one another, nodded and then looked ahead to wait for the lights.

As soon as they went out, I made a blistering start, passing five other riders on my way to Coppice. Vanessa had also made a good start and was right behind me, keeping up before passing me cleanly on the approach to the Gooseneck. I kept the gap between us short but she was soon getting ahead and that was it. Again, I'd let myself down through not concentrating.

Armchair critics seem to think that all a racer has to do is keep the throttle open and get round the track. I recalled the comment Vanessa's husband Mark had defended us at our last Cadwell meeting when a spectator had criticised the back markers. Even from a rookie's perspective, there's way more to it than that. On track, you're surrounded by thirty other riders, all aiming for the same piece of tarmac at high speed. Everyone, including back markers must be on their wits; a harsh lesson learned by four riders at this morning's Minitwin warmup.

I watched in dismay as Vanessa smoked me again, her bike peeling into Coppice as I was approaching the start/finish line. Determined not to let her get too far ahead, I got my head down and wrung Sylvie's neck. I took Coppice nice and wide and then swung to the left of the track for Charlies 1 and 2. I went into the second apex at Charlies 2 way too hot and rode straight onto the grass again. Managing to keep Sylvie upright, I rolled off the throttle and bounced back onto the tarmac about two thirds of the way up the track. I leant over into Park corner and saw a waving yellow flag, just as two riders flew past me.

"Hey, fellas! Yellow flag!" I shouted. I assumed that the flag was for my off-road incident and gave the guys the benefit of the doubt as I may have inadvertently cut into their line. I settled down and got Sylvie back into thrash mode, desperate to catch Vanessa.

Where the hell was she? She had been consistently quicker than me all season but at every race we'd done so far, I had at least been able to keep her in sight, even if it was in the distance. She must really have got into a groove. The race continued with me pushing as hard as I dared but I didn't see her again.

There was, of course, a reason for that. The yellow flag I'd seen wasn't for me at all but for Vanessa. She had gone off at Chris Curve, almost saving it but, unlike me, when she hit the grass, her line was taking her straight to the tyre wall. Rather than trashing her bike, she slowed up and laid it down. When Mark pushed it back to the paddock, it didn't look too bad, although the fairing looked distinctly off-centre. Fortunately, the damage was mostly cosmetic and Mark soon had it looking much better.

Vanessa, on the other hand, hadn't faired so well and emerged from the medical centre, her left arm in a sling and her right hand holding a "Not fit to compete" document. It could have been a lot worse but she had landed awkwardly after her dismount and broken her wrist. For her, this was a double blow. Not only was her race weekend over but she would also not be allowed to ride in the Dan Thomas tribute lap on Sunday. She had asked if she'd be allowed to ride pillion with someone but was told it was race bikes only. Instead, she had to take a ride in the course car. It wouldn't be the same but she would at least take part.

In the meantime, Simon had got the result sheets from the race office. My time? I had improved again, with a best lap of 2:09.674. I was getting back on target.

Dan's Tribute Parade Lap

Following Dan Thomas's death at Brands Hatch, Bemsee had obtained a new trophy in his memory for what would become the Dan Thomas Memorial race, run at Brands Hatch in October.

Stickers had been produced and sold to fund the trophy. They would be applied to most of the Minitwin and Thunderbike Sport bikes (a number of riders, including me, would also wear them on their helmets). For the Minitwin and Thunderbike Sport classes, a lunch-time parade lap around Cadwell had been organised. We met in the collecting area where, before going out on track, we all revved the bikes to provide 34 seconds of noise, in recognition of Dan's race number. Due to the proximity of Sylvie's fairing to the exhaust and, never having been revved for that long while stationary, she started smoking like a chimney, as bits of the fibreglass started burning off. I assured riders around me that all was well and, once I'd stopped revving, the smoke cleared.

After the 34 seconds, we rode on to the circuit, two abreast. Vanessa was up ahead in the course car but Simon and I agreed to stay together throughout the lap. Passing through the woods, we continued around the circuit, being acknowledged by flag-waving marshals and spectators. It was a moving occasion but, as we approached the Mountain, we were waved through to do a second lap. It was at this point I choked up, realising how much I still missed my friend. Getting through that second lap was difficult but, true to his word, Simon stuck with me all the way, both of us swapping positions at various points before being let off the circuit at the foot of the Mountain. Even then the applause didn't stop, with spectators clapping and patting bikes and riders as we returned to our pit spaces. By the time I returned, I was emotionally drained. It had only been a few minutes but it had felt like a lifetime. We had given the most appropriate salute to our fallen colleague and for Vanessa, Simon and me, it felt good to honour our friend.

Race 3: Minitwins
(Row 12, Grid 35)

This was going to be a difficult race for me, as my usual grid mate Vanessa would not be there. Had she not crashed and been declared unfit to race, she would have taken her place directly in front of me. As it was, there was just an empty slot. This would at least give me a clearer view ahead and an opportunity to make a good start. As far as points were concerned, there were still fourteen rookies taking part this time, rather than the usual ten. Assuming I finished, it would be lower in the order. Even with Vanessa being out of the picture, I couldn't catch her in the championship table but I was now in danger of losing my seventh place in the championship. Still; I had to get on with the order of the day and that was racing.

An uneventful warm up was followed by a mostly uneventful race, for me at least. Another great start was ruined when my sensible head stepped in at Coppice. A rider I had passed at the start was on my left shoulder as I tipped in, so I lifted Sylvie a little but didn't change down a gear, meaning I was going uphill too slowly. All those places I had taken were lost as the riders passed me and I berated myself for not racing properly. I stayed with the pack as far as Chris Curve but then returned to my standard "Steve's on a track day" mode.

Riding alone did have an advantage, though and allowed me to spend more time with the throttle pinned against the stop and taking corners in a manner that at least felt faster and smoother. When Simon slapped the result sheet on my gazebo table, it showed a best lap time of 2:07.795. I had taken another two seconds off my fastest time so far and couldn't help but smile. Not having Vanessa to chase down had been a negative but seeing that time made me glad to have made the trip to Lincolnshire.

Race 4: Thunderbike Sport
(Row 9, Grid 25)

Another Thunderbike race and a second race without my usual rival. I wasn't enjoying the Thunderbike races but was still determined to give it my best shot. I was higher up the grid and would be starting against the pit wall again. Ahead of me, to my right, I could see Michael Armani's CBR 600 in its distinctive Stars and Stripes livery. He had looked pretty useful on track but I thought I'd at least see if I could get a better start than him.

I did exactly that, firing Sylvie off the start line like the proverbial overheated feline. I had been happy with my starts for a while; I just had to work on consistency and confidence on the corners. Passing another six riders, I held station around Coppice, making myself wide enough to make approaching riders think twice before trying to pass. I knew that I was ahead of Michael but didn't worry about who was where; I just wanted to get round Charlies and be able to hammer down the Park Straight.

I lifted Sylvie into Charlies 1, remembering to drop down a gear, keeping the revs up and the momentum going. As soon as I was on the Park Straight, I stamped the gear lever quickly into fourth, fifth and finally sixth gear but even with her new-found power hike, Sylvie struggled to keep everyone behind. Going into Park, there were still three riders behind me until I got around Barn. Once on the start-finish straight, those last three slipped by and I found myself in familiar, tail-end Charlie territory. Michael Armani was the last of the three.

I was gutted. It had only taken a lap but I persisted, hanging on to Michael's tail round Coppice, following his line and closing in as we rounded Charlies. Once back onto Park straight, however, the superior power-to-weight ratio of his four-cylinder Honda played its card and he was gone. I persisted but pushed a bit too hard in places, finding myself in the wrong gear at Mansfield and the chicane.

Swearing, I regained my composure. The front wheel lifted again as I topped the Mountain but wheelies were not scaring me now and I grinned broadly as the front landed and I flicked Sylvie through Hall bends. Again, everything was clicking; the bike felt smoother and faster but only the results sheets would confirm that.

Back in the paddock, I popped Sylvie on to the stand and went down to the race office for the result sheet. There it was: 2:06.089. Another tenth and I would have broken into the 2:05 territory. I had to check the sheet again, as I couldn't believe what I'd read. Sure, I was still slower than the rest of the pack but I reminded myself that when I had first gone round Cadwell in that April qualifier, it had taken me 2:32 to complete a lap. Here I was now, a full twenty-seven seconds faster. While I couldn't expect that sort of time-tumbling rate to continue, there was every chance that a two-minute lap could be achieved with training, practice and improved cornering.

It had been quite a weekend. I had mostly maintained my "Couldn't organise a piss-up in a brewery" reputation but I had also found new levels of riding that had improved my confidence no end. It was getting harder to use the "I'm old, scared and useless" excuse now, even if I was. I was still too slow but I had made progress at every meeting.

I went to thank Dan Singleton for his help. He had rebuilt Sylvie, teasing another ten ponies out of her but, more significantly, he had poured gallons of confidence into my head. The utter joy of racing at this level is that everyone wants you to do well. They don't want you to do better than them, of course but even the top racers acknowledge that the also-rans form an important part of the grid and, without them, races lose some of their value.

The postponed Minitwin race had been put back to be the last race of the day. I had already elected not to enter; Cadwell is a good six-hour drive from home and, once the race was over (at about 5:30), packing up would take a good hour and a half before I could leave and I'd not be getting home until past midnight. So, it was decided - I would pack up and then watch the last Minitwin race instead.

Cue my next regret. I was not the only rider missing the last race and there were only eighteen on the grid, of which only seven were rookies. I was kicking myself. Finally, I had an opportunity to get at least eight points (there would have been eight rookies if I had turned up) yet I had chosen to opt out. In the end, there were only five rookie finishers. Had I been there and finished, I would have got at least sixth rookie spot; my highest placing and ten points. As it was, I got a DNS. I had to remind myself that I was shattered and that, for Brands, I would withdraw my entry for the Thunderbike Sport class. I wasn't going to get any useful points there and I was more confident with my knowledge of the little Kent circuit layout, so would rather keep the remaining money in my pocket for next time.

Next time; there was a thing. There was only one more round left to go and then the annual dinner. After that, the 2019 season would be over. I could apply for my Clubman licence but now had a new dilemma.

My initial goal in March had been to enter and survive one race meeting. It had soon become clear that one weekend was never going to be enough, nor would it prove whether I had the staying power to remain on the grid for more than one occasion. As the season progressed, so had my confidence and speed. I had enjoyed nearly all of it but of course, Dan's death had dealt a heavy blow to us all and certainly had me thinking a lot more.

Of the Minitwin rookies I shared this season with, Simon, Vanessa, Alan and Matt, I thought only Matt would continue full-time in 2020. As the likely 2019 Rookie Minitwin champion, he would be more than capable of challenging the main riders. We all reckoned that he would be fighting for the main championship. For the rest of us, a return in 2020 was looking shaky.

Alan was not coming back, as racing had fulfilled a bucket list item. He had been very successful, winning a number of pots and had given the other rookies a major run for their money. With Dan gone, Alan and Simon would be fighting for third place in the championship. Not bad for a 60-year-old with no previous racing experience.

Simon had also won trophies and had been closing in on Alan in the rookie championship. He would consider local rounds but, with Lyndsay expecting their first child, that was likely to be it.

Vanessa had embarrassed many of us and shown that she was just as good as the other rookies. She had got faster as the season progressed but that Cadwell crash had cost her points and dented her confidence. She was well out of my reach as far as points were concerned, though. Dan's death had a profound effect on her, too and had made finishing the season more of a chore than it should have been. 2020 was looking unlikely for Vanessa, too.

If our little clique ended, returning would be difficult. I'd make new friends if I carried on but it wouldn't be the same as racing against the mates I had joined with. Matt was in a completely different class, so I'd see as little of him on track as I did this year. By the time he completed the 2020 season, he was likely to have achieved a National licence. This was a known target for him and he was hoping to be taken on as a Bemsee instructor.

The five of us would discuss it at length come Brands Hatch. It had been a huge part of my year, providing massive highs and deep, dark lows, all of which had provided an undiluted, heavily concentrated dose of life. I reckoned that the others shared the same feelings.

None of this would have been possible without the unwavering support of my Cheryl, of course. She's never been a bike racing fan but had cheered me on at Brands and was in my head for every race. She worried every time I went out, only relaxing (a little) when I sent word on returning after each race.

At this point, I could never say never but it would be a sad end if none of my rookie mates returned to fight together next year.

I'd have liked to have been better. I'd have liked to have been faster and more confident. Most of all, I'd have liked not to have come last every time. Perhaps there was still unfinished business after all.

Results (Minitwins):

Qualifying: 2:14.352
Race 1: 2:09.716
Race 2: 2:11.181
Race 3: 2:07.795
Race 4: DNS

Results (Thunderbike Sports):

Qualifying: 2:13.047
Race 1: 2:11.164
Race 2: 2:12.035
Race 3: 2:09.674
Race 4: 2:06.089

Chapter 11:
Final Round Preparation

There was a long break between Cadwell and Brands for the Minitwins. Some of the other classes had an additional round at Snetterton and at the Sidecar Revival meeting at Cadwell Park but Minitwins miss both rounds, which meant a six-week hiatus.

I already missed racing but a conversation with Mark and Matt had me on a "No Limits" track day at Brands Hatch on the Wednesday before the final round. Funds were tight but I had just enough to cover the day, so I made my booking. I chose not to pay for instruction; not because I didn't think I needed it but because I wanted to use the day to re-familiarise myself with both Sylvie and the circuit.

I arrived just after 7:30. Matt was already on site but Mark and Vanessa were yet to arrive. Vanessa and I had both booked for an intermediate group, me in purple and Vanessa in yellow. Matt and Mark were with the orange advanced riders. I'd only seen Mark ride on the road; a far cry from hooning on a track-prepared SV. This was going to be interesting.

The advanced group was out first, so Vanessa and I watched from the pit wall. Matt was blindingly fast but it wasn't long before Mark was matching his times. Mark was really making that little Minitwin hustle. Fifteen minutes later, both men were back in the garage and I was off to pit lane, having my wristbands checked and the sighting lap sticker signed.

Getting back on a track was fantastic and I recalled my first outing on the yet-to-be-named Sylvie in 2017. Back then, I had been excited about taking a racing bike onto a track, only to be disappointed when I had all those issues. Now, bike and rider had been transformed. I still had work to do but Sylvie ran like a dream.

We had come such a long way and only now was I feeling confident enough to take on another season.

The aim of the track day was not to smoke the opposition but to get reacquainted with both bike and track. My goal was to get confident with my lines and work out where I needed to point Sylvie at each corner. I would later find out how much I had learned when I did the track walk at the race meeting with Jeremy.

We went out in groups of eight at a time from pit lane, on to Paddock Hill. The Indy circuit is only 1.2 miles long, so I would need to complete a couple of laps before the tyres were up to temperature.

Peeling right into Hailwood Hill, I crossed to the left to take the tight Druids hairpin wide. Driving on towards Graham Hill bend, I moved Sylvie over to the right, so I could open up along the Surtees straight and into McLarens, Clearways and back onto the Brabham start/finish straight.

I opened Sylvie up, getting into the habit of being in sixth gear before I had reached the start line light gantry, dropping two gears to get round Paddock Hill. Staying in fourth down Hailwood, I dropped down one more as we rose, taking Druids in third gear, getting over to the left on the approach and finding the apex about two thirds of the way around the very tight corner.

That apex allows you to take a natural line over to the left, about halfway back down the hill before swinging right, aiming directly for the 100m braking marker, leaning hard on the left and clipping the kerb on the inside left side. Position yourself correctly and the bike heads straight towards the right-hand side rumble strips. In the dry, clipping the kerb is fine, if bumpy but the paint is very slippery when wet, so kerbs are best avoided if there's any rain.

Heading up the Cooper Straight (staying on the right side of the track), you lean left towards the Surtees/McLaren's left-right curves. The best and fastest way to get through that is to make it a straight by cutting the middle corner, heading towards the rightmost orange marshal marker point.

McLaren's and Clearways combine into one long sweeping right hand curve but, with its negative camber, Clearways catches a lot of riders out who can easily end up in the enormous gravel trap. I kept to the middle of the tarmac until I could see the pit lane entrance, keeping a tight line near the pit wall and opening the throttle as soon as I reached the marshal post. I was trying to work out which gear I was in and realised that I was probably in too low a gear (third) for Clearways the first few times I circulated.

Approaching Paddock Hill, I got into sixth, so I knew where I was. Rapidly shifting down to fourth by the time I had reached the pit lane exit point and getting over to the left side of the track, I pulled hard on the front brake and tipped right, getting both Sylvie and my body over the inside kerb where it ran out.

I was now going fast enough to feel my stomach coming into my mouth as I hit the dip and shot back up towards Druids. I had now steered Sylvie to the left of the track, close to (but not on) the kerb, ready to drop down and take Druids in third gear.

I kept her in third down the hill, around Graham Hill bend, along the Cooper Straight and round Surtees, going around McLarens on an open but neutral throttle, gradually opening up as I entered Clearways. Fourth gear was selected as I passed a white line (my new marker point) and, as soon as Sylvie was upright, quick-shifting up to fifth and then top gear to start all over again.

Matt and Mark were now competing with one another for times, both getting under the 60-second racer's target for the Indy. Vanessa and I were happy to circulate around the 1:10 mark. Neither of us expected to match Matt's times and neither of us wanted to risk trashing our bikes by trying too hard just ahead of the final race meeting.

So the day continued in a similar vein; me repeating my lines and doing laps by rote, not worrying about times (Mark reckoned my best was about 1:08); just being comfortable with the direction I was going. I didn't do the final session, having achieved what I wanted to for the day. Sylvie had behaved impeccably and I was really happy with everything. I still needed more speed but that was not the point for today. I packed the van, said my goodbyes and made the journey back down to Hastings.

Chapter 12:
The Big Finale (Brands Hatch Indy)

Friday: Test Day

So, it was finally here; the closing round of the BMCRC 2019 Championship. My rookie friends and I had spent the last eight months learning how to race and trying hard to move up the results table. I had stayed in seventh place for the last few rounds but another rookie, Simon Garner, had raced at Cadwell and his results there had demoted me to eighth place. OK, so it was still a top ten place but I really wanted that seventh place back.

I had entered the Thunderbike Sport class again for this round, as additional track time was always useful. I wouldn't get any points in that class but I like Brands, so was happy to get out more often.

I had a commitment to make on Friday morning and issues at the delivery location meant that getting to the afternoon test session was going to be tight at best. I'd brought the caravan up on Thursday evening and dropped Sylvie off in the garage (Simon had specifically asked for Garage 7), so all I needed to do today was turn up, sign on and get out on track. I hadn't booked instruction, having only recently attended the track day. I just wanted to practise my lines, so to speak.

To be at the circuit in time for testing, I needed to leave the house by 11:00 at the latest but the venue where I had to take some equipment would not be able to receive it until 10:00. As it was, by the time I'd got back home, it was nearly midday. So it was that I resigned myself to losing practise time (and money). By the time I finally arrived at the circuit, I had missed two sessions. I still had to get Sylvie noise tested and get myself changed so instead spent the afternoon getting set up and prepared for Saturday. I had lost the £85 test fee but was happy to chill and catch up with Matt and Alan, set up in Garage 9.

Simon arrived at about 3:00 and I helped him get his bike and gear set up in his corner of the garage. It seemed strange being back in Garage 7; the last time we were here, it had been with Dan. Simon and I took up our corners as we had in July and Vanessa would probably set up where she had last time. The last corner, previously home to Dan, would be taken by Vanessa's friend Sylvie Botquelen, who was riding her GSX-R600 in the Thunderbike Sport class. Neither Vanessa nor Sylvie were due to arrive until evening, so it was just Simon and me for the day.

Before leaving the house, I had printed a poster of Dan to place on the wall where he had last been resident back in July. On the way up, I bought a bouquet of roses, mounting them next to Dan's photo. The poster read, "Dan: still with us in spirit #34"; a simple message but heartfelt. I still really missed my friend and this weekend was going to be difficult for us all. Dan was still in third place in the Rookie Minitwin championship but Alan or Simon would pass his score come Sunday. While they were both happy to have progressed so well, neither wanted to get third place this way. Alan had been eleven points behind Dan after Cadwell Park and Simon thirty points further behind Alan. Had it not been for Simon's two DNFs at Cadwell, he would have been considerably closer, as he was now getting regular podium places and points. Unfortunately for him, it looked like it would be too late to oust Alan from third in the championship now.

Once Simon was set up, we took our bikes and gear down to scrutineering, ahead of the crowds that would go down tomorrow morning. When we got there, it appeared that the world and his wife had made the same decision. It was heaving with bikes so we sat patiently, waiting for our turn.

I got waved through and found myself facing Mark Dent, Chief Tech. Of all the people, I had the most senior member of staff giving Sylvie the once-over. Still, I wasn't worried. She'd performed perfectly well on Wednesday and had no issues that I was aware of.

Mark took my inspection card and instructed me to hold Sylvie's tail while he checked the front suspension, brake, wheel and head bearings. So far, so good. Mark tugged on the fairing, foot pegs and rear brake and then went around the back, asking me to hold on to the handlebars.

"What the? Bloody hell, Steve; looks like your wheel bearing has collapsed. I'll keep your card for now. Go back and check that out but please; ride it carefully. I don't want any accidents before we've even started."

I couldn't believe it. Those bearings had been changed at Cadwell Park, after the first set had spat out their innards at Charlies. To have a set go after only a couple of rounds was a disaster. I got back on and rode Sylvie carefully back to the garage where, once on the paddock stand, I found the problem.

As I put the socket onto the wheel spindle nut, I found it was only hand tight, so the wheel had been running loosely. I was lucky not to have lost the nut and that the spindle hadn't detached, along with the catastrophe that would have followed. I tightened the nut back up, held on to the wheel and pulled it left and right. I could feel no axial movement, so took Sylvie off the stand and rode back to scrutineering.

I found Mark, explained what had happened, that I had changed from the wet back to the dry wheel and had simply not torqued the nut up properly. After a suitable amount of piss-taking from everyone in scrutineering, Sylvie passed. My riding gear had no issues, so both bike and I left with test stickers applied. I was happy to get over that hurdle but it felt as though I was at my first meeting again, rather than the last of the season.

As I pulled away, Vanessa arrived. Her truck was too high for the pit lane tunnel so she would have to wait before she could get to the garage via the track crossing. Simon and I recommended that she got her bike and gear checked now, rather than wait until the morning so there would be one less job to worry about. We got her bike out while she changed, Simon took the paddock stand to the garage and I waited with Vanessa, holding her bike while she had her riding gear checked.

I looked at Vanessa's bike. Her husband Mark had prepared it very well and, compared to my Sylvie, looked like a works bike. I had already decided to enter at least one meeting next year, so I could race without my orange bib. Sylvie had served me so well during the season that I felt she should get both some proper maintenance and some upgrades, including the bodywork that Vanessa had let me have earlier in the year, a repaint (red and yellow beckoned) and getting the wheels powder coated. I had already decided to make my dry wheels yellow and the wets black. All these jobs could be sorted in the winter. I was inordinately envious of bike #70 but for next year, hoped that bike #20 would look as good.

We were now all ready for qualifying. All that remained was to get back into civvies and attend the track walk at 6:00.

About thirty people were waiting on the start line for Jeremy. He soon arrived, astride his massively-tyred mountain bike. The walk was as informative and entertaining as ever and I was delighted to find that those lines I had been practising earlier in the week were indeed about right. All except Clearways where, although my initial approach was acceptable, I was turning in too early and needed to get over to the right by aiming for the marshal tower, rather than the pit lane entrance. Other than that, it all seemed all right.

Once the track walk was done, I took Jeremy to one side to ask about his references to trail braking. As a road rider, I thought of trail braking as light use of the rear brake as you go round a corner. Knowing that rear braking is an almost exclusive no-no, I asked for clarification. Jeremy explained.

"Where a corner demands it, usually the long, sweeping kind of corner, you should be braking hard on the approach, front wheel only but, as you start to apply the gas, so your braking should slowly come off. Trail braking lets you keep the bike stable on the lean as you bring the power back on, preventing any wobbles or high-sides."

I thanked him for the explanation and then went on to analyse my season. I knew that I was slow but felt my times were improving. However, I was still worried that I was getting in the way.

"Actually, I'd been meaning to talk to you about this," he replied. Uh oh - here it comes…

"There have been a few riders who were concerned. Not because they thought you were unsafe but they could see when you lost confidence because you'd take a line but thought you'd not make it and so changed direction. That was a worry because they weren't sure how best to pass you. We have been watching you and your progress has been phenomenal. You've cut huge amounts off your time from the start of the season. Sure, some may have gone from shit to bad but I looked at your Cadwell times and you've taken about twenty seconds off. While you're still a way off the main pace, your confidence has grown, you've taken instruction and it shows you've been listening. We've had riders who we thought were really a danger to themselves and others on the track. So much so that, in one case, we had to tell a rider that he'd not be allowed to race that weekend. He took it very well, had a full day's instruction with us and went out on the next round a transformed rider.

"At no point have I felt the need to pull you from a race. You're aware of what's going on around you and you've held your line. Remember you saying how you'd see the pack coming around Paddock as you approached Graham Hill? I told you not to worry about them but to just get your head down and have your own fast ride out. I've watched you doing that as the season has progressed and you're a much, much better rider today."

"Well," I replied. "If I come back next year…"

"What do you mean 'if'? You are coming back. You know you are. You'd better. After all, why would you want to waste all that learning? Come back and ride without the bib and then see what more progress you can make."

"OK, assuming I come back, what I will do, whenever I can afford it, is a full day's testing and ask for instruction. I do want to get faster and I really want to be able to lean further and get my knee down."

"That's more like it. Taking the full test day is perfect. You'll get as much instruction as you need and, if we think you need more, we'll chuck you into another group to increase your track time and learning opportunities. Trust me, mate; you are really a much better rider than you give yourself credit for. You've definitely come to the right club. Everyone here wants you to become a better racer."

I was struck by Jeremy's genuine praise and enthusiasm. He loves his sport and he loves bringing riders on. His greatest pleasure is derived from watching terrified newbies develop into proper racers. I liked him a lot.

I walked back to the garage with a renewed spring in my step, joined Simon, Mark and Vanessa for a cheeky beer and dinner before settling in for the night, ready for tomorrow's qualifying.

Saturday: Qualifying/Race Day 1

The weather was looking good when I woke. The forecast was for a dry day today but rain was due on Sunday, which wasn't good. I had a set of dry and wet wheels and could do wheel changes pretty quickly now, so it shouldn't be an issue. Little did I know how the day would pan out.

Vanessa, Simon and I had each got two practice passes, one for Minitwins, the other for Thunderbike Sport. For my second series, I had to run under number 120, because 20 was taken elsewhere. I therefore fashioned the extra digit from some black gaffer tape.

At 9:00, qualifying began. Thunderbike Sport riders would be out first but only those who had it as their main class. Those of us having it as an extra class would be out in the seventh group, followed by Minitwin qualifying in group 9. Sylvie Botquelen set off to the collecting area while the rest of us checked fuel levels, tyre warmers and pressures ahead of our own qualifying sessions.

At 10:30, we rolled up to the collecting area. Rather than go through the normal entry point at the back of the grid, we joined at Surtees, riding round McLarens and Clearways before opening up on the Brabham straight. Peeling into Paddock Hill, I became aware of what felt like a little wobble. Sylvie settled down as we approached Druids though, so I ignored it.

The first lap passed without issue and I caned Sylvie as I exited Clearways. That second lap felt pretty good and I settled down to get myself a decent qualifying time. Sylvie was performing well and I was putting Jeremy's advice into practice. Coming round for the fourth lap, I got my head down and veered left as I braked for Paddock Hill. I lifted Sylvie up at the exit, when the wobble returned with a vengeance.

I raised my arm and coasted to the left edge of Druids, stopping in the gravel. I dismounted as the marshals dragged Sylvie to safety behind the fence. A marshal approached.

"What happened? Do you need the van?"

"Front end got wobbly. I'm worried that the wheel is loose or a bearing has failed." I replied.

"Can you ride it? If so, get down to the pit lane marshal exit and get off there."

As soon as the chequered flag announced the end of the session, I remounted and rode back to the garage. As soon as I got in, Mark come over.

"Are you all right? I saw you only did a couple of laps."

"Front wheel felt wrong and was all over the place. I'm going to check that nothing's come loose."

Sylvie was on stands now so, as I started to work on the front wheel, Mark went to fit the rear tyre warmer.

"Er, Steve..."

We looked at the rear wheel to see no wheel bearing, or at least only the inner and outer races. The ball cage and balls had all disappeared. It was Cadwell Park all over again.

The Minitwin qualifying was next out, as soon as the current group had finished. I didn't have time to get to Rod Harwin to change tyres over, so took the risky decision to run with a wet rear wheel. The dry track would wear a wet tyre out quickly but the track temperature was still cold, so tyre damage would be limited. Besides, there was no time for other options. I had the only curvy SV in the garage and the wheels are not interchangeable between Gen 1 and Gen 2 bikes, so I couldn't even borrow Vanessa's spare dry wheel.

With a new wheel fitted, I had enough time to get a mouthful of water before the call for Minitwin qualifying was made. Simon and I rolled out towards the collecting for qualifying.

Halfway along, Simon stopped and turned back. He'd forgotten his practice pass and was desperately trying to perform a multiple point turn to get back to the garage. I smiled briefly before realising I'd made the same mistake. Like Simon, it seemed to be an endless number of manoeuvres made before Sylvie was point back to the garage. As I rode in, Mark looked at me. Confused.

"Practice pass!" I shouted. "Top drawer of my tool box."

After he'd stopped laughing, he handed me the pass and I charged back to the collecting area. As Simon and I arrived, the group was let out. We'd made it by the skin of our teeth. I knew to take it steady for at least two laps to allow the rear tyre to get some warmth but then got my head down on lap three.

As I approached Surtees, a faster rider passed on my right. I followed his line to see if it would help get my time down, even if

I only followed him for one corner. This turned out to be a big mistake on my part.

As I took his line, I realised I was going round Clearways much faster and wider than I intended. I leaned Sylvie down lower but the combination of excessive speed, lack of nerve and a cold, wet weather tyre had me stand the bike up as I hit the outside kerb and charged full tilt into the gravel. I knew I was going to lose it and before I could react, both Sylvie and I were sliding on our sides through the gravel towards the air fence.

I was gutted. I had survived an entire season without a crash (the beaching incident at Druids in July didn't count) and here I was on the penultimate day of the final round, picking myself up out of the dusty gravel. It all happened so fast that I had no time to react. One moment I was up, then I was down. The bit between upright and being flat on my back completely eluded me.

I couldn't have chosen a better crash site though as, standing with the Clearways marshals was doctor Rosie Dent, the very person who had helped me get my licence in the first place. She and the marshals were keen to make sure I was all right (I was, ego aside) and I assured them that the only damage was to my pride. I'd taken a minor knock to the head as I went down but I was already well into the gravel by the time that had happened so no damage had occurred.

Sylvie looked a bit sorry for herself, though. Her entire right side was now scarred by the dragging impact, the brake lever guard had snapped and I couldn't see the clock. As riders were going around, many were pointing to something black in the middle of the track. I was worried it might have been my clock but Rosie assured me that it was a knee slider; one they'd seen come off another rider who was currently parked up by McLaren's having tumbled the lap before me.

That still left the mystery of the missing clock but there was no time to worry about it now. The qualifying session was over and, having been given the all clear by the marshals (I wouldn't have to go back to scrutineering, as the damage was very light), I pushed Sylvie back onto the track and returned to the garage. I only hoped I had at least got a qualifying lap in. Things surely couldn't get any worse.

Once back in the garage, Mark and Simon got to work removing the fairing. Inside, the belly pan was filled to the brim with gravel, along with much of the engine casing. They started clearing it all out and I took the wheel out and carried it and the wrecked wet wheel over to Rod Harwin to get the tyres swapped so I would at least have a dry tyre on for the races.

Rod was not happy. "That tyre has had it," he said. "You really shouldn't be riding on it."

I told him that I was down to my last £20, £5 of which would be spent on the tyre swap and potentially another fiver swapping back if it rained on Sunday.

"Which it will," Rod offered, helpfully. He made the change and told me that, if I intended to continue racing, I really needed to budget better (or find another sport). He was right, of course. I told him that, if I returned, I'd set up a race account to cover such incidents. I then took wheels and tyres back to the garage.

I picked up a copy of the qualifying results sheet. My time? 1:14. God, that was awful and no better than my first outing in March. I noticed that Keith Povah, running second in the main Minitwin championship hadn't qualified; he was the McLaren's crasher. He'd not completed his first lap, so would be starting from the back of the grid, directly behind Vanessa. This was a potential source for trouble. When someone as fast as Keith starts at the back, that rider will charge through the back markers like a hot knife through butter, with the added risk of hitting them as they go through. Vanessa was worried about this but said she would see how best to deal with it on the grid.

Back at the garage, Simon had reassembled the fairing. I re-fixed the left-hand side and then got back to fitting the wheel. I was struggling to get the spindle through, when Benn Ridgewell appeared to ask how I was. Benn was another Minitwin rookie who I had met at Cadwell Park. I told him what Rod had said about the tyre.

"Would you like to have mine? I've got a scrub you can have."

"Have?" I asked. "What, for nothing?"

"Yes, for nothing. There's life in it but I was going to bin it. You'll save me a job."

Of course I would have it, so I said I'd see him in a while. In the meantime, there was the matter of replacing the brake guard and finding the missing clock.

I had a spare guard in the tool box. I wasn't prepared to race without one now, so removed what was left of the original and fitted the replacement. I reached into the nose of the fairing and found the clock hanging by its lead. The mounts had snapped in the crash but I was able to reattach it with a few cable ties. During the winter months, I had arranged to see Steve Weeden to fit the Triumph fairing that Vanessa had given me. We could look at a new mount for the clock at the same time.

After chatting with Simon and Mark, both suggested that, if Rod wasn't happy with my tyre and I was being offered another, I really should take up the offer. There was plenty of time before the race, so it would be better to do it now while I could.

I found Benn in the lower paddock. When I arrived at his gazebo, Benn gave me not one but both tyres, which I strapped precariously onto Sylvie's screen. I thanked Benn and promised to return the favour if I could before riding back to the garage.

Simon helped me unload the tyres. I loaded the wheel and Benn's tyre into my van and drove back to Rod Harwin. He looked at the new tyre and said, "That's a bit better," took my fiver and made the change. With the wheel fitted and the bike refuelled, I made a couple of final checks before finally getting the opportunity to relax. Cheryl would be coming to watch and was due at the circuit just before my first race.

Racing is great but it's so much better if you have support. By her own admission, Cheryl is not a bike racing fan and constantly worries about my safety (getting those phone calls at Cadwell hadn't helped) but she is my most ardent supporter, so I was really looking forward to having her at the circuit.

The announcement for the Thunderbike Sport race went out before she arrived, so I gave my phone to Theresa, Sylvie's wife, asking her to answer it if Cheryl rang. I then joined everyone in the collecting area.

Race 1: Thunderbike Sport.
(Row 12, Grid 36)

Here it was; first race, first day and the last meeting. I was at the back of the grid but really didn't mind. For most races, my starts were good. All I needed to do was to capitalise on them and not be in last place by the second corner. The start marshal waved his yellow flag and we were off on the warm up lap. Sylvie was running sweetly and I stayed with the pack all the way round. Granted, we weren't going at race pace but it was good to be with everyone for once. Perhaps I had finally upped my game.

We returned to the start and I rolled Sylvie to the line. Something didn't feel right...

As I rolled forward, I noticed that the brake lever didn't come back fully. I pushed forward but it felt like the brake was binding. I rolled back and the brake freed up. I shrugged my shoulders and waited for the lights.

Red lights on. Wait. Wait.

Red lights off. The pack shot off towards Paddock Hill. Vanessa was already ahead of me, so I opened the throttle fully to catch up. As I did, I could feel the bike slowing, rather than accelerating, coming to a dead stop at the top of Paddock Hill, in the centre of the track. The red flags came out immediately as a pair of marshal came running over.

"The brake has locked on!" I shouted. The two marshals told me to get off and tried to move the bike. There was no hope, so the recovery van was called out. It took four men to drag Sylvie into the van, with the front wheel in the air. I was told to sit in the back as they drove me back to the garage.

I was gutted. Not only had I failed to start, I had caused a red flag and delayed the race. There was no time for reflection, though. I need to sort it.

Ricardo Branco was set up on the other side of the garage. He came over to ask what had happened, knelt down to look at the brake and then jiggled the caliper. He withdrew his hand immediately.

"Geez! That's red hot!" We need to get those calipers off now!" he said.

Donning gloves, we removed both calipers and took out the pads. They looked all right, albeit glazed but Ricardo said I should not change them. I had a replacement set but the new pads were Performance Friction units, whereas those in the calipers were SBC pads.

"Performance pads are great," said Ricardo" but they need bedding in. The first time you use them, you'll think you have no brakes unless you've run abrasive across the faces first. I'd stick with what you have for now but we need to strip the calipers, as the slide pins are jammed. Get the rubbers off, clean them out with WD-40, wipe them scrupulously clean and refit everything."

Between us, we had both calipers rebuilt and mounted in ten minutes, by which time the calipers and disc rotors had cooled sufficiently to handle. I tested the feel of the lever once everything was back in place and was astounded at the difference. The problem had been purely down to lack of maintenance and another vital lesson had been learned. I knew that I would need to carry out some serious servicing work in the winter months if I was to return in 2020. Having seen how easy it was to sort the calipers out, I was confident that I could do the job myself.

With Sylvie back together, I had time to find Cheryl, who had heard the commentator say, "A back marker has stopped in the middle of Paddock Hill. That's not a clever place to be." Yeah, right; my stopping there (and causing the red flag) was a planned manoeuvre. Ah well; infamy again.

She may have missed my first race but so had I. When the other riders came back in, we all just got on with preparing our bikes for the first Minitwin outing. For me, that meant just double-checking the tyre pressures. I'd not used any fuel to speak of, having only done a slow warm up lap and I'd put in six litres anyway. We had worked out that we would use about 0.2 litres per lap. The Saturday races were ten laps, plus the warm up and warm down laps, so twelve laps at 0.2 litres per lap meant I needed 2.4 litres, plus a minimum of 2 litres at the end of the race meant that I only needed 4.4 litres in total.

In no time at all, the call came out: "Race 10 - MRO Minitwins and Rookie Minitwins. First call." I started to take the tyre warmer off but Mark stopped me.

"Keep them on as long as possible. We're close to the collecting area, so don't take them off until at least second call." I left the warmers where they were and waited. The second call went out so Simon, Vanessa and I made our way over to the collecting area.

I was first to roll up. Collecting area marshal Leah walked over to me, checked the transponder and said, "Hello, Twenty. Row 11, grid 33, please."

I lined up to my marker and Vanessa rolled her bike next to me. Once in place, she turned around to see Keith Povah pull up behind her. As a title contender, we knew Keith would get past us quickly so Vanessa indicated that, for the race, he should pass on the left. She'd keep out of his way. Keith put his thumb up in acknowledgement. Vanessa and I tapped gloves, ready for the signal to join the grid. As the previous racers peeled into the garage lane, we peeled out to the grid.

Race 2: Minitwins
(Row 11, grid 33)

I was a little apprehensive, due to Sylvie's earlier braking issue but I had made a point of applying the front brake regularly as I rode to the collecting area and onto my place on the grid. It felt much better, so I told myself to relax. The marshal waved his flag and we went off on the warm up lap. Again, I kept up with the pack all round and only lost them in Clearways. Riders were still settling as I pulled up.

I selected first gear, held the clutch in and let the revs rise. The marshal pointed to the lights, which illuminated, stayed on for what seemed an eternity and then went out. I got a blinding start, passing both Vanessa and Chris Cowan ahead of me before the world suddenly went mad.

Behind us all, Keith Povah had made an even faster start, passing Vanessa, Chris and me in a flash. Ahead, however, Wil Green, who had gridded 16th, had a problem. His arm was up but by now, Keith was accelerating fast and directly towards Wil. Keith braked hard, forcing the back end of his bike up. The bike fell and folded before slamming into the back of Wil's bike, sending both riders and bikes down the track. Chris Cowan had nowhere to go and his bike also dropped. Chris was sent tumbling to the left, ahead of Keith, who was still lying on the circuit. Both Chris and his bike collided directly with Wil, who remained motionless.

Chris's bike was now pirouetting on its footpeg and, having hit both Wil and flying over his bike, was now spinning out of control towards me. I didn't dare brake, for fear of losing control, so closed the throttle and flicked Sylvie left then right, around the stricken bike, which had now come to rest against the pit wall, broken pieces of bodywork scattered everywhere. By this stage, Vanessa had caught me up, the red flags were out and we all rode as far as the start of the Cooper straight, where a marshal held us all back.

Vanessa pulled up next to me. "Fuck! FUCK!"

I looked across. "Bloody hell. You OK?"

"Yes," she said but I could see she was shaking. "Was that Wil?"

I didn't know. All I knew was that at least three bikes were down and that a white bike had landed directly in front of me. I hadn't wanted to go left because I knew Vanessa would be coming through and I didn't know where the other fallen riders were.

The marshal told us to switch our bikes off. We were held for about twenty minutes before being told to ride back to the pits. Mark Gillam was at the fence looking down at us and Vanessa tried to relay to him what she had seen. This was not good; the last two times such an incident had occurred were at Cadwell, when Hayden Killworth had gone down and the terrible time when we lost Dan at Brands.

Vanessa looked ahead and saw Matt, Alan and Simon but not Keith (Povah). We didn't know who the third rider was at the time but could see that Wil was missing. Vanessa had watched the mayhem unfold in front of her and knew Will had been hit by at least one bike and feared the worst. We were sent back to the pits to wait for an announcement. We would now race towards the end of the day or be first out on Sunday. Either way, it would be a while before we would be racing.

The announcement came out that the Minitwin race would be slotted in between the MZ/Blue Haze race and the EDIasia Formula 400 race. In the meantime, the word went out that the air ambulance was on its way. To keep occupied, I checked the fuel (still plenty) and Cheryl and I got some lunch. As we ate, the air ambulance arrived and touched down at the medical centre.

The sidecars were out next, followed by the 600s, Thunderbike Sport, Team Green Junior Cup and finally the Blue Haze races. The Minitwins were called back to the collecting area as the two-stroke bikes returned to the pits. The marshals told us we were being held back to allow the helicopter to leave and we were all encouraged to wave to Wil as he was flown to Kings Hospital in London. It would have been a surreal sight for anyone looking down to see 31 riders looking up and waving maniacally but we all wanted to show solidarity to our friend.

We lined up for the race, did our warm up and then set off. I got a good start but was soon passed by the three riders I had got ahead of. I completed the race but it all went in a blur and I don't recall any of it. What I did know was that I came home as eighth placed rookie, which got me eight points and meant I had reclaimed my seventh place in the rookie championship. If I finished all my Minitwin races, my scores would continue to rise. Chris Cowan, who had been one of the start line fallers, wasn't present as his bike was too badly damaged. Chris was a rookie, so my worst result as a rookie finisher would earn me eight points per race, which should give me a total haul of 32 for the weekend, so long as I didn't have any other moments of madness.

I had decided to drop the Thunderbike races. The additional track time would have been useful but I needed to concentrate on the Minitwins and didn't want to risk jeopardising anything there. I'd crashed in qualifying yesterday and wasn't going to add any more risk to my weekend. I'd already lost my money for not doing the test day and, with no more to be spent for the season, I was happier to lose that than to risk losing anything more with Sylvie.

Simon went to the race office to get the results sheets. He passed me a copy and I looked down the list. I couldn't believe what I read but there it was: 1:06.793. I had taken just over four seconds off my best time from Round 1. I was getting closer to the magic 60-second mark and could barely contain my excitement. All the worry about the start line pile-up was temporarily forgotten.

We later learned that Will had got away with the luckiest of escapes. He had remained conscious throughout, although he later told us that he couldn't remember anything from about an hour before the race. The first fear was that he had sustained a bad head injury and the photo he posted of his crash helmet would have surprised anyone that he had even survived, let alone walked away (eventually). There was then a concern that he may have broken his pelvis or leg, as he could not move either. That concern turned out to be unfounded but he had suffered massive bruising and was very sore.

Wil is a very quiet, unassuming young man. He provided me with endless advice on where I could improve (thus "endless" advice) but also gave me encouragement by telling me how much I had improved since I had started. Wil typifies the Bemsee club member. He had already decided that 2019 would be his final year of racing but he assured us all that he wasn't going anywhere. He wouldn't race any more but had planned to join race control, which would allow him to remain an active member of the Bemsee family. We were all delighted for him.

Race 3: Minitwins
(Row 11, grid 31)

I had gained two places in the grid, courtesy of the loss of Wil and Chris. Keith Povah had gridded behind me, so his not being on the grid this time made no difference. While you never want to gain by virtue of another rider's misfortune, grid 31 put me on the left side of the track; a much better place to be, as you want to be on the left for Paddock Hill. Starting on the left means there's no crossing in front of anyone else as you head for that first corner.

Warm up complete, we lined up for our last race of the day. The lights went out and we were off. Being on the outside of the track gave me a clear route to Paddock Hill and I stayed with the pack as we all peeled right. I was aware of how tightly packed we were and later recalled how far I'd come. When I did this back in March, I felt myself screaming inside, terrified that I'd be hit. Now, I simply followed everyone else, laughing as I went and we all got round. It was brilliant.

Sadly, as soon as I reached the dip of Hailwood Hill, I was losing ground. Sylvie by now had plenty of poke but I knew I was still the weak link. We got round Druids and I looked at the lines that the riders ahead were taking. There were so many different routes being followed, so I stuck with the one I'd been following so far; entering Druids on the left (outside line), cutting across about two thirds of the way around and getting over to the left again to approach Graham Hill bend. As I went down the Hill, I swung to the right, aiming for the 100 metre board before leaning hard left to go up the Cooper straight.

I became aware of two things in this race. Firstly, everything was being done robotically without conscious thought and secondly, I was breathing. I knew this, as I was talking to Sylvie and laughing as I circulated. When I did mess a line up or find myself in the wrong gear, I was apologising to my bike. What was that all about? I did know that I was trying harder because the rev limiter light was on almost permanently. I was in lower gears for the corners and back straight and changing up earlier as I rounded Clearways. It occurred to me as the chequered flag came out that I was still laughing. I wasn't sure whether that was elation or some kind of euphoric release but, as I came to Cooper on the warm down lap, I saw Cheryl waving from behind the fence and my heart swelled. This was AWESOME!

What was even more awesome was reading my result. By now I was beyond caring about finishing last and had accepted my lot (mostly). What did made me smile was seeing a best lap time of 1:04.213. Not thinking too much while out had paid dividends. If I just got on with the job and didn't constantly analyse what I was doing, the times would drop of their own accord.

In this case, that was another two seconds wiped off. I was still away from the magic sub-one minute mark but hey, comparing this round to Round 1 was astounding. Even my fellow, faster racers acknowledged that tail end Steve had come on in leaps and bounds. Cheryl applauded me as I returned to the garage and gave me a massive hug when I got off the bike. What a brilliant day.

Sunday: Race Day 2

I was woken at 5:00 by the sound of rain falling steadily on the caravan. This wasn't good but I was awake, so grabbed a shower and breakfast. I'd eaten well yesterday but today's egg and bacon sandwich went down very well. I was glad that I had elected to bring the caravan; it meant I could shower, prepare meals and have more comfortable sleeping arrangements. Taking the van only to Cadwell was easier (and cheaper) but Brands, as my local track, was only an hour's drive and was less of an issue.

I went into the garage and removed the rear wheel so I could get it to Rod Harwin first thing. Unless the weather changed, wets would be the order of the day. Rod was convinced that would be the case but I said I was going to try and get the other wheel repaired, just in case.

"You won't need a dry set up," Rod said. "This rain won't let up any time today. I'll get this fitted as soon as I can. Give me time to open up properly first."

I handed over another fiver and then drove back down the pit lane tunnel. As I did, Glynn Davies, Minitwin championship leader, was walking up with a pair of wheels in a wheelbarrow. I pulled up and opened the van window.

"Sorry, Glynn. If I had seen you, I'd have offered a lift. Are you taking those to Rod?"

He was, so I offered to bring him back when I collected my wheel. It was a long walk, so Glynn accepted happily.

I gave it fifteen minutes before driving back. I picked up my wheel and waited for Glynn. As he arrived at Rod's gazebo, the handle of his wheelbarrow had fallen off, so he was even more willing to take me up on my offer of a lift. Frankly, I was just happy to be able to help another rider for once. We drove back to the garages and Glynn asked how I was getting on.

"It feels like I'm back in Round 1, to be honest. My times are better, even if they're still bad but the reason I was with Rod was because I'd lost a wheel bearing and so didn't have a spare wheel any more. If I come back next year, I'll make sure to get better prepared in the winter months."

"That's all it needs," said Glynn. "A lot of it is in your head but a bit of preparation goes a long way. If you've got the money in place and you know you're prepared, you can relax more and everything else will come. Thanks for the lift."

Back in the garage, I fitted the rear wheel as Mark Gillam appeared. He started checking Vanessa's bike straight away before sitting down and going through her telemetry data again. Vanessa may well be an amateur but Mark runs a tuning company and loves poring through data. He had worked out the fuel usage for every circuit Vanessa had ridden and determined which gearing worked best for her level of performance. By this final round, he had amassed a considerable amount of information.

Simon and I were interested in finding out the fuel usage. In my case, I had filled Sylvie before arriving on Thursday and had two full 20 litre jerry cans. As I'd missed both testing and all the Thunderbike races, I had used hardly any of my fuel. Knowing each race would use about three litres, plus the mandatory two remaining post-race, I had more than enough.

I walked towards the noise testing area, as I knew Rob Cameron was set up there. Rob had provided me with a set of bearings at Cadwell, so I asked whether he had another pair again. He only had one but was happy to let me have it. Again, all he asked was that I replaced it with an identical bearing.

While one of the bearings was ruined, the other was still serviceable, at least for this round, so I could get away with just the one replacement. I took it back to the garage to offer it up to the hub. I then realised that the outer race of the destroyed bearing was still fitted. Mark came over to have a look.

"Would you like me to sort out a new fitting for you? He asked. Thinking he meant doing the work while we were on track, I said yes. I was very keen to have the wheel sorted, as it would be far quicker to swap wheels than to go back to Rod Harwin to swap tyres, especially if the weather changed just before a race. Mark took the wheel and the new bearing to put in his truck. He looked at the wheel.

"Where's the spacer? There should be a spacer that supports the inner faces of the bearing races. I'm not surprised it collapsed, if there was no spacer."

I looked at the wheel. Sure enough, the section of tube that forms the inner support for the bearings was missing. I had got the previous bearings fitted at that first Cadwell round at the end of April. I can only imagine the wheel had run without the spacer since then. I had been lucky that the bearings hadn't collapsed earlier; luckier still that the wheel itself hadn't been destroyed.

I checked my tool cabinet. The first rule I had started to apply was to have all the wheel maintenance-related equipment in the top drawer. Sure enough, there was the spacer. I can only imagine it was missed at Cadwell because of the mad panic we'd had when the wheel had first gone. I was aware that I had needed to tighten the rear wheel at every round but hadn't made the connection. Each time I had tightened the wheel spindle, I had been putting additional stress on the bearing faces. I had indeed been extremely lucky but would learn from this. As soon as the season was over, the wheels would be stripped, the hub bearing mounting faces checked and, so long as they were good, new bearings and spacers would be fitted. I would also make sure to have at least one spare set of bearings available for each wheel in the tool cabinet, plus the equipment to change them on circuit if necessary.

In the meantime, my friend Mark Lucas had arrived. Seeing immediately that things were not as good as they could be, he rolled his sleeves up to help sort out the wet rear wheel.

"You get on with the front. I'll fit the back," he said. Both were on in a trice and I relaxed. We looked outside. The rain had stopped but it was still very overcast. Mark looked at the forecast.

"Looks like it's going to dry out. Rain isn't forecast until about 6:00." he said. I had hoped that wouldn't be the case, what with my now limited wheel set up. There were bikes circulating on the track now, so we walked up to the pit wall to take a look. Sure enough there were two clear dry lines. If the rain held off, by the time the Minitwins were out, a dry set up would be needed.

I didn't want to have to do another tyre swap, so ask Mark Gillam whether he'd be able to have the wheel ready before the race.

"What? No! I wasn't planning on doing it today. That bearing will need heat soaking before it comes out. Besides, there's a good chance that the wheel is buggered now."

Seeing my look of resigned disappointment, he went back to his truck and retrieved the wheel and bearing. "Come on, then. Have you still got the spacer?"

I handed it to him and between them, Mark and Ricardo removed the old bearing, leaving the wheel ready to take the replacement. It wasn't going to be perfect (I would buy new rear wheels when the season ended if they were deemed unusable) but it would survive a couple of short races. I loaded the wheel and Benn's donated tyre into the van and charged down to Rod Harwin's gazebo. Rod threw me a wry smile and took my last fiver. Five minutes later, I had a dry rear wheel set up again.

Everyone looked up and agreed that it would stay dry, at least for our race, so I set to making what I hoped would be the final wheel swap. I checked and re-checked the rear wheel for alignment and, satisfied that everything was in order, fitted the tyre warmers. Now I could properly relax. I got into my leathers and waited for a call from Cheryl, who was on her way.

There had been more incidents, so the timetable was running a little late. The first Minitwin race would be the inaugural Dan Thomas

Memorial Trophy race; a race we all wanted to be in. Dan's wife Lorne would present the winner's trophy at a special ceremony and would then come over to Garage 7, where she and I had prepared our own presentation event. After a brief chat, she was called over to the race office to discuss the sequence of events for Dan's race. In the meantime, Cheryl had arrived but was struggling to find a parking space. I walked through the tunnel to meet her and we found a spot in the lower paddock.

I couldn't believe how packed it was but the final round was always going to be popular. We walked back to the garage via the pit entry tunnel, where Cheryl said hello to my fellow residents as the announcement for lunch was made. She had timed her arrival perfectly; we would be first out after the break.

Race 1
(Row 10, grid 30)

"Race 11, MRO Minitwins and Rookie Minitwins. This is your first call. Please make your way quickly to collecting, as we want to get a prompt start."

Mark Lucas got the rear warmer off and took the rear paddock stand away. I got a hug from Cheryl and made my way to the collecting area.

Leah, the collecting area marshal, looked at her clipboard and then at me. "Row 10, grid 30, please".

With Keith, Chris and Wil out of the race, I had gained a hitch up the order. We rolled out to the start line and took our places. I saw Cheryl out of the corner of my eye as she looked through the gap in the pit wall fence.

The start marshal waved his flag and we were off on the warm up. Or at least, everyone else was. I managed to select second gear and stalled Sylvie off the line. Shaking my head, I pulled in the clutch, restarted her, selected first gear and joined the pack.

It was important for me to complete this race. I wanted to add to my points haul but more importantly, I really wanted to have my name shown as a competitor in the results table of the first Dan Thomas Trophy race. The revs rose and, as the marshal pointed to the lights, they illuminated, went out and we were off.

I got a blinding start and threaded my way through about five riders by the time I got to Paddock Hill but lost it all by allowing myself to wonder where they all were. I had forgotten that first rule of racing - "it's not your responsibility to get out of the way but for approaching riders to pass safely."

So it was that Vanessa slipped past me on the approach to Druids and once again, I took up my post as tail end Charlie. I did pick up my pace, though and kept up with the pack for the first couple of laps but it wasn't long before that gap started to widen and I was once again circulating alone. It was a twelve-lap race but my pace was that poor that I was passed on lap four and again on lap nine, so only ended up completing ten.

It was on lap four that I made another schoolboy error. Coming out of Druids, I lined Sylvie up to aim for the 100 metre marker, that same marker I had been successfully making all weekend but this time I went in way too hot. Suddenly, I found myself back on the grass on the right side of Graham Hill bend. I hadn't even started to lean Sylvie over as I approached and had gone straight up the grass embankment. Trying to keep a relatively level head, I carefully steered Sylvie around and coasted back down towards the Cooper straight, where I saw Simon get his first lap over me as he bore down on a mid-pack group of riders. Keeping everything on a neutral throttle, I checked that there were no other riders in the immediate vicinity and rejoined the track at the Cooper pit entrance point. I could see a marshal put his thumbs up at what was presumably considered a decent save and got my head back down to continue the race. My reputation as a foolish racer remained.

Vanessa had done somewhat better than me, managing eleven laps, so I was grateful not to have been lapped by her. Even my off-road excursion hadn't allowed her enough time to catch me though. That would have been a humiliation too far, although I wouldn't have begrudged her the result.

The race over, we were directed back to pit lane, rather than the garages and told to line our bikes up on the wall in order that the Memorial trophies could be awarded immediately. A large crowd of Minitwinners and their supporters gathered around the podium where Glynn Davies, Dave Twyford and Tommy Downes were awarded first, second and third places respectively, along with Tommy also getting first rookie with Matt Wetherell and John Reynolds taking second and third places.

Following the presentation, Lorne paid a very emotional tribute to Dan, the Minitwinners and Bemsee for putting on such a great show, encouraging us all to "keep it pinned to the end of the race". Rapturous applause, cheers and tears followed as she stepped off the podium. A very emotional moment for us all.

I went to the race office to get the results sheets. Collecting sets for Simon, Vanessa and me, I looked down the list. I'd managed another 1:04 lap although, at 1:04.831, it was 0.6 seconds slower than my previous outing. Still, I was really pleased with the result, which showed consistency if nothing else and was way ahead of that tortuous first meeting.

We returned to the garages where Lorne was waiting. I found Alan and Matt and asked them to come over to Garage 7. With us all gathered, Lorne stood on a chair and addressed the group.

"This year has been an eye opener for all of us. Everyone will have learned things about themselves that they didn't know before (apart maybe from Matt. He knew he'd win all along). We've all learned race craft, we've learned about competition but we've also learned about life and about friendship. Those outside the protective, close circle that is the paddock will never truly understand what it means to be a part of such a group and what a privilege it is to have such friends. Once seeing it in action, even those supportive loved ones who may not get or like bike racing at least understand why racers get such a buzz and form such loyal friendships.

"Irrespective of your age, this year proved that you're never too old to learn. Every one of you has come such a long way, irrespective of your results. Whether you were fulfilling a bucket list item, wanting to get your Clubman licence or simply wanting to finish the season, every one of you will have come out as a different person, a better person than the one who first rolled up at Brands Hatch back in March. Dan may not be here with us in person but we all know he's here with you in spirit and every time you line up on the grid. Some of you have told me as such, so I know it's true. He'd be as chuffed and proud of you as I am.

"Some of you have won trophies from Bemsee but in my eyes, you are all winners. Because of that, I felt it was important that you were recognised as such. Therefore, it gives me great pleasure to be awarding these one-time only "2019 Garage Seven Plus" special award trophies.

"First up is Matt, the demon of the rookies. From round 1, there was never any doubt that he would wipe the floor with the lot of you. Fearlessly competitive, it looks like his "Watch it, Sonny - I'm a hard-as-nails copper" attitude would, if not win you all over, would at least win him a pot or two. That's a trophy, Matt, rather than any illicit drug. So, for you, I am awarding the "Get Out Of My Way, I'm Coming Through, Ya Bastards" trophy.

"Next up is Vanessa. Good on you for showing the boys how to do it. Once on track, of course, everyone is equal, even if some are a little more equal in terms of trophy hauls. Only Steve had the regular joy of being able to watch you from behind (sorry, Mark), as he was always the slowest on track (except at Cadwell, of course. Sorry about that, too) but you learned as quickly as everyone else (and much quicker than Steve), having seen your times drop each time you went out. Of course, sometimes the lesson learned by even the quickest of learners is that a track can bite back. Therefore, in recognition of your Cadwell adventure, the award that is uniquely yours is the "Chris Curve 'Not As Flexible As You Thought You Were'" trophy.

"This next trophy goes to our favourite fly-boy. While he hasn't attended as many meetings as some of you, his presence has always been memorable, even if sometimes it's for the wrong reasons. No one but no one has been able to trash a bike so efficiently yet still walk away wearing a massive grin. To that end, the "Eddie The Eagle Binner Winner" award goes to Sam.

"I can't help but feel this next award is a bit personal. Someone in the room clearly holds a grudge but hey; a trophy is a trophy, right? On the surface, this rider is the quiet one of the group but, once on track, he's as keen as the rest of you (except maybe Steve) to get to the front. From what's written on the plaque, I guess this has been a regular occurrence. So, with tongue firmly in cheek; the "Most Annoying Last Lap Lapper" award goes to Simon.

"The next award may cause a few mental images that, once seen, are unlikely to ever be unseen. Even reading the plaque made me smile, imagining what the other blokes in the garage were thinking. The women, of course would have to be dragged away for fear of being overcome with lust. Anyone coming into the garage anything up to about fifteen minutes before the first call to arms will have risked seeing this sight and I'm hoping we won't need to see it again for a while at least. You can get too much of a good thing, you know. Again, the recipient has won a fair few pots from Bemsee but these are our trophies so that makes them more distinguished and personal. The 2019 "Best Underwear Model" goes to Alan.

"So far, all the awards have been given out to you heroes (and heroine) who put it all on the line in the pursuit of a small piece of shiny plastic. A racing team isn't just the racer, of course, even if it is the racer that goes for all the glory. In many cases, without the backroom boys and girls, a lot of those racers wouldn't be out there at all. The winner does, however, tower over the rest of you in one very specific department. Like the other trophies awarded here today of course, this winner won't be walking away with anything sensible or "normal". No, the 2019 "Best Crew Chief/Best Eyebrows" trophy is awarded to Mark.

"Our last award goes to the slowest tryer of the bunch. Despite all advice and encouragement from everyone, this rider has steadfastly ignored all of it and thus maintained his Tail End Charlie position. With a few exceptions, when either his bike was misbehaving, or his brain hadn't engaged, he has always been the last-placed rider. His screw ups in the paddock, on track or even between rounds (at least you found the caravan keys) are now legendary. Or infamous, perhaps. Last placed maybe but at least a finisher. So, the 2019 "Least Likely To Successfully Organise A Piss Up In A Brewery" award goes to Steve."

Lorne and I had arranged this awards ceremony after the Cadwell round and managed to keep it quiet until today. It had gone down very well and once again, hugs all round between riders and with Lorne, who was by now overcome with it all. It had been an emotional day for us all but for her it must have been especially difficult. Every one of us felt for her.

All that remained was the last Minitwin race and, for three out of four of the Garage 7 group, one more Thunderbike race. Again, I would watch from the Cooper Straight fence, not worried about taking part but happy to cheer on Simon, Vanessa and Sylvie.

Race 2
(Row 9, Grid 27)

I rolled up to my grid spot after the warm up lap, next to Vanessa and directly behind Alan. At the start of the season, when I had visions of passing at least a couple of riders, Alan had always been a target. With Dan Thomas no longer featuring, Alan had secured third rookie spot. Any delusions I had of getting past him had evaporated long ago. Today, I just wanted to keep up.

The lights went on and then out and we were off. I made a terrible start and, although I hadn't stalled this time, I had been concentrating too much on not stalling and had missed the initial off, so I was on the back foot immediately. However, for once, I ignored that error and pinned the throttle, actually catching the pack as we all dropped down Hailwood Hill. Vanessa was taking the standard wide line for Druids, keep well to the left so she could clip the apex on the return downhill section. Seizing the opportunity, I dived on the inside and got round ahead of her.

I couldn't believe it. I had finally made my first genuine overtake and I had made it stick. Well, sort of. So pleased was I with that manoeuvre that I didn't block Vanessa at Graham Hill bend. Again, I took my usual line, sweeping wide to the right at the 100 metre marker so as to run along the outer kerb. Vanessa wasted no time in returning the favour and shot off on my inside. By the time I realised what had happened, she had left me for dead.

I was livid with myself and proceeded to cane Sylvie within an inch, the rev limiter light being almost constantly lit. The problem with riding with a red mist attitude is that errors can creep in. As a result, I missed a few apexes in my desperate desire to reach Vanessa, who continued to make progress, oblivious to my attempts to catch her. Once again, I was double-lapped, only completing ten out of the possible twelve laps but then, so had Vanessa. I didn't care now, though; I had got my final eight points and had achieved a season total of 146 points to finish the year in seventh position.

Epilogue

So, what had it all been about? What was a 57-year-old man doing racing a motorcycle for the first time? Well, that was simple: despite the lows, he was having fun with a capital "F".

I'd learned so much about myself and learned some major life lessons along the way. I had made some fantastic, supportive friends; friends that I will likely have for the rest of my life.

Even at my pedestrian level, I learned that anyone with the desire to achieve a seemingly unreachable ambition really can do it. In the rookie group that I joined, one rider showed how brilliant he was (which is why he won the rookie title), whereas the rest of us, while not world-challenging racers, all proved that we could race at a respectable pace and push ourselves further than we ever believed possible. Racing helped build my self-confidence no end and made me reassess much of my life, in terms of what matters and what doesn't. Racing is on the "matters" list.

I did take some painful financial lessons too and learned that, even at this level, racing cannot be done on the cheap; not if you want respectable results. Plenty of planning and having plenty of money is a prerequisite. Sure, you can race on a (relative) shoestring like I did but what that comes with is the frustration of watching everyone else leave you in the dust as you potter around on a bike that doesn't perform properly, with tyres that have seen better days (and better grip).

I had gone from petrified newbie at that first Brands Hatch round in March to far more confident rider on my return for the final meeting in October. While there were a few low points, the euphoria I felt after finishing a race was priceless. I won no trophies but won a wealth of experience.

So, what should you do now? If you have read this far and still feel the pull, get yourself to a club race meeting. Meet the racers, talk with them and find out more. There are clubs that allow you to rent a bike for a meeting if you don't have the money to buy a bike; all you'll need is the gear and an ACU licence. The Bemsee Minitwin championship is one such class that has a rental bike.

Go on; you know you want to. I had wanted to for 40 years and my only regret was leaving it so long. I also only expected to do that one meeting yet by the halfway stage, I was already planning my first non-rookie year. Racing is a drug and I am an addict.

Today, I am a racer.

Appendices

1. Costs (2016-2019)
2. 2019 rounds
3. Circuit maps
4. 2019 Rookie Minitwin Results
5. Acknowledgments & thanks

Appendix 1: The Costs

Part 1: Getting ready for the first season

Starting out with nothing but a few scrappy tools, this is what I spent to get on track.

1. 2000 MY SV650: £1400 (March 2016)
2. Sorting electrical gremlins: £800
3. Replacement forks: free (if you discount the dead road bike)
4. New wheel bearings: £24
5. Replacement wheel spacers: £38
6. Front fork emulators: £300
7. Chain and sprockets: £120
8. Brake lever guard: £30 (compulsory from 2020)
9. Shark fin (chain guard): £25 (compulsory)
10. Rain light: £20 (compulsory)
11. Spare rear hub: £30 (second hand, to mount spare rear sprocket)
12. Gen 2 clutch cover/front discs: £50 (second hand)
13. Carb kit, oil, filter, plugs: £90 (Wemoto)
14. Replacement wheel bearings: £30
15. Transit van: £2800 (original purchase, service and MOT. Since replaced with a newer van)

16. Leathers: £100 (PSI, second hand)
17. Boots: £120 (Frank Thomas)
18. Gloves: £80 (Frank Thomas)
19. Helmet: £120 (HJC)
20. Generator: £150 (second hand)
21. 6 kg fire extinguisher: £30 (compulsory for 2019)
22. Gazebo: £500 (Surf 'n' Turf. c/w side panels and weights)
23. Tool cabinet: £150 (Machine Mart)
24. Various tools: £200 (approx.) so far.
25. Spare wheels: £100 (second hand)
26. Used scrub tyres: £100

27. Tyre warmers:	Donated (but usually about £80)
28. Track days:	£600 (4 at roughly £150 each)
29. ACU assessment:	£150
30. ACU licence (annual fee):	£50
31. Bemsee annual membership:	£35
32. Eye tests (annual for over-50s):	£50
33. Dog tag:	£10 (compulsory)
34. Back protector:	£100 (compulsory).
35. Insurance (loss of income):	£1000 (not compulsory but sensible. Vital if self-employed)

Total spend before Round 1: £9402.

Part 2: 2019 season race entry costs (assumes only entering one class. Add about £90 per round for an additional class)

1. Bemsee membership renewal: £35
2. ACU membership renewal: £52
3. Eye test (annual for us oldies): £10
4. Round 1 (Brands Hatch Indy): £385 (£300 racing, £85 test day)
5. Round 2 (Oulton Park): didn't enter
6. Round 3 (Cadwell Park): £375 (£290 racing, £85 test day)
7. Round 4 (Donington Park National): didn't enter.
8. Round 5 (Snetterton 300): £399 (£314 racing/marshal contribution, £85 test day)
9. Round 6 (Brands Hatch GP): £360
10. Round 7 (Cadwell Park): £445 (Minitwin & Thunderbike Sport)
11. Round 8 finale (Brands Hatch Indy): £464 (Minitwin & Thunderbike Sport)

Total entry fees: £2525

Part 3: 2019 costs (excluding entry fees)

1. Bike fuel (high octane, unleaded petrol. About £1.30/ltr):
    a. Brands Indy: £30
    b. Cadwell Park: £60
    c. Snetterton 300: £60
    d. Brands GP: £60
    e. Cadwell Park: £90 (testing plus two race classes)
    f. Brands Indy: £60 (testing (aborted) plus two classes (TBS aborted)

Total: £360

2. Van fuel (diesel. £1.30/litre):
    a. Brands Indy: £30
    b. Cadwell Park: £90
    c. Snetterton 300: £65
    d. Brands GP: £30
    e. Cadwell Park: £90
    f. Brands Indy: £30

Total: £335

3. Expenses as the season progressed:
    a. 5 litre fuel jug: £15
    b. Fuel siphon: £5
    c. Wheel bearings: £48
    d. Front brake pads: £80
    e. Replacement front brake guard: £30
    f. Wet weather tyres: £250 (fitted)
    g. Tyre changes at circuit (£5 per wheel per change): £30
    h. Roll of yellow vinyl for number background: £10
    i. Black vinyl for numbers: £10

Total: £478

Total spent from start (buying the bike) to finish (end of season): £13,100. This was entirely self-funded over three years, working on a very tight budget and buying used equipment or accepting donations wherever possible.

What if I continue racing?

Having spent a season racing with a novice bib, I really wanted to do at least one race without that piece of orange fabric. To run a second year and, if I wanted to do better, I'd have to buy more tyres and travel further afield. However, the larger cost items have already been covered. A second season would need:

1. Club and ACU membership renewal - estimate £80-£90
2. Tyres. Assume two new dry sets and a new wet set. £750
3. Fuel (bike & van) - estimate £600 for the year
4. Entry fees: estimate £3000, assuming seven rounds
5. Food: £200
6. Replacement wheels and bearings (if rear wheels are too damaged). Estimate £200
7. New front disc rotors: £200

Estimated 2020 racing costs: about £5000 to complete all eight rounds

To cover this, I would have to put away around £500 per month in a specific racing account. If I am unable to do that, I would reduce the number of rounds I entered. Silverstone has been added to the 2020 calendar, which would definitely be on the bucket list. Currently, there are eight rounds planned but at least one will not have a Minitwin race.

The calculation works out at £600 per round but if I only entered seven rounds, that monthly savings requirement could drop a little.

Appendix 2:
2019 Bemsee Race Calendar

Round 1:   Brands Hatch Indy, 9-10 March

Round 2:   Oulton Park, 29-30 March*

Round 3:   Cadwell Park, 27-28 April

Round 4:   Donington Park National, 18-19 May*

Round 5:   Snetterton 300, 8-9 June

Round 6:   Cadwell Sidecar Revival, 22-23 June**

Round 7:   Brands Hatch GP, 13-14 July

Round 8:   Cadwell Park, 3-4 August (Minitwins & Thunderbike Sport)

Round 9:   Snetterton 300, 14-15 September**

Round 10:   Brands Hatch Indy, 5-6 October (Minitwins & Thunderbike Sport)

* Not entered.

** No Rookie Minitwin round

Appendix 3: Circuit Maps

Although I didn't attend every round in my first, 2019 season (I missed both Oulton Park and Donington Park meetings) but felt it would be useful to include maps of all the circuits that were used for the 2019 season. These maps have been kindly provided by TSL Timing, whose copyright is gratefully acknowledged.

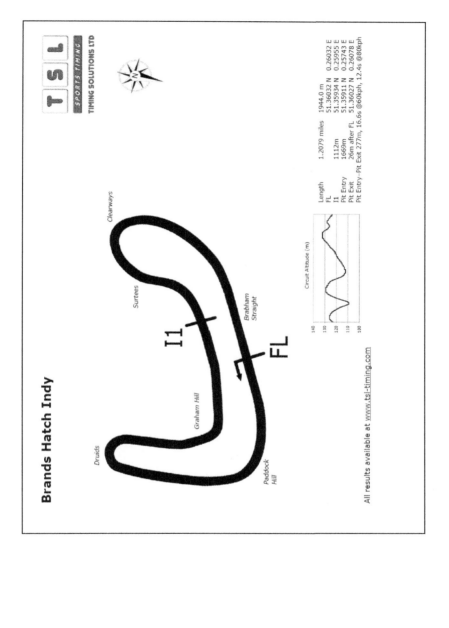

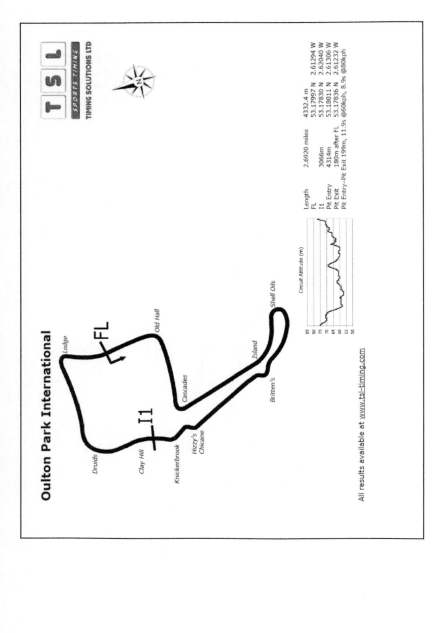

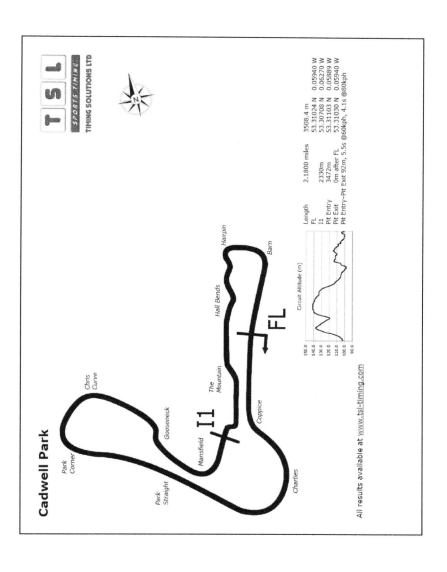

Donington Park National

Length	1.9790 miles	3185.0 m
FL		52.82971 N 1.37867 W
I1	2096m	52.82978 N 1.36508 W
Pit Entry	3100m	52.82951 N 1.37832 W
Pit Exit	229m after FL	52.82996 N 1.38205 W
Pit Entry–Pit Exit 287m, 17.2s @60kph, 12.9s @90kph		

All results available at www.tsl-timing.com

TSL SPORTS TIMING
TIMING SOLUTIONS LTD

Snetterton 300

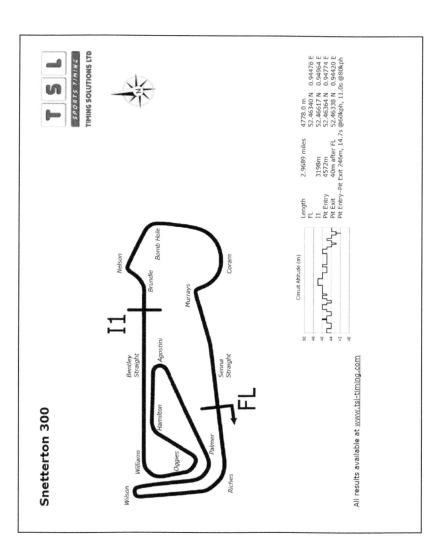

Length	2.9689 miles	4778.0 m
FL		52.46340 N 0.94476 E
I1	3198m	52.46617 N 0.94964 E
Pit Entry	4572m	52.46364 N 0.94774 E
Pit Exit	40m after FL	52.46338 N 0.94420 E
Pit Entry - Pit Exit 246m, 14.7s @60kph, 11.0s @80kph		

All results available at www.tsl-timing.com

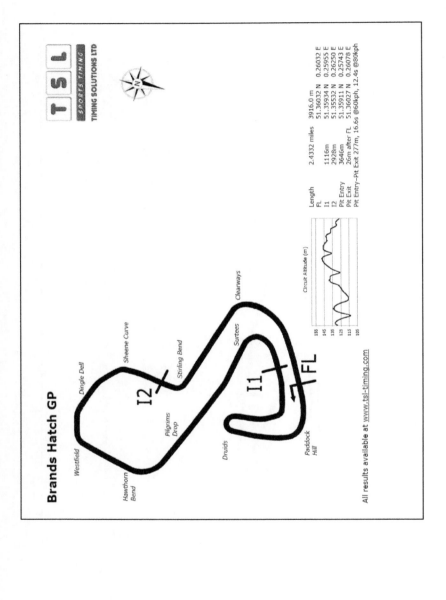

Appendix 4: Rookie Minitwin 2019 Results

Pos	Name	Total	Brands Hatch Indy 9-10 March				Oulton Park 29-30 March		Cadwell Park 27-28 April				Donington National 18-19 May		
			1	2	3	4	5	6	7	8	9	10	11	12	13
1	Matt Wetherell	635	20	25	25	25	25	25	25	25	0	25	20	20	25
2	Tommy Downes	561	25	20	20	16	0	20	20	20	25	20	25	25	20
3	Alan Hensby	286	10	11	11	11	16	13	10	9	10	10	8	8	10
4	Simon Wilkinson	273	11	13	13	13	0	0	11	10	11	11	0	0	0
5	Daniel Thomas	258	16	16	16	20	20	16	13	16	16	16	16	16	16
6	Vanessa Gillam	190	0	10	10	10	13	11	8	8	9	8	7	7	9
7	Steve Male	146	8	9	0	9	0	0	7	7	8	7	0	0	0
8	John Reynolds	127	0	0	0	0	0	0	0	0	0	0	0	0	0
9	Simon Garner	120	0	0	0	0	0	0	16	13	20	0	0	0	0
10	James Nagy	102	0	0	0	0	0	0	0	0	0	0	10	11	0
11	Michael Noah	95	0	0	0	0	0	0	0	0	0	0	13	13	13
12	David Curtis	76	0	0	0	0	0	0	0	0	0	0	0	0	0
13	James Chapman	75	0	0	0	0	0	0	0	0	0	0	9	9	11
14	Hayden Kilworth	56	0	0	0	0	0	0	0	0	0	0	0	0	0
15	Ashley Mitchell	48	0	0	0	0	0	0	0	0	0	0	0	0	0
16	Sam Kent	48	13	0	0	0	0	0	9	0	0	9	0	0	0
17	Dean Holland	37	0	0	0	0	0	0	0	11	13	13	0	0	0
18	Jamie Patrick	34	0	0	0	0	0	0	0	0	0	0	11	10	0
19	Thomas Corthom West	30	0	0	0	0	0	0	0	0	0	0	0	0	0
20	James Careto	15	0	0	0	0	0	0	0	0	0	0	0	0	0
21	Martin Tomkins	9	9	0	0	0	0	0	0	0	0	0	0	0	0

Pos	Name	Total	Snetterton 300 8-9 June				Brands Hatch GP 13-14 July				Cadwell Park 3-4 August				Brands Hatch Indy 5-6 October			
			14	15	16	17	18	19	20	21	22	23	24	25	26	27	28	29
1	Matt Wetherell	635	0	25	25	25	25	25	25	20	25	25	25	25	20	20	20	20
2	Tommy Downes	561	20	20	0	20	20	20	20	25	20	20	20	0	25	25	25	25
3	Alan Hensby	286	10	10	9	10	10	10	10	9	6	7	7	11	10	10	10	10
4	Simon Wilkinson	273	13	11	16	16	13	16	13	13	9	0	8	0	13	13	13	13
5	Daniel Thomas	258	25	0	20	0	0	0	0	0	0	0	0	0	0	0	0	0
6	Vanessa Gillam	190	0	0	0	0	8	9	8	8	5	6	0	0	9	9	9	9
7	Steve Male	146	9	8	7	8	7	8	0	0	3	4	5	0	8	8	8	8
8	John Reynolds	127	0	0	0	0	0	0	0	0	16	11	16	20	16	16	16	16
9	Simon Garner	120	11	9	13	11	0	0	0	0	8	9	10	0	0	0	0	0
10	James Nagy	102	0	13	11	13	0	0	0	0	0	0	0	0	11	11	11	11
11	Michael Noah	95	0	0	0	0	0	0	0	0	11	16	13	16	0	0	0	0
12	David Curtis	76	16	16	10	0	0	0	0	0	10	13	11	0	0	0	0	0
13	James Chapman	75	0	0	0	0	11	13	11	11	0	0	0	0	0	0	0	0
14	Hayden Kilworth	56	0	0	0	0	9	11	9	10	7	10	0	0	0	0	0	0
15	Ashley Mitchell	48	0	0	0	0	16	0	16	16	0	0	0	0	0	0	0	0
16	Sam Kent	48	0	0	8	9	0	0	0	0	0	0	0	0	0	0	0	0
17	Dean Holland	37	0	0	0	0	0	0	0	0	0	0	0	0	0	0	0	0
18	Jamie Patrick	34	0	0	0	0	0	0	0	0	13	0	0	0	0	0	0	0
19	Thomas Corthom West	30	0	0	0	0	0	0	0	0	0	8	9	13	0	0	0	0
20	James Careto	15	0	0	0	0	0	0	0	0	4	5	6	0	0	0	0	0
21	Martin Tomkins	9	0	0	0	0	0	0	0	0	0	0	0	0	0	0	0	0

Appendix 5:
Acknowledgements & Thanks

Where to start? This story has been forty years in the making but the season was over way too quickly. So much effort (well, not a lot on my part) was expended and so much money spent but with it came highs and lows, the likes of which I have rarely experienced. My journey was not made alone, though and without the help and support of so many people, the story would never have been told.

None of this would have been possible through my efforts alone. If I'm honest, I'm just too lazy to follow many things through. With racing, that's not possible. Completing tasks (and properly) is imperative if you are to get anywhere and if you want to keep risks to a minimum. I was never under any illusion concerning my racing ability or my mechanical knowledge. I can say that I have learned a huge amount over the season and the two years leading up to my first race.

A number of people have been instrumental in getting me on circuit. It may have been me who actually raced but these people made it a little less painful and I thank them all.

Heading that list is my late father, Bob Male. It was his enthusiasm for bikes, albeit for British ones, that first got me hooked. Post-divorce, Mark Lucas got me back into bikes and racing in particular. Once drawn into the Bemsee paddock, Mike Wake was instrumental as Head Badgerer, even if he didn't really approve of my final choice of bike, what with him being a Yamaha Past Master racer.

Once I was finally up and running, the following people and organisations helped keep me going:

EVERYONE at Bemsee. I knew I had chosen the right club the moment I joined. It may be the oldest, it may be the largest club in the world but it is still run like a big, friendly family and has an enviable reputation for looking after its riders. From CEO Mike Dommett down to all the staff, everyone mucks in as they need to ensure riders get the best out of every meeting. The club caters for our prima donna needs, provides access to amazing tracks (the only amateur club that is allowed to race on the Brands Hatch GP circuit), has marshal and medical teams that are second to none, instructors (all racers themselves) who can show even a talentless racer like me how to go fast and safely and a backroom team of admin and technical staff that, without any of our knowledge, make it all look so easy with an ethos that positively promotes riders of all abilities. I don't know how other clubs work but I know this one is run phenomenally well.

Individual recognition goes to:

Tracey Ringrow. The long-suffering Bemsee Secretary certainly suffered long at my incompetent hands, providing endless patience when I screwed up during my first few rounds as I found my feet. An absolute credit to the club, Tracey knows pretty well all the riders in all classes; a considerable feat. She is friend, counsellor, mum and general embodiment of efficiency.

Mike Dommett. The CEO of Bemsee, Mike has a wealth of knowledge and runs a very efficient but friendly team. A dry wit and a very good sense of humour is vital here. Mike has that in spades.

Jeremy Hill - pint-sized racing god/chief instructor. Jeremy's track walks are legendary (as are his track walk group selfies) and, for newbies and experienced riders alike, he is a vital part of the learning experience. He spends most of his time instructing, providing pep talks and imparting years of racing wisdom with more than a few dodgy anecdotes along the way.

Dan Singleton - Thunderbike Sport and Minitwin racing god and bike builder extraordinaire. Dan breathed those additional ten horses of new life into Sylvie, turning her from so much scrap metal into a fire-breathing contender, even if her rider still needed more go in him. A fiercely competitive racer but a patient, learned teacher who wants nothing more than to show riders how to improve. Dan's insights saved me from myself a number of times and made me a far safer (and faster) rider. Dan retired at the end of 2019 as Thunderbike Sport champion and third placed rider in the Minitwins championship; not a bad legacy.

"Dyno" Dan Beighton, who watched my progress on an originally terminally asthmatic Sylvie and, after that magical touch from Dan Singleton, handed me a performance chart that showed a massively improved and perfectly fuelled bike. Dan would often comment on my progress and gave excellent insight into what was needed for me to up my game.

Ben Rothwell. Ben took me around that monsoon-drenched Snetterton track and had me prove that I could go faster in the wet than I had dared believe; faster than I had gone in the dry, as it happened. Excellent guidance and endless patience from Ben boosted my confidence no end.

Rosie Dent. Had I not been introduced to Doctor Rosie (thanks to Mike Wake (see later)), my racing would not even have started. Rosie fought my corner when the ACU initially refused to issue a licence, due to a previous heart condition that I had been given the all-clear from ten years ago. She also did my medical for me, asking only that I make a charitable donation for doing so. I made a payment to MacMillan Cancer in payment for Rosie's service.

Kevin Lilley. Kevin drew the short straw as my paddock buddy for the first round at Brands Hatch and must have despaired at my lack of preparation. Patient to the last, he never abandoned me (except when he had to go for qualifying when my rear wheel had seized), he provided wisdom, race craft, paddock stands, spares, maintenance advice and so many other things, none of which I would be able to pay back properly. A true star.

Steve and Sarah Jordan and the staff at Steve Jordan Motorcycles. Sarah's initial help had me bring the yet-to-be-named Sylvie to Leatherhead on a number of occasions to be sorted. Steve's team rebuilt the wiring loom and suspension, and sorted the fuelling, all of which transformed Sylvie. Every time I took her on track following a visit to Dr Jordan, it was like riding a brand-new bike. The depth of knowledge that the staff have, particularly where the SV650 is concerned, is without parallel.

Steve Shrubshall. I met Steve through the Bemsee Facebook page and learned that his company, Bexhill Gearboxes, was only a couple of miles from my house. Steve entered a Minitwin race in the summer of 2018 and we became firm friends. The evenings spent in his company workshop meant that, over a number of months, we were able to sort out a long list of issues ahead of that first round at Brands. Steve helped rebuild the carbs, fitted the new forks when the original ones were found to be bent like a banana and carried out countless other jobs to keep me going. All for the price of a few pizzas. Top man (and not too shabby a racer himself). Sylvie is more complete thanks to Steve's initial work.

Steve and Tom Weeden. Rather ironically, Tom Weeden (2016 Senior Manx Grand Prix Champion) and his dad Steve have supported my endeavours in getting on track, despite having to cope with a full-on race season themselves. From providing a pair of old (but still perfectly serviceable) tyre warmers, selling me a cheap (but otherwise way beyond my means) set of leathers and loaning me a generator for the final Cadwell meeting, plus endless encouragement (and piss-taking where necessary), they helped make my first racing season a joy.

Mike Wake. I've known Mike for about sixteen years, when we met through the Shane Byrne Fan Club. Mike became a YPM racer and I would watch him race at Bemsee. It was Mike who put me onto Doctor Rosie back in 2018 so I could ultimately get my provisional Clubman licence. He also came to my opening and closing rounds at Brands, providing both practical assistance and feedback for that woeful first round.

Next, my fellow rookies:

Matt Wetherell. The 2019 Rookie Minitwin title winner, Matt was demonically fast from the off. There was never any question that he would win the rookie championship, other than maybe in his mind. Despite that, he would also give me more than just the time of day and was always willing to give advice. Coming from a police motorcycle instructor, I knew I was in good hands. Always first with the acerbic comments, Matt is, by contrast, modest of his own achievement, very generous with his praise of other riders and fiercely protective of his fellow rookies.

Alan Hensby. Eventually securing third place in the 2019 Rookie championship, Alan proved to me that being even older than I am is no barrier to racing success. His size belies his speed and he finished the season with an armful of pots. Matt's best mate and paddock space cohabitee, Alan was the only rider to enter and complete every single race in Minitwins; no mean achievement.

Simon Wilkinson. Undoubtedly the quietest one in our little clique, Simon came very close to taking the championship third place off Alan. Only a few DNFs prevented him passing his senior competitor. Quiet perhaps but another very good racer and a very capable engineer, Simon was always at hand to come up with ideas for making ingenious improvements to his bike or ours.

Vanessa Gillam. Vanessa proved that gender is no barrier to success; she beat me at every single round where we raced together. It was only her Cadwell crash that allowed me to get more points than her on that one occasion. Otherwise, she smoked me every time. Even if my starts were generally better than hers, it is a matter of extreme personal shame that I only ever got to overtake her once all season. Even then, she got past me at the next corner.

Always level-headed, even when she broke her wrist after that lapse in concentration at Cadwell, she made sure she was healed in time for a charity race at Donington Park a couple of weeks later. A racer throughout and a fantastic paddock buddy, whose coffees are legendary.

Mark Gillam. Vanessa's husband Mark may not have raced with us but he proved how fast he was at a track day ahead of our last round. Mark was Vanessa's crew chief but didn't limit his services to just working on his wife's bike. He lent me the hex tool I needed at the first round, lent me a rear wheel at Cadwell and rebuilt mine at the final Brands Hatch round. A great sense of humour (as is the case with anyone who wants to enjoy racing), between him and Matt, I became the butt of a season's-worth of ribbing but done with genuine warmth. I think.

Sam Kent. Our favourite fly boy could crash like no one else but always walked away with a huge grin. No one but no one could destroy a bike as comprehensively as Sam and his once beautiful, fully-faired bike ended up looking more bobber than Minitwin but still he'd come back for more. Very down to earth, Sam is always up for a laugh and was happy that he learned from those endless crashes. Well, we think he learned.

Dan Thomas - for a while, Dan looked destined for racing greatness until fate dealt him the worst possible hand. A self-confessed coffee snob, we could all guarantee getting a classy caffeine hit from Dan that would have us wired for an entire race weekend. He was warm, funny and very generous with his time. He was also very fast. We all liked him immediately and he will be greatly missed.

My fellow garage buddies shared all my 2019 season highs and lows. We laughed together, raced together and grieved together; all knowing how it felt to be part of a unique, tight-knit family. It wouldn't be glib to say you had to be in it to have really felt it. My new paddock mates felt it through and through. We became the closest of friends from Round 1 and will likely remain so for the rest of our lives.

Other riders who influenced my season include:

Wil Green. This quiet, unassuming young man was often the first to come into our garage to ask how we all got on. Very generous with his time and knowledge, that relaxed demeanour was instrumental in calming my initial nerves and the private conversations we had got me through some tough times, on and off the track. After his horrific start line crash at Brands, Wil had the dubious honour of being the first rider that Bemsee can remember being back at the circuit after being airlifted to hospital. Quiet he may be but he's tough as old boots.

Charlie Crawt. The catwalk model of the paddock (and 2018 Minitwin Rookie champion), Charlie was, like everyone else in the Minitwin paddock, more than willing to help with gear and advice whenever called upon. Easily spotted on track thanks to his lairy pink leathers, Charlie was always happy to give me pointers on getting my speed and confidence up. For such a young man, he has provided a wealth of experience.

Rob Davie. A seasoned racer, Rob shared a garage with Simon, Dan and me at Snetterton and, while not a rookie and not part of our clique, settled in with this group of wannabes very quickly. A regular mid-pack runner, Rob still lapped me at every race but provided plenty of intelligent advice, including having me talk him through the route and lines I would take around Cadwell Park. Honest and frank, he was always genuinely interested in helping me improve, which makes him a very typical Bemsee racer.

There are so many other people who influenced my year; far too many to recall here and I apologize for those names that I have missed. I must, however, include everyone who is a member of the Orange and Red Army; that great bunch of volunteers who make up the marshalling and medical teams. Racing is a very selfish luxury, even at club level. Without that dedicated team of men and women, none of us Valentino Rossi wannabes would be out there doing our prima donna thing. They are out there all weekend, in all weathers, keeping a protective, watchful eye on us all, springing into action as soon as we do something stupid. I was grateful to have only needed their very welcome assistance three times throughout my rookie season.

Without the constant pushing, cajoling but genuine warmth of everyone in Bemsee, whether that be officials, marshals, fellow racers, friends, families and spectators, neither my ambition to race would not have been fulfilled and this book would not have been written.

I leave my final acknowledgement for the beautiful and wonderful **Cheryl**, my long-suffering other half. Cheryl has never been much of a racing fan and was certainly not happy about me taking up the sport. At no point did she stop me, though and when she was able to attend a race meeting, she was my most enthusiastic and loyal supporter, shouting encouragement during a race and waving frantically to me from behind the fence when it was over. Having her at a meeting made the participation all the better and without her support, neither my racing nor this book would have happened. She is truly one in a million.

Dan Thomas - A Tribute.

Racing comes at huge risk and there is the very real danger that you will not go home. Of course, everyone mitigates against that; for the venue owners, their circuits are far safer these days, with more runoff and air fences are commonplace. The clubs provide marshals (hundreds of them in the case of Bemsee), medics, recovery vehicles and ambulances. Technical rules are in place so that bikes are inspected closely to ensure they all are track-worthy and safe to ride, while riders' gear is also checked over to ensure it is up to the job. The one thing we cannot protect ourselves against is the freak incident and that is why this section has been included.

I met Dan in February 2019 at a Brands Hatch track day, just before the Bemsee race season started. We had got in touch through social media in 2018, where I learned he lived down south like me and would be starting his rookie year with Bemsee in the same series as me. We hit it off immediately and arranged to meet up at that track day. I was really looking forward to finally meeting this unassuming guy, see what he was all about and see whether he was any good. I needed to up my game and had joined the Intermediate group for the first time but Dan, who had ridden in the intermediate group for some time, was with the advanced boys and girls. This was great because I could see how well he was doing. By comparison, he was able to point out where I could improve. From that first meeting, we became the best of friends.

It became clear very early into that friendship that, while he was the nicest, quietest man you could wish to meet in the garage, once out on the track, his "race demon" switch flicked on and he was phenomenally fast. And talented. I had spent forty years riding bikes and, while I considered myself fair to middling, Dan was a natural and I was inordinately envious.

At that first Brands Hatch race meeting, Dan got the first of what was to be many trophies. I hadn't seen a great deal of him at the first round, because I was set up in the lower paddock, whereas Dan had got one of the garages. We agreed to share a garage whenever we were at a meeting together and when garages were available.

As far as his trophies were concerned, I was always genuinely happy for his wins (with a character like his, how could anyone not be?) and for my part, was pleased if I hadn't been passed by him until the penultimate lap. It would often be much earlier.

Dan and I got on famously and, along with Simon Wilkinson and Vanessa Gillam, we soon formed our own little Rookie clique. We supported one another, from saving spaces in the paddock when we'd not booked a garage, to stripping bikes, sharing coffee, beer, tools and parts or simply bolstering each other if a race didn't go to plan. When Dan received a technical disqualification from that Snetterton race, Simon and I helped him get it ready for the next day's racing.

Dan would always come in from a race beaming, following another tussle with Matt Wetherell and Tommy Downes. He would often tell us, with his trademark grin, how he "So nearly passed Tommy again but still got beaten to the line."

When the weather turned at Cadwell, we liberated some timber to reinforce Dan's gazebo, as it slowly but inexorably collapsed. By the end of the weekend, the gazebo had to be scrapped and returned the timbers. Dan would have had probably the only half-timbered gazebo in the country.

Dan always had a pot of seriously strong coffee on the go, which certainly kept me on my toes, or wired at least. "I'll compromise on some things but never on decent coffee," was his mantra. He seemed to be in competition with Vanessa and Mark for the best coffee in the garage. That made us winners all round. What with all that coffee, along with his wife Lorne's peerless flapjacks and brownies, we were living the dream on track and the café lifestyle (well, partly) in the paddock.

Track walks with Dan were *de rigueur*. He may have been a rookie but when I listened to his advice on what lines might work best (based on track days he'd done in the past), I found the sweet spot almost every time. When I didn't, I knew that it was my speed or lack of confidence that was to blame, not Dan's advice.

Away from the track, he was a true gentleman and a gentle man. His wife Lorne was as down to earth and as much fun as Dan and her presence lit up the garage. After winning three trophies at the first round, Lorne had said, "You've got to enter as many rounds as you can. You're in with a great chance of a placing." No one would have disagreed with that and, by the mid-season round at Brands, he was third in the Rookie championship, where his pace was improving even more. Tommy Downe's second place in the championship was then at serious risk.

Dan got his first genuine win at the Brands round in July, in the first Thunderbike Sport race; something that was too long in coming but I was delighted that he finally got the accolade he so deserved. Again, we were all genuinely delighted for him. We all believed that he could only go up from here. The irony is that he never actually lifted that winner's trophy.

Tragically, it was not to be. In the next Minitwins race, he was involved in a high-speed chase. Heading down Pilgrims Drop towards Hawthorn Bend, he collided with another rider and locked his front wheel when his brake lever was hit. The red flag had gone up immediately and by the time I had reached him, his bike was in the middle of the track and he was being attended to on the grass. He was airlifted to hospital for what turned out to be his final journey.

We all make friends in the paddock but our little quartet was very tight. I honestly believed that these would be my friends for life. With Dan, that became the case but much earlier than any of us would have wanted.

We all mourn him and I feel absolutely empty. He was my racing partner, my better rival but more than that, he had become my close friend. I will miss him terribly.

Printed in Great Britain
by Amazon